Instrumental Teaching

Oxford Music Education Series

Series editor: Janet Mills, *Research Fellow, Royal College of Music, London*

The *Oxford Music Education Series* presents concise, readable, and thought-provoking handbooks for all those involved in music education, including teachers, community musicians, researchers, policy-makers, and parents/carers. The series encompasses a wide range of topics and musical styles, and aims to provide 'food for thought' for all those looking to broaden their understanding and further develop their work. Written by acknowledged leaders of education who are passionate about their subject, the books present cutting-edge ideas and aim to stimulate good practice by showing the practical implications of research.

Recent titles in the Oxford Music Education Series

Instrumental Teaching

Janet Mills

MUSIC DEPARTMENT

OXFORD
UNIVERSITY PRESS

OXFORD

UNIVERSITY PRESS

Great Clarendon Street, Oxford OX2 6DP, England
198 Madison Avenue, New York, NY, 10016, USA

Oxford University Press is a department of the University of Oxford.
If furthers the University's aim of excellence in research, scholarship,
and education by publishing worldwide in

Oxford New York

Auckland Cape Town Hong Kong Karachi
Kuala Lumpur Madrid Melbourne Mexico City
Nairobi New Delhi Shanghai Taipei Toronto

With offices in

Argentina Austria Brazil Chile Czech Republic France Greece
Guatemala Hungary Italy Japan Poland Portugal Singapore
South Korea Switzerland Thailand Turkey Ukraine Vietnam

Oxford is a registered trade mark of Oxford University Press in the
UK and in certain other countries

British Library Cataloguing-in-Publication Data
Data available

Library of Congress Cataloging-in-Publication Data
Mills, Janet.
    Instrumental teaching / Janet Mills.
        p. cm.
    ISBN-13: 978-0-19-335908-6
    1. Instrumental music–Instruction and study.   I. Title
    MT170.M43 2007   2007033471
    784.071–dc22

10 9 8 7 6 5 4 3 2 1

Typeset by RefineCatch Limited, Bungay, Suffolk
Printed in Great Britain by Ashford Colour Press Ltd

Foreword

In this entertaining and very readable book, Janet Mills brings a lifetime of experience to bear on one of the most intriguing and elusive subjects within music education: the instrumental lesson. Her broad sweep covers a huge variety of perspectives, whether that of a child nervously taking a first lesson, an experienced teacher, a parent wondering how to give support, an advanced student, or many more. One thing that makes the discussion so rich and appealing is that Janet has herself taken a number of the roles she examines, as both a learner and a teacher, over many years. Those roles she has not taken herself are probably few in number. However, in all cases she supports her discussion with entertaining and apposite quotations and examples drawn not only from her own experience but also from that of other musicians, music teachers, learners, and parents from all walks of musical life. She is not afraid to consider examples of bad as well as good practice; and she never pulls her punches when it comes to criticizing the former.

Mills is quick to dispel a number of what she refers to as 'myths', including the idea that instrumental teachers do not think about what they are doing, but simply repeat whatever methods they were themselves brought up with. Whilst, as she says, there are few grounds to support that claim, the life of the instrumental teacher—even in today's self-consciously research-and-development oriented society—is nonetheless relatively lonely. Most work away from the eyes and ears of colleagues, particularly when they are engaging in that most crucial point of their teaching activities—the lesson itself.

In this book they will find immeasurable companionship. The book gives the opportunity for instrumental teachers from any background to get that much-desired look over the parapet of their own practices, and learn about what others do. No teacher reading it will, I am sure, be able to resist considering their own practices in a fresh light, and in relation to a range of other possible approaches, however experienced they are.

The book will also prove helpful for those many parents who wish to support their children through instrumental learning. Large numbers of adults today have sad and negative memories of where their own instrumental lessons went wrong when they were children; and for reasons which Mills illustrates with abundant examples, many have been left with the enduring impression that they were 'unmusical'. The world of instrumental tuition must be bewildering for parents in such circumstances. But in these pages they will find ways of interpreting their own past experiences constructively, perhaps understanding anew what may have gone wrong—or right—and how to foster more positive experiences for their children.

Nearly three decades ago I was a young teacher tentatively taking her first few piano students to support herself through post-graduate study. Despite having a Bachelor's degree in Music Education, and despite the fact that I was focusing my continuing studies on music education, when I approached my first few lessons I became aware that I had a great deal to learn about the practicalities as well as the theory behind both content and method. Teaching the piano, despite my previous knowledge and experience, seemed to be a bit of a leap in the dark. I made many mistakes, and the memory of some still makes me wince. I also think I got some things right, although I wish I had been more conscious of how and why I was doing so at the time. There was little critical, enquiring literature available to a young instrumental teacher in those days. Today, more and more publications are appearing which will inspire teachers to consider their practices in a more self-conscious, balanced, and open manner than used to be the case. I wish *Instrumental Teaching* had been available to me then.

Readers may not agree with every argument or conclusion that Janet Mills puts forward in these pages. But as she herself makes very clear, agreement is not the point. Rather, it is the opportunity to explore and challenge oneself as a music teacher and a perpetual music learner.

Lucy Green
Institute of Education, University of London

Acknowledgements

This book owes much to the initiative and enthusiasm of over 1,000 instrumental teachers whose group and individual lessons I have observed. I watched them teaching in schools, universities, conservatoires, and the community. Many also spent time talking to me about the lessons that I had seen, and the lessons that some of them also gave in their homes. Some of them were teachers with a wealth of experience and educational qualifications; others were undergraduates who were taking their very first—in some cases tentative—steps as instrumental teachers. I thank them all for the positive contribution that they made to this book.

The many colleagues, friends, and relations who helped me to shape my thoughts as I worked on this book include David Acheson, George Adamson, Lydia Bunn, Karen Brock, Delscey Burns, Rosie Burt, Kim Burwell, Chris Collis, Ben Couldwell, Alan Dobson, Caroline Hunt, Anthony Phillips, Geoffrey Reed, Andrew Scott, Fred Seddon, Steve Tommey, Maurice Walsh, Charles Wiffen, and Mary Worthington. Some colleagues provided text, and this is attributed to them as it occurs. Mary Worthington read the entire text several times, and made many helpful suggestions.

My thanks to those who contributed photographs for the cover of this book: Karen Brock (Tower Hamlets Arts and Music Education Service), Steve Tommey (Bishop Perowne Church of England College, Worcester) and Hamstead Hall School in Birmingham. Mayomi Anuwe and his team at the RCM kept my fragile computers working. Kristen Thorner and David Blackwell, in particular, at OUP showed sustained support of this project.

I sincerely thank them all.

About the author

Dr Janet Mills began her career teaching music (and mathematics) in a comprehensive school in Keighley, West Yorkshire. She soon found herself additionally teaching violin and viola to groups of students at lunchtimes, and 'privately' at home during the evenings. Subsequently, she was a teacher educator at Westminster College in Oxford and the University of Exeter. Her work as an HM Inspector of Schools, for more than ten years, included observation of more than 1,000 instrumental lessons, and the development and implementation—with instrumental teachers—of the first national system for inspecting Local Authority Instrumental Music Services. Along the way, she learnt violin and singing from instrumental teachers, and taught herself to play instruments including recorders, piano, classical guitar, folk guitar, bass guitar, trombone, and French horn. She is a Research Fellow at the Royal College of Music in London, and continues to work widely in schools, colleges, and the community.

Janet Mills is author of *Music in the School* (2005), *Music in the Primary School* (1991), and many articles in books, magazines, and research journals. She has given talks on instrumental teaching throughout the UK, and overseas. She studied music and mathematics at the University of York, trained as a teacher at the University of Leeds, and completed a DPhil at the University of Oxford. In 2004 she won a National Teaching Fellowship.

Contents

Figures and tables

Figures

Tables

List of abbreviations

ABRSM	Associated Board of the Royal Schools of Music
DfE	Department for Education (now Department for Children, Schools and Families)
DfEE	Department for Education and Employment (now Department for Children, Schools and Families)
ESRC	Economic and Social Research Council
FAQs	frequently asked questions
FMS	Federation of Music Services
HE	higher education
HEFCE	Higher Education Funding Council for England
ISM	Incorporated Society of Musicians
LEA	Local Education Authority (now Local Authority)
NC	National Curriculum
NIAS	Northamptonshire Inspection and Advisory Service
Ofsted	Office for Standards in Education
PGCE	Postgraduate Certificate of Education
QAA	Quality Assurance Agency (for Higher Education)
QCA	Qualifications and Curriculum Authority
RCM	Royal College of Music
RNCM	Royal Northern College of Music
RSAMD	Royal Scottish Academy of Music and Drama
TLRP	Teaching and Learning Research Programme (of ESRC)
YPMPP	Young People and Music Participation Project (of ESRC)

Chapter 1

Introduction

Elizabeth began to play. Mr Darcy, as always, listened to her with admiration, for though she was not the most proficient player, few things gave him greater pleasure than to hear the vibrant music her graceful fingers managed to extract from those simple ivory keys.

Mr Darcy admires the pianistic skills of Miss Elizabeth Bennet.

Pride and Prejudice (Austen 1813)

Instrumental teaching—a challenge

Mr Darcy reminds us, if obliquely, that learning to play an instrument (a term that, in this book, always includes learning to sing) is not only a matter of 'standards', 'grades', or international concerto appearances. People also learn instruments for social or cultural reasons, to get a little closer to playing music that they love (but may never be able to play well), to work partly through their dreams of being a great player, or simply to have fun.

There is, in my view, nothing wrong with different students wanting to learn an instrument for different reasons, or with individual students changing their reasons from time to time. And if some instrumental lessons are taking place entirely at the expense of the student, with absolutely no call upon the public purse (not even through the provision of space or time in a school or a community centre, for example), it is possible to argue that the aims and content of these lessons are the business only of the teacher and the student (although surely everyone who describes themselves as a 'teacher' will want to teach in a way that is as encouraging and well informed as possible). But there is a sense in which the discretion of students to say what they want to learn from instrumental lessons, and of teachers to say what and how they will teach is both a curse and a blessing. It is a blessing that students may, in principle, take instrumental lessons just for the fun of it (provided that someone is willing to pay for this!). It is a curse because this very blessing may mask teaching that is lacklustre. When students cease lessons, their departure may be attributed too frequently to a supposed waning of interest, rather than any deficiencies in the ways in which they were taught.

The world of playing an instrument is, for many people, one of unrequited dreams. Mention to anyone that you work in music—or are studying it or enjoy it—and the chances are that they will immediately and enthusiastically ask 'do you play a musical instrument?' And that if, like me, you answer 'yes', and speak a little of the playing and singing that you do and have done, your questioner will come over a bit misty, and say that they wished they played and sang too.

Playing instruments and singing are central parts of the music education and musical activity enjoyed by many people of all ages, and of people with infinitely varying experiences of music and life, around the world. Although we may at times think of instrumental lessons primarily as a feature of western classical music, they are also found in many other musical contexts. For example, I recently observed sessions in Bali, where gamelan have been set up in some community centres, so that groups of students of all ages can receive expert tuition in traditional playing. The large groups of students whom I saw in their lessons were very enthusiastic. I left with a strong sense that traditional forms of gamelan playing were being both preserved and invigorated through the instrumental teaching that was available.

The value of instrumental teaching for young people is endorsed by some national governments. In England, for example, playing instruments and singing—that is, performing—are compulsory parts of the national curriculum for music that was introduced, in its first version, in 1992,[1] and must be followed by all students aged 5–14 who attend maintained[2] schools (DfEE and QCA 1999). More recently the government's endorsement of performing has moved beyond the basic requirements of the national curriculum for music, which is designed normally to be taught—like that for other subjects— by a single teacher working with a class of around 30 students. In 2000, the government pledged that 'over time, all primary school pupils[3] who want to should have the opportunity to learn a musical instrument' (UK Parliament

---

[1] The national curriculum for music in England was revised in 1995 and 2000, and the part of it that relates to students aged 11–14 years is being revised again as I write. All of the versions of the national curriculum have included composition and listening, as well as performing.

[2] These are the schools that many other countries describe as public schools, because they are run at public expense. In the UK, the most expensive schools in the land are generally known as 'public schools', and so I avoid this term in this book.

[3] Children become 'primary school pupils' at the age of 5, and 'secondary school pupils' in the September after their eleventh birthday. Pilot schemes for giving all students their first experience of instrumental teaching have typically provided this when they are aged around 8–9.

2005)[4] and made some funding available for this purpose. These sorts of lessons are typically taught to groups with far fewer than 30 students per teacher.

The use of the phrase 'opportunity to learn', above, is interesting. Although the text shows, through its references to schools and pupils, that this initiative is essentially about 'music at school', rather than 'music out of school', the phrase 'opportunity to learn' (an instrument) belongs to the world of private instrumental lessons, rather than that of school. In school, 'learning' is about progress. If we say that we are 'learning chemistry' at school, then we are thought to be attempting some progress in chemistry. Out of school, however, 'learning' can be synonymous with 'doing' rather than 'progressing'. If we say that we are 'learning flute' out of school, we may be thought to be referring to our experience of going to lessons, whether or not progress is made. Because the government scheme utilizes public funding, 'learning' takes the same meaning as in chemistry. Experiences of going on this scheme should build on students' previous earlier progress in music, and lead them towards further opportunities for progress that are available.

As I write, the government has moved forward with fulfilling its pledge—particularly in some regions of England.

While many people who do not play instruments wish that they did, and governments may provide endorsement of this activity, some important aspects of instrumental learning are often much misunderstood. Instrumental lessons are sometimes spoken of as though they were the only music teaching that students in maintained schools ever receive. In fact, of course, students also follow the national curriculum, may participate in extra activities such as choirs, and typically listen to music for much of the time when they are not at school. Instrumental lessons are sometimes planned in a sort of vacuum, as though students do no other music in the rest of their lives. Assumptions are sometimes made that 'having lessons' is the only way of learning an instrument, when there are many examples of people learning successfully through other means, including on their own.

As well as being misunderstood, instrumental lessons sometimes go wrong. Vast numbers of students 'give up' lessons each year, under the mistaken impression—sometimes shared by that of their parents or carers—that they are 'no good'. Moreover, adulation of instrumental skills is fickle. Blind admiration of people who play instruments rather well—and possibly also have many other skills—can turn rapidly to blind derision when a prominent public

---

[4] Although the source of this quotation relates to the UK Parliament, the pledge relates only to England.

figure, who happens to play a musical instrument, puts a foot wrong in another field. While Tony Blair was initially praised as 'in touch', and 'cool', for having a hobby of playing guitar when he began as Prime Minister, the same hobby is now as likely to be interpreted as 'fiddling while Rome burns'. See, for example, the following parody of William Blake's 'To a Sick Rose' (Keynes 1932: 71; Coren 2006: 21):

The Sick Rose

Oh, Rose, thou art sick!	O Rose thou art sick!
The invisible worm	The invisible worm
Might be a suitable symbol	That flies in the night,
For the party.	In the howling storm,
But I'd prefer something cooler	Has found out thy bed
Like a plectrum	Of crimson joy,
Or a football.	And his dark secret love
	Does thy life destroy.
Walter de la Blair/Giles Coren	**William Blake**

On the other hand, at times it appears that people will believe almost anything favourable that they are told about music! Note the care taken to ensure that readers of the following article—which appeared in the same issue of the *The Times* as that above—understood that it was an April Fool:

Chip 'n' SING, the new way to beat card fraud
By Alexi Harpor

Today it is 'chip and PIN'. Soon it will be 'chip and sing'. Britain's banks are developing a system of credit card security that uses the voice's tonal range. Rather than needing to recall a PIN, you will need to remember a line of a song.

Fraud has fallen since chip and PIN became compulsory, but customers struggle to remember their numbers. Ellis Bastan, chief technical spokesman of the British Banking Federation, said: 'High street transactions have been suffering, so we have been looking at alternative methods of identity verification. Optical scanners are too fallible, and standard voice recognition too easy to mimic electronically. But no two people sing the same way.'

Tills and cash dispensers are to have microphones. However, Mr Bastan adds, 'if people struggle to recall a PIN, there is every chance they will also forget which song they are meant to sing. You might get some poor old dear belting out *My Way* in her local Co-op, when she is supposed to be doing *The Hallelujah Chorus*. That wouldn't do at all. There has to be one universal song, for everybody.'

The search for one continues. Technicians developed the system using Parry's *Jerusalem*, but dropped it to mollify Scottish and Welsh nationalists.

The new technology will be equally secure over the telephone or, where computers are fitted with a microphone, over the internet.

The Lyrical Input Elocution System looks set to be commonplace by April 1, 2009. (Harpor 2006: 12)

There are some lovely examples of potential musical misunderstanding in this writing. The term 'tonal range' is thrown into the melee without explanation of what it might mean. The notion that people sing any song—let alone one that may not be a natural part of their repertoire—with sufficient repeatability to make this technique feasible appears risible. The notion that *Jerusalem* could be found acceptable as a 'universal' song by UK citizens who are not Scottish and Welsh nationalists is also rather troubling. And how could one person sing *The Hallelujah Chorus*? I could continue . . .

What are instrumental lessons for?

So, given this confused and confusing picture, what is the purpose of instrumental—including singing—lessons? Opinions may differ on this as on most other matters, and I am not sure that you and I need to agree entirely in order to have a useful 'conversation' about instrumental teaching through the pages of this book. However it seems right that I should 'lay my cards on the table' in these early pages, and share a personal statement written as a consequence of what I have thought and done, so far, when involved in or considering instrumental music, as a student, teacher, researcher, and inspector. This personal view of instrumental teaching underpins the whole of this book.

I see instrumental lessons—wherever and to whomever they are taught—as:

- *a process of enquiry in which instrumental teachers, and increasingly also their students, observe and analyse each student's music-making and musicianship, and develop ways—that they evaluate—of moving these forward.* There are no foolproof 'methods' or approaches that work for everyone when learning an instrument;

- *contributing importantly to the musical lives of the students who take them.* But I do not see them as being the sole component of these musical lives, or the only worthwhile part of these musical lives, or a separate constituent of these musical lives that only comes out on 'guitar lesson day', or when the guitar case is opened for 'practice' between lessons. Every instrumental student has musical interests that extend beyond their instrumental lessons, and instrumental teachers will wish to show that they acknowledge and respect the whole of students' musical lives, and offer to build links between instrumental lessons and students' other musical interests, if that is what the students wish;

♦ *assuming differing levels of relative importance in the musical lives of different instrumental students, and possibly also differing levels of relative importance in the musical lives of individual students over time.* There are some students for whom instrumental lessons may clearly be so important that these lessons drive the whole of their musical lives. There are other students for whom instrumental lessons may, at least at times, be a means to an end in their musical lives. I am thinking here, for example, of some students at Ernesford Grange School and Community College, in Coventry, who were taking lessons from a classical singing teacher, and also singing in the school choir, with a view to improving their singing in the student bands that were central to their musical lives (Mills 2005*b*: 54). The classical singing teacher viewed these students as no less worthwhile to teach than had they been intending to train as professional classical singers;

♦ *taught with care for the self-esteem, and self-respect of students. It has become a cliché to say that, as an instrumental teacher, one teaches students, rather than bass guitar, for example.* But the philosophy that lies behind this cliché is an important one. No student who invests self-esteem in taking up instrumental lessons should have this betrayed through an educational experience that leaves them feeling that they are 'no good';

♦ *taught so that students who embark upon instrumental lessons want to continue taking them—or ultimately decide to leave their instrumental lessons behind—nevertheless feeling that they were pleased to have taken part.* A survey of instrumental teaching in local education authority music services throughout England during 2005 reported that 10 per cent of students who began instrumental lessons at the beginning of the academic year had given them up within six months, and cited 'loss of interest' as the most usual reason for this (Hallam, Rogers, and Creech 2005). (It is not clear that the cause of this massive 'loss of interest' in provision that young people had initially entered into voluntarily, and probably with considerable excitement, and that typically also involved substantial investment by their parents, has been investigated.)

- *not only about, literally, learning to play an instrument.* Instrumental lessons are also about being creative, imaginative, resourceful, self-evaluative . . . They provide a distinctive, and potentially very valuable, opportunity for one or more learners to engage musically with a musician, and musical role model, who shares their enthusiasm for a particular instrument;

- *not only about meeting the needs, as initially expressed, of the person who is paying for the lessons—typically parents in the case of students who are children.* Instrumental teachers, as professionals, have a responsibility to help to shape these needs. For example, instrumental teachers can guide any parents with a particularly limited—possibly 'exam-bound'—view of instrumental lessons as to the wider range of opportunities that is available to their children.

Further, I see instrumental teaching which takes place within the school system—including local authority music services—as:

- *organized so that instrumental lessons are available in principle to all students who would like to take them, with no sense that they are open only to students who are thought to have particular 'abilities';*

- *linked with the music curriculum of schools but offering something extra, for students who would like this, through:*

  o focusing on performing music, rather than composing it or listening to it, and giving correspondingly greater attention to interpreting music, rather than creating or responding to it

  o making a virtue of the fact that this tuition is optional

  o exploiting the autonomy of instrumental teachers. Instrumental teachers in the UK have greater autonomy than class teachers when it comes to shaping their teaching. For example, they are not required to cover the whole of the national curriculum, and they have choices as to whether or not to prepare (all) their students for graded performance examinations.[5]

We will return to each of these points, in greater detail, later in this book.

---

[5] Graded performance examinations for different instruments are run by UK examination boards including the Associated Board of the Royal Schools of Music and Trinity Guildhall. The basic system runs from Grade 1 to Grade 8, and the overall standards of the different grades have been agreed between the examination boards, and are linked to the National Qualifications Framework.

This book

Instrumental Teaching is a companion volume to *Music in the School* (Mills 2005*b*),[6] which was published in 2005. *Instrumental Teaching* is organized so that readers can work through it either before, or after, reading *Music in the School*. It includes reprints of almost all of one chapter of *Music in the School* that relates particularly to instrumental teaching—chapter 6: 'Teaching instruments musically'—and the four sections of the original chapter

An emphasis on performance

The instrumental curriculum and the school

The optional instrumental curriculum

The autonomy of instrumental teachers

are reprinted as sections of Chapters 5 and 3 respectively of *Instrumental Teaching*. These reprinted sections all fall close to the end of a chapter of *Instrumental Teaching*, and each is demarcated clearly, so that those who have already read *Music in the School* can pass over them if they wish.

Instrumental Teaching aims to build upon the strengths of current practice in instrumental lessons, mainly through disseminating good practice by instrumental teachers and managers whom I have worked with over the years. It draws upon my experience as an instrumental teacher, class teacher, teacher educator, and inspector. It greatly extends and develops the content of the chapter on instrumental teaching that I included in *Music in the School*. It is intended for everyone who is, or is thinking of becoming, an instrumental teacher—and also for everyone else who is interested in this subject.

Following Chapter 1, this introduction, Chapters 2 and 3 are 'teacher-centred' in that they ask 'why teach an instrument?' Instrumental teachers in the UK are not required to be qualified; we consider the advantages—for teachers and taught—of nevertheless participating in training. Chapter 4 centres on students, and asks 'why take instrumental lessons?' Chapter 5 considers why people begin lessons on one instrument, rather than another, and whether this matters. Chapter 6 sets instrumental lessons in the context of students' broader music-making, and their life. Chapter 7 addresses 'the first instrumental lesson'. Chapter 8 turns to 'planning a programme of lessons'. Chapter 9 is concerned with the thorny issue of what is generally known as 'practice', that is, the reinforcement of our teaching that many of us encourage students to undertake between lessons. Practice is frequently something that teachers recommend, but students avoid. If we believe that practice is important, how

---

[6] *Music in the School* was the first publication in the Oxford Music Education Series.

can we make it more appetizing? If we don't think that it is important, why bother with it? Chapter 10 addresses some of the myths that are associated with instrumental lessons. Chapter 11 concludes the book. The appendices include one, written in the form of 'frequently asked questions' (FAQs), that focuses on important practical matters, and which was prepared mainly by Charles Wiffen, pianist, teacher, and colleague at the Royal College of Music in London (RCM), who is Course Director for Music at Bath Spa University.

While this book focuses on the dissemination of good practice, it also, like *Music in the School* (Mills 2005*b*), contains some examples of bad practice. As in my earlier book, the decision to include examples of bad practice was not taken lightly. Few of us would suggest that we have never made any mistakes in our own teaching. Many of us, including me, would argue that a teacher who does not do anything wrong also does not do anything that is dramatically right, as they are not taking the calculated risks with their teaching that lead to outstanding practice when they come off. I, for one, have learned much from watching other people's mistakes, as well as their successes, over the years. The present book promotes and spreads successful teaching through publicizing it, discussing it, relating it to relevant findings from the vast research literature of music education, and sometimes by giving counter-examples: examples of teaching that, for one reason or another, was not successful. There are many successful programmes of instrumental teaching.

Like other books that I have written, this is not a recipe book. Teachers will not find lesson plans or units of work that they can apply directly to their students, because such an approach could not promote high-quality teaching that is tailored to the purpose of the tuition, its students, its teachers, and its resources. They also will not find text that deals systematically with the techniques of particular instruments. No book of this modest length could possibly deal comprehensively with the technique of all instruments, and there are other materials that may help teachers here.[7] If an analogy with food is appropriate at all, this book aims to provide food for thought. It encourages teachers to view instrumental teaching as a form of enquiry. Questions that instrumental teachers may wish to address, through this enquiry, may include, for example:

> What forms of teaching best suit the (usually) small groups of students that are 'time-tabled' for my instrumental lessons?

---

[7] For example, readers who work for Local Authorities in England may be familiar with *A Common Approach 2002* (Federation of Music Services (FMS) et al. 2002*a*). This is a published curriculum framework (not a published curriculum) that reflects the distilled thoughts of hundreds of instrumental teachers in the UK. Further references to *A Common Approach* can be found in the index.

> Would it be helpful for this range of teaching to be expanded, perhaps particularly for some students, or on some occasions?
>
> How can I encourage students to want to work hard on their instruments for years on end?
>
> What does it mean to be an 'effective instrumental teacher', and are there ways in which I, as an individual teacher, could further enhance my teaching?

The list of questions that individual teachers might seek to answer is very large, if not infinite.

This book is intended primarily for those who describe themselves as instrumental (including singing) teachers, whether they work in schools, music services, youth services, the community, private practice, or other settings. It is written also for all those who are interested in instrumental teaching, including individuals who are considering beginning work as instrumental teachers, class teachers who work with instrumental teachers, university and conservatoire students who are taking courses in music education, community musicians, and parents and carers. The book focuses on learners who are roughly of an age to be at school, and who may have been learning for only a few years, because this is true of most instrumental tuition—but the book relates also to learners who are older, younger, total beginners, or very advanced. It seeks to help instrumental teachers teach music in a manner that is true to the nature of music and what musicians do, in other words to teach instrumental music musically.

Chapter 2

Why teach an instrument?

You ask which comes first, the words or the music. I will tell you, the phone call.

Sammy Cahn, song writer (Leigh 2005)

To be honest it's been financial need that pushed me to start teaching now, but I love doing it . . . The feeling you get when you help someone learn something new or increase their confidence is wonderful.

Louise Brown, viola

Why teach? Early days

There is, in my view, nothing wrong with taking up instrumental teaching primarily because one is in need of, or would like to earn, some money. People in all occupations, around the world, take up work for exactly that reason. It would be odd if they didn't.

But there are also many other reasons for being an instrumental teacher, not least the buzz that you get from sharing your love of music with others, the illumination about your own playing that is gained through analysing, and working out how to solve, the playing problems of others, and the individual contribution that you make to developing and rejuvenating the world of music.

Music, as a field, has never stood still, or looked only towards the past: through working as an instrumental teacher, you can help to shape the progress that music, and the ways in which music is taught, make in the future. This is not only through helping to train the musicians of future generations, important though this is.

Our students can help us to develop our own musical knowledge and ideas. Through engaging, as teachers, with the musical interests of our students, we learn much music, and information about music, that is very useful to us. For example, Lynne Buckley, a class teacher at St Saviour's and St Olave's School—a girls' comprehensive (i.e. all-ability secondary) school in

Southwark, London—has written of how the gospel music that her students brought from the community soon influenced her own thinking, and permeated the curriculum of much of her school (Mills 2005*b*). And my own appreciation of how much can be expected from well-motivated young brass players, and my love of brass-band music, were ignited when I met my first brass-band players at the second school where I taught, in Brighouse, West Yorkshire. Inspired by the role models of outstanding local brass bands, including Black Dyke Mills and Brighouse and Raistrick, and surrounded by Brighouse and Raistrick trophies, as we rehearsed in that band's hall for our school concerts (the school had no hall of its own), young female players of cornet, tenor horn, or baritone from my school, who had trained in local junior bands, continually amazed me by reading almost any music I could give them—totally accurately and with A1 quality of sound, concentration, and posture, at sight.

Being a teacher can also change repertoire. Like many other teachers, I constantly arranged and composed new music for my students to play—music that I hoped would challenge every individual, and which I also hoped they would enjoy playing. Some of the students also started to compose items for us to play. Rather more famous examples of teachers shaping the music we play now, through writing that was initially at least partly pedagogical, include Benjamin Britten (e.g. *Noye's Fludde*), Carl Orff (*Carmina Burana*) and Béla Bartók (*Mikrokosmos*). There are countless further examples from many—possibly all—fields of music.

There are further benefits to be gained from being an instrumental teacher. Instrumental teachers who also perform—in any context, paid or unpaid—speak of the symbiotic relationship between these two activities. For example, the instrumental teachers—themselves also performers—who studied and now work at the Royal College of Music in London (RCM), and who often also enjoy teaching students who are younger, older, or more, less, or differently musically experienced or motivated than those at the RCM, report that:

- Explaining things to someone else promotes personal understanding. Hearing someone else's playing makes it easier to diagnose and solve one's own similar problems—and helps in 'the quest to play things in the most simple way possible' ([graduated in] 1966);

- It is the 'explaining to someone else that proves whether what you say about how you sing is accurate' (1988);

- Stopping students making mistakes similar to one's own shows up the worst aspects of one's playing. 'You have to teach students how to teach themselves, and this helps with teaching yourself' (1983);

- Teaching is more intellectually demanding than performing, and so teaching helps one to be less frustrated by some performing work. Teaching firms up a teacher's understanding of technique, and raises their expectations of the technical possibilities of the instrument, and its optimal sound. One [RCM instrumental teacher] thinks of teaching as a form of continual enquiry: 'students have different problems, and that is part of the fascination of teaching' (1983);

- 'One feels under pressure to play in concerts with the same concentration and rigour as one has made students play with during lessons that are still uppermost in one's mind' (1981);

- 'Teaching is a form of sharing that differs from performance, but that nevertheless helps to develop performance communication. It also requires one to learn new repertoire' (1979);

- 'One learns new repertoire from [students]' (1976);

- 'Teaching clarifies one's understanding about the possibilities of technique. For example, one might advise a pianist that they can only play fast octaves with a loose wrist, and then someone comes in and plays them superbly with a stiff wrist. It can also freshen one's enthusiasm for some repertoire that one has known for a long time.' Teaching leads this [instrumental teacher] to explore new repertoire that he would not know about otherwise. For example, a student introduced him to a sonata by Stuart Macrae, and he recently played it at a recital (1973);

- 'The more I teach, the more I pick up. The more I see the problems, the more I learn about my own problems, and how to solve them' (1982);

- Teaching has impacted more on one [instrumental teacher's] playing since he became chairman of his orchestra, and has had less time for practice. Using his instrument in lessons helps. He has become more aware of the need to play as well when teaching as he does on stage, and so lessons contribute to his practice, as well as revealing points that he needs to work on during his limited practice time (1991);

- Teaching has helped [an instrumental teacher] to get better at turning down performing work that he does not have time to prepare for: there is nearly always a former student [listening and evaluating] in the audience (1983);

- 'When teaching I look at my own playing through that of the student. It is too claustrophobic to look directly at one's own playing' (1969)' (Mills 2004*d*: 193–4; Mills 2004*c*).

Finally, one of the—literal—joys of working in music is that we 'earn money' through engaging in music, through working alongside other people who love music as much as we do, and through sharing our love of music with students. It is very rare to find a music teacher, not least an instrumental teacher, who does not love, and is not moved by, music. How often could one say something similar of the teachers, or other practitioners, of almost any other subject or field? Teachers of mathematics, geography, or business studies, for example, have often spent three years focusing on these subjects at university, and may have chosen to study them initially because they liked them more than any other subject. But that isn't quite the same. . . How many mathematics teachers, or geography teachers, or business studies teachers, for example, now spend as much of their leisure time doing mathematics, geography, or business studies as music teachers, including instrumental teachers, spend doing music?

Our personal engagement with music means that we naturally want to teach it 'musically'—in a manner that is 'of music'. In *Music in the School* I suggested that music teachers who are teaching musically build on students' musical achievements so as to:

draw in students with their different enthusiasms and backgrounds, and leave each of them at least slightly better for having been to a lesson. [The teachers] teach through music (not just about music): students spend lessons making music, listening to music, and reflecting on music. The teachers understand that all forms of notation are only a means to an end, that many ends do not require notation, and that some ends would be compromised by it. They have high expectations of their students: they organize lessons so that the sky is the limit, and do not oversimplify their teaching material. Their lessons are ones that they, personally, would quite like to attend. They are observant of the response of their [group], and continually fine-tune their lessons to maximize the benefit to students, adjusting their expectations upwards, where this is appropriate. (Mills 2005b: 20)

Instrumental teachers have the opportunity to exemplify all of this to their instrumental students.

Instrumental teachers also provide an ideal context for further developing some aspects of being a musician that I have said, in *Music in the School* (Mills 2005b: 15), I would hope all school students would experience, in some context or other, including:

♦ *creating, interpreting, and responding to music* (see also Mills 2005b: 33–47). This aspect overarches everything else on this list. I am suggesting that a basic test of whether a particular activity could or should feature in an instrumental lesson is whether or not it contributes to students' ability to create, interpret, or respond to music. I have some doubts here about activities that are billed as 'warm-ups', but that do not seem to lead anywhere. Warming up students for musical activity that is going to take place is a valuable way of using their time. Filling their time with 'warm-ups' that do not warm them up for anything, either because they are poorly planned or occupy too much of a lesson, would not be:

At the end of a musical . . . activity, an instrumental teacher can always answer the following two questions with answers other than 'none' or 'I do not know':

o What music (for example, composing, performing, or listening) did the students do?
o What music did the students learn?

They can sometimes also answer a third question:

o What else (other than music) did the students learn? (Mills 2005*b*: 33–46)

◆ *joining in performances that everyone feels proud of*. Performance is a fundamental activity of all musicians, whatever their musical fields and interests. Some educators with interests broader than music, including Tim Brighouse (Birmingham City Council 1996*a*; 1996*b*), believe that providing opportunities for young people, in particular, to take part in memorable performances benefits them personally, for example through developing self-esteem and enjoyment, and not only musically. However, it is possible to overemphasize some more limited forms of performance within an instrumental music curriculum. Keith Swanwick has commented that, in those American middle and high schools where the music curriculum consists of several band rehearsals each week, 'students tend to get a limited view of what music is and how it functions' (Swanwick 1999: 103). A curriculum that focused on rehearsal of staff-notated published music, and that used a very limited range of teaching strategies to help students improve their performance (such as 'playing slower and then gradually speeding up', or 'practising parts separately and then combining them') could shrink in on itself, so that it ceased to be creative, imaginative, or enjoyable.

◆ *feeling 'musical'*. Feeling that we can do music contributes to our ability to do it. Students who have what some psychologists describe as 'self-efficacy' (Bandura 1997) in instrumental music are more likely to feel able to participate in it, and make a success of it. Motivation is 'an integral part of learning that assists students to acquire the range of behaviours that will provide them with the best chance of reaching their full potential' (O'Neill and McPherson 2002). I believe that there is no such thing as a 'non-musician', and no such thing as a 'non-singer', 'non-guitarist', or 'non-composer'. Whether one feels able, and the degree to which one *is* able, to do any of these things depends on the encouragement and support that has been received. Graham Welch agrees with at least the first part of my proposition here when he writes of everyone being 'programmed' for music (Welch 2001). Instrumental lessons are not only for those who want to make playing an instrument their career. We do not speak of 'non-geographers' or 'non-artists'—why should we talk of anyone as though they were some sort of 'non-musician'?

John Holt, author of *Why Children Fail* (Holt 1984), which has inspired several generations of teachers around the world, and across the curriculum, wrote: 'If . . . people, or most people, do not become musical, the problem is not with lack of innate ability, but something else, probably many things, including the kind of music teaching they run up against' (Holt 1978: 102). I am not entirely comfortable with John Holt's suggestion that people have to become musical, as I believe that everyone is born that way. But this is a semantic difference, and John Holt's sentiments here strike me as spot on.

◆ *being moved by music.* This is part of understanding music's 'evocative power'. One cannot understand the evocative power of music unless one is paying attention to it, and instrumental lessons provide an ideal context for this. John Paynter has written of the differences with which audiences listen in theatres and concert halls. Commenting on observations made by the American composer William Schuman, he writes:

> In the theatre, as the lights are dimmed, people sit up in their seats and lean forward attentively, eager to see from which side of the stage the actors will enter and anxious not to miss the opening lines of dialogue. But in the concert hall, as the conductor lifts his baton, the audience tend to sink back into their seats, waiting for the music to drift over them! (Paynter 1997: 6)

This differs markedly from the total concentration on music and musicians that can be seen at some pop concerts.

Being moved by music is an experience that it is hard—probably impossible—to ensure that all our students receive. But we can help to establish conditions in which it is more likely to occur. Part of this is to do with respecting, and building upon, signs that students are becoming moved by music, even if this is music that we have ceased to regard as particularly profound—or never liked much. I recall visiting the house of a friend when her daughter, aged 9, was practising Elgar's *Salut d'amour* full throttle on her violin. The mother explained that the daughter had 'discovered' this piece a few days previously, thought that it was 'wonderful', and had been working on it incessantly. It must have been very tempting for any of the adults living within earshot of this student, including her mother, to suggest that the student tone down the intensity of her performance, or practise some other pieces. But they left the 9 year old to her own devices, and she presumably did not suffer musically from her, arguable, overdose of one of Elgar's less weighty pieces, as in due course she became an international concert soloist.

One person's meat is another person's poison, as they say, and a piece of music or a particular performance of a piece of music that once entranced can, in due course, start to pall. Teachers take care not to, however unintentionally, criticize a student's taste in music. We might, in a teacherly way, offer students a related (but in our view better!) piece of music to listen to or play, but that is as far as we can go in seeking to comment upon students' taste.

Adult, and not only child, students can have favourite pieces of music that grate with us. Radio stations of all musical persuasions invite listeners to vote for their favourite pieces, and reinforce the popularity of these pieces by playing them frequently. When Sue Lawley, who used to front BBC Radio 4's *Desert Island Discs*, which interviews 'persons of achievement' about their choice of eight pieces of music selected for an imaginary sojourn on a desert island, stood down in 2006 after an 18-year stint, she expressed some frustration about the frequent repetitions in the lists of music that 'castaways' chose. In particular she had become frustrated by being asked to play Frank Sinatra's *My Way* on what seemed to her like almost every programme (Hattersley 2006). I wonder whether 'persons of achievement' really would want to play *My Way* repeatedly on their desert island, or whether they would soon learn how to play it in their heads, and seek more demanding listening material. Nevertheless, should a (miraculously) rescued 'castaway' appear on one of our door steps, and request some instrumental lessons with the aim of learning to play *My Way*, I guess that most of us would rise to the challenge of teaching *My Way*, and also moving students on to some other, possibly more demanding, repertoire.

We cannot guarantee that students will be moved by the same musical experiences that move us. Some of the music that moves me, almost regardless of circumstance, does so partly because of my extra-musical associations with it. Some of the musical experiences that have moved me, when an adult visiting a school, have probably done so partly because of the youth of the musicians generating them. Readers who, like me, watched the 2006 television series *The Choir*, which charted the progress of a choirmaster in building a four-part choir in a secondary school of mainly disadvantaged students with no previous experience of choral singing may, again like me, have been moved by their final performance. I doubt that any of us was moved by the quality, in absolute terms, of the choir's performance as this was only modest, but the performance was moving because the choir had improved so much—socially as well as musically—since we first saw and heard them.

In this case, the choir—and not only the audience—were moved by the performance. They showed this in their faces. But this open display of response does not always occur, either because it is not present, or because it is suppressed through convention. I, for one, do not subscribe to the view of some psychologists that musical performances move their listeners because the musicians who performed them are moved, and successfully transmit this experience to their audience. In the case of western classical music, this idea places composers—who originated the music that is doing the moving—in an odd position. And it also is at variance with the anecdotal comments of performers that they must keep their emotions in check if they are to recreate, during a concert, a performance that they want an audience to find moving.

Sir Thomas Beecham, conductor, was not amused when a concert pianist became so moved during a performance that he actually stopped playing:

Pachmann was playing with that felicity of touch now legendary; and I was conducting as well as it is humanly possible to conduct a Chopin Piano Concerto . . . In the middle of the slow movement, Pachmann stopped dead, stopped playing, and, leaning over the keyboard towards toward me, said, 'Isn't it lofely?' And I replied, 'Indeed it is lovely, M. Pachmann—but would you mind going on?' (Cardus 1961: 47)

Hindemith is among other musicians who have observed that the whole matter of being moved by music is much more complex than it might at first seem:

There is no doubt that listeners, performers and composers alike can be profoundly moved by perceiving, performing or imagining music, and that, consequently, music must touch on something in their emotional life that brings them to this state of excitation. But if these mental reactions were feelings, they could not change as rapidly as they do; they would not begin and end precisely with the musical stimulus that aroused them . . . Thus these reactions may, within a few instants, skip from the most profound grief to hilarity . . . Dreams, memories, musical reactions—all are made from the same stuff. We cannot have musical reactions of any considerable intensity if we do not have dreams of some intensity, for musical reactions build up, like dreams, a phantasmagoric structure of feelings that hits us with the full impact of real feeling. Furthermore, we cannot have any musical reactions of emotional significance, unless we have once had real feelings, the memory of which is revived by the musical impression . . . If music did not instigate us to supply memories out of our mental storage banks, it would remain meaningless; it would merely have a certain tickling effect on our ears . . . If music we hear is of a kind that does not easily lend itself or does not lend itself at all to this connection, we still do our best to find in our memory some feeling that would correspond with the audible impression we have. (Hindemith 1952: 38)

Yes, it would be nice for students to have the experience of being moved by music, and if this happens through their instrumental lessons all well and good. But the conditions under which this happens, or does not happen, are both fickle and tremendously complicated.

◆ *understanding how some music is put together.* Activities that are routine parts of learning and memorizing repertoire—for example noticing patterns such as riffs or sequences in a part being learnt, or spotting the differences between parts being played by other students—all contribute to this. Further, students, particularly students who work in groups, can use their instruments for composing-based activities that develop their thinking about the compositional possibilities of their instrument, and how music is, and could be, put together (see also Mills 2005*b*: 57–61; Paynter 1992; Paynter and Aston 1970).

◆ *waking up in the morning with music playing in their heads.* This may not happen literally to some people. But in *Music in the School* I wrote:

> Playing with music in your mind—carrying out thought experiments to change melodies, or improve them, or to work out new ways of combining them—is part of composing, and part of the mental rehearsal that many performers undertake . . . If you have worked at learning pieces of music until you can replay them in your head, either in their entirety or from any point that you choose, and possibly even discovering something new about a piece as you replay it in this way ('I did not know that the horns were playing there . . .'), you will know how seemingly infinite the mind is in this respect. (Mills 2005*b*: 61–2)

◆ *sometimes turning off background music because it draws them in so much that they cannot concentrate on what they are supposed to be doing.* This is an exciting, and musically valuable, feeling. We could not stop those of our students who experience music passively for much of their waking lives from doing so—even if we thought that it might be musically appropriate for us to seek to do this. But instrumental lessons introduce students to alternative ways of using music that demand their total attention.

◆ *wanting to listen to new music that they have never heard before, as well as their old favourites; wanting to think about the role of music in, and beyond, their own culture.* Learning to play, and understand, new types of music—and not only music that is familiar or of a familiar type—is an important aspect of instrumental lessons. The initiative for this can sometimes come from students—or from the need to cover a range of music to meet the requirements of an examination syllabus—rather than from an instrumental teacher, for example:

> My private teaching includes a woman in her 60s who has been learning with me since 1980 and who will say: 'I heard some Martinu at a concert. Is there any that I could play?' She is a very fulfilling student to teach. (Mills 2004*d*: 192)

To train, or not to train?

> We new girls were to be cultivated into teachers and only after three years of residential study would be ready for release into the schools of Jamaica . . . Like butterflies, we new girls dazzled in our white gloves, our pastel frocks, our pretty hats. Girls from good homes from all across the island. Girls who possessed the required knowledge of long division, quadratic equations. Girls who could parse a sentence, subject, object, nominative, and name five verbs of manner. Girls who could recite the capital cities of the world and all the books of the Bible in the perfect English diction spoken by the King.
>
> Hortense, in the novel *Small Island*, explains something of her teacher training in Jamaica in 1948 (Levy 2004: 62)

Teachers who work on the staff of maintained schools in England are required to have qualified teacher status (QTS). This is the case whether you work in a primary or secondary school and whether or not you specialize in teaching a particular subject, for example music, to classes of students.

It currently takes at least five years to gain QTS after leaving school yourself. Schoolteachers who presently teach class music to students aged 11 or over in secondary schools typically gained QTS by committing three years to taking a degree in music, followed by a further year on a PGCE (Postgraduate Certificate of Education) training course, and then a further probationary period of at least a year. Schoolteachers who presently teach class music to younger children have committed as many years to gaining QTS, but their training—like that of Hortense—has usually addressed many more subjects, so that less time was spent on music.

Many instrumental teachers in England invest as many years in their initial teacher training as class teachers. Overall, 74 per cent of the teachers who work full-time for 149 local authority music services[1] have QTS (Hallam et al. 2005). And while 78 per cent of the teachers who work for local authority music services for at least part of their working week are not full-time, many

---

[1] Until 2005, 'local authority music services' were known as 'local education authority music services'. There were a total of 150 local authority music services throughout England, and their work focused—and continues to focus—on instrumental teaching.

part-time teachers also have QTS. A survey carried out in 1999–2000[2] suggested that around 60 per cent of the instrumental teaching provided by local authority music services is taught by teachers with QTS, although there was wide variation in this figure around the country (Mills 2000*a*). Further instrumental teachers with QTS work in settings where this qualification is not assumed, such as conservatoires, universities, community music, and private practice. And increasing numbers of serving instrumental teachers, including private instrumental teachers, participate, like class music teachers, in professional development courses that help to hone their skills. Some of the courses run mainly for private instrumental teachers are very substantial, requiring significant commitments from them in terms of time, effort, and finance.

However, there remains something potentially intriguing about a situation in which schoolteachers must train for many years after leaving school, and pass many tests in teaching competence, before gaining a post, while instrumental teachers could—in theory—just open for business. Some instrumental teachers in many countries begin teaching while they are students at university or college, and others while they are still students at school. And some students who are investing several years in training to be class teachers carry out some instrumental teaching 'on the side', without training. What is it about instrumental teaching that makes some people feel that they can do it without any training (Fredrickson and Brittin 2006; Mills 2004*a*; Mills 2006*a*; Mills and Jeanneret 2004)? What is it about instrumental teaching that leaves some parents content to buy it for their children from a person who is untrained, when they expect their children to be taught mathematics and so forth, at school, from someone who is qualified, and who may have independent checks made of their teaching quality quite frequently? As instrumental teachers, are we happy with what the answers to either of these questions may say about the status of instrumental teaching?

While it does not follow that an instrumental teacher without training or qualifications would necessarily be any less effective than one with QTS and a

---

2 This data was based on inspections by Ofsted of 11 local authority music services (then called local education music services) during 1999–2000. Almost 60 per cent of the 501 instrumental lessons that were observed and evaluated during these inspections were taught by teachers with QTS, but this proportion ranged from 10 per cent in one service, to 90 per cent in another.

The Office for Standards in Education (Ofsted) is a non-ministerial department of the UK government that was established in 1992, and its responsibilities include the inspection of schools in England.

long list of letters after their name—just as it does not follow that a primary schoolteacher who has trained to teach many subjects will necessarily be any less effective at teaching music than one who has trained to teach only that subject (Mills 1989*b*; 1991*a*; 1994; 1995/6; 1997; Mills and O'Neill 2002)—the situation is nevertheless an interesting one. Researchers in the US (Henninger, Flowers, and Council 2006) have found differences in the methods used by music undergraduates, and those used by experienced teachers, to teach a simple melody on a wind instrument.[3] It would be surprising were this not the case.

It goes without saying that the responsibility of being a teacher is a huge one whatever subject, or in whatever context, a teacher works. But when learning or lessons go wrong, for whatever reason, say in English or science at school, students can rarely 'give up' the subject in question, and parents will often urge the school to find another teacher for their child: one who will meet their needs more effectively. This is rather less likely to happen in instrumental music. We have already learnt (see Hallam, Rogers, and Creech 2005) that 10 per cent of the students who began instrumental lessons with local authority music services in September 2004 had given them up by February 2005, with 'loss of interest' cited as the most usual reason for their departure. How much of this 'loss of interest' was entirely independent of the nature of the instrumental teaching that they were receiving, and the way that it was organized? Might a different, or more varied, approach to teaching have helped? Why is the responsibility for the 'giving up' of instrumental teaching being placed so firmly at the door of the students, when so much of the responsibility for failure in education more generally is—rightly or wrongly—placed with teachers? Will the former instrumental students bounce back from this experience of failure, and try other instruments or teachers, or different types of music-making in due course, or will they—and their parents—now see themselves as 'unmusical' or musical failures?

The answer is that while some students do bounce back in due course, many do not. Among the success stories are an organ student at the Royal College of Music who generously told the whole of his year group, during one of my

---

[3] The experienced teachers gave their students more feedback in the form of statements of approval and disapproval, made less use of their instrument to demonstrate, and gave their students more opportunity to talk. There are few absolutes about how to teach anything effectively but I, for one, would not argue that making less use of one's instrument to demonstrate is necessarily an endorsement of quality—although clearly it would not be constructive for teachers to spend so much time demonstrating that their students had little time to play. This research related to the teaching of a single melody to students—and was not set in the context of a whole lesson, or a course of lessons.

teaching sessions, that his lessons on piano were discontinued when he was aged 6, because his piano teacher persuaded his parents that he was not 'musical'. He recalls a piece called *Soldiers*, which required him to play with both hands at once, as the cause of his disgrace. This student fell in love with a new instrument—the church organ—when he was 13, his parents gave him another chance with instrumental lessons, and he is now a successful player.

But he is unusual. Instrumental teachers—trained and not trained—take on a significant responsibility for peoples' musical future whenever they take on a student.

Music undergraduates as instrumental teachers

David Baker (2006) has reported that instrumental teachers in their early twenties, working for a particular local authority music service, tend to reject training in teaching as unnecessary. He argues that this is because they had their most significant childhood experiences of music outside school, developed 'idealistic teenage career trajectories' based on becoming performers, and disregarded the possibility of becoming a music educator until, essentially, they found themselves working as one.

While there doubtless is some of this about, as otherwise David Baker would not have found what he did in the music service that he researched, the picture that emerges when we start to ask musicians who are music undergraduates about working as instrumental teachers is markedly more positive. For example, undergraduates training as performers have typically thought hard about the instrumental teaching that many of them have already given, want to continue this work—alongside performance—when they graduate, and are conscious that training will be of help to them.

In 2003, a cross-sectional group of 61 third-year undergraduates training as performers at the Royal College of Music filled out a questionnaire that investigated their experience as instrumental teachers, and their attitude to working as instrumental teachers when they graduated (Mills 2004a). As is usual on research projects, the questionnaire was completed in confidence. It had been developed in consultation with another, smaller, group of RCM undergraduates, and so it asked questions that RCM undergraduates felt were relevant to them. The RCM is an international community of musicians: around a third of the undergraduates completing the questionnaire had attended schools outside the UK.

Forty-seven (77 per cent) of the RCM undergraduates had already worked as instrumental teachers, of whom 23 (49 per cent) had begun teaching before they even entered the RCM. The 29 (48 per cent) RCM undergraduates working as instrumental teachers when they completed the questionnaire had on average six current instrumental students, worked with them mainly individually rather than in groups, and taught for an average of three hours each week.

The 28 attitudinal questions that RCM undergraduates answered are listed in Table 1, together with their responses. These questions fall loosely under eight headings, although these headings were not included on the questionnaire in order to reduce the English text that RCM undergraduates with a first language other than English needed to read. The questions were answered using a 7-point scale running from '1' (strongly agree) through '4' (no opinion) to '7' (strongly disagree).

The RCM undergraduates emerge[4] as young musicians, often already experienced as instrumental teachers, who both expect and hope to include instrumental teaching in their career, do not expect to be bored by it, consider that teaching will improve their playing, think that they need to be trained as teachers, do not think that good performers always make good teachers, look forward to working out how to improve their teaching and seeing their students progress, and want their lessons to be fun. They also agree, but less strongly, that they would like their teaching to include composing and improvisation as well as performing, reject the notion that performance is improved best through repetitive drill, and want to teach students to be expressive from the earliest stages of learning a piece. Male RCM undergraduates are significantly[5] more likely to aspire to teach conservatoire students,[6] advanced students, or students who find music easy, consider that staff notation should be introduced from a first lesson, and favour repetitive drill as a means of improving performances.

Through identifying with educational views that are generally more conservative than those of their female peers, the male undergraduates may—ironically—be decreasing their suitability to teach at a conservatoire in future. Conservatoire teachers emerge from earlier research (Mills 2004d) as examples of the type of

---

[4] The criteria being used here for general agreement, or general disagreement, with a statement are 2.6 or 5.4 respectively.

[5] $p < 0.05$, t test

[6] Currently, it is more realistic for male than female RCM undergraduates to aspire to teach at a conservatoire in due course. Males remain more likely than females to enter conservatoire teaching throughout the UK. The gender index, defined as the quotient of the proportion of male tutors and the proportion of male students, is 1.46 across the nine conservatoires in the UK, and ranges from 1.26 to 1.96 in individual institutions (Federation of British Conservatoires 2003).

expert that Bransford and Brown (2000) denote as 'accomplished novices', rather than 'answer-filled experts'. 'Accomplished novices' are rightly proud of their achievements, but constantly strive to know more, and to push out the boundaries of their expertise. By contrast, 'answer-filled experts' know and communicate the information associated with their expertise in a more self-contained way. These ideas of what might be called 'expanded', or 'expansive', learning are developed in Chapter 6.

Perhaps particularly in the case of the female undergraduates, but also more generally, I feel that their views represent a healthy attitude to beginning as an instrumental teacher. The RCM undergraduates appear poised to become 'performer-teachers'—performers for whom instrumental teaching is integral to how they see themselves professionally: performers for whom the instrumental lessons that they give are 'meetings between two parties [i.e. teacher and student(s)] who really want to be there' (Mills 2004c: 259).

At the RCM, we have subsequently used the questionnaire shown in Table 1 on optional music education courses, to help undergraduates and postgraduates monitor their learning, and so that they can compare their attitudes and learning with those of their peers.

We have used it also for further research. In particular, it has been completed by four groups of music undergraduates outside the RCM:

- 73 performance degree undergraduates at a conservatoire in Australia that also trains teachers (education undergraduates) (AU Con Perf)

- 26 education undergraduates at the same Australian institution (AU Con Ed)

- 26 education undergraduates at an Australian university that does not train performers (AU Un Ed) (Mills 2006a)

- 100 performance degree undergraduates in two US universities (US Con Perf) (Fredrickson and Brittin 2006).[7]

All the eight conservatoires in England and Wales focus on training performers and composers: they do not have undergraduate courses for aspiring teachers. We chose the first three of our comparison groups, in Australia, above, in order to investigate whether UK conservatory undergraduates would feel:

- more positive about including instrumental teaching in their portfolio of work

- more persuaded that training in instrumental teaching would be of value to them

---

[7] There were some minor changes to the wording of some questions to account for differences in terminology used by British/English and American/English speakers.

Table 1 RCM undergraduates as instrumental teachers

1 = agree strongly, 4 = no opinion, 7 = disagree strongly	Average (arithmetic mean)
(a) Teaching and my career as a performer	
Q1. I expect that I will do some instrumental teaching when I graduate	1.5
Q2. I hope to do some instrumental teaching when I graduate	2.1
Q3. If I do some instrumental teaching, this will be mainly because I want the income	3.0
Q4. I think that I would find instrumental teaching boring	5.7
Q5. I hope that I will only teach for a few years, and then perform full-time	4.7
Q6. One day, I would like to teach at a conservatoire	2.8
(b) The relationship between my teaching and playing	
Q20. Giving instrumental lessons would help me improve my playing	2.5
Q27. My teacher often talks to me about how teaching helps him/her to improve his/her playing	4.3
(c) My need for teacher training	
Q15. It is obvious how to teach: I do not need to be trained	5.4
Q16. A good performer will always be a good teacher	6.1
Q17. I would teach my students exactly the same way that my best teacher has taught me	4.8
(d) The students I would like to teach	
Q7. I would particularly like to teach beginners	4.1
Q8. I would particularly like to teach advanced students	2.6
Q9. I would particularly enjoy teaching students who find music difficult	4.3
Q10. I would particularly enjoy teaching students who find music easy	2.9
Q11. I would particularly enjoy teaching young children	3.6
(e) Why I would enjoy teaching	
Q12. I would enjoy seeing my students develop into better musicians	1.4
Q13. I would enjoy working out how to improve my teaching	1.6
Q14. I would enjoy working out ways to help students understand a particular point	1.7
(f) My responsibility for students' learning	
Q18. When a student gives up, I will worry that my teaching was not good enough	3.8
Q19. If students do not practise enough, I would think that this was my fault	5.0
(g) Teaching styles and curriculum	
Q21. I would want my instrumental lessons to be fun for my students	1.6
Q22. I would want my students to take all their 'grades' from 1 to 8	4.4
Q23. I would teach my students to improvise and compose—not just perform	2.8
Q24. I believe in getting the notes right first, and adding expression later	5.0
Q25. The best way to solve a problem with a difficult passage is to keep on playing it again and again—until it is always right	5.2
Q26. I think that it is important to start teaching students to read music from their very first lesson	3.8
(h) The status of instrumental teaching as an occupation	
Q28. Instrumental teaching is a career that is valued by the community	3.5

- less wedded to (arguably) conservative educational approaches such as reliance on staff notation, or 'getting the notes right first and adding the expression later'

were they to mix socially and academically with undergraduates who have committed to teaching, rather than performance, as a career. The conservatoire in Australia was a natural choice of an institution with education undergraduates for comparison with the RCM. Like the RCM, it is internationally prestigious and English-speaking, and the systems of school music, instrumental tuition, and conservatoire education in England and Australia have similarities. The university course in Australia provided for comparison with the education course at the conservatoire in Australia.

The American group provides a welcome and helpful basis for further comparison.

Fig. 1 summarizes the findings for all five groups:[8] one in the UK, three in Australia, and one in the US.

Teaching and my career as a performer

Like the performance undergraduates at the RCM, the performance undergraduates in Australia and the US were positive about the role of teaching in their career. However, they were more likely to think that teaching might bore them, and to hope to give up teaching and perform full-time after a few years. The education undergraduates also looked forward to doing some instrumental teaching when they graduated, but were motivated more strongly by money. This is not surprising: they have committed, through their choice of university course, to class music rather than instrumental music.

The relationship between my teaching and playing

The findings from all five groups were very similar. The music undergraduates generally consider that giving instrumental lessons would help them improve their playing, but this issue is not discussed, as a matter of course, in the instrumental lessons that they themselves receive.

My need for teacher training

All the groups consider that they need training as instrumental teachers, and are certain that good performers are not invariably good teachers. The RCM undergraduates were least likely to want to teach their own students using exactly the same approaches that they recalled their best teacher used to teach

---

[8] Differences are reported descriptively here. However, the data for the four groups in the UK and Australia were entered into a single data set, and the significance of differences was calculated, and is reported elsewhere (Mills 2006a).

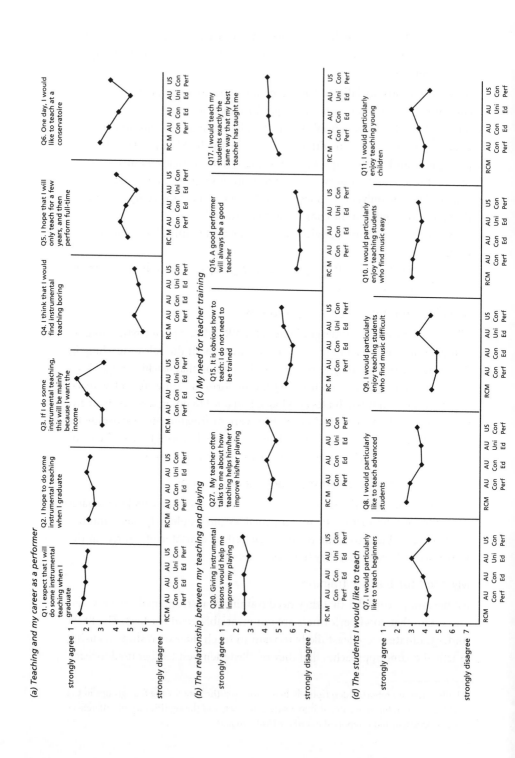

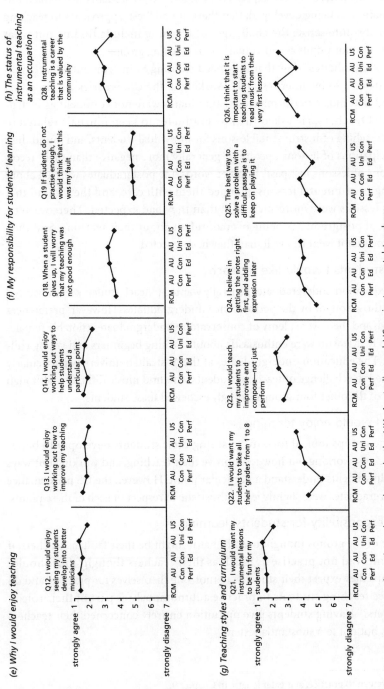

Fig. 1 Comparison of music undergraduates in the UK, Australia, and US as instrumental teachers

them. This reflects a view, expressed by several RCM students when the questionnaire was being developed, that there are no 'best' approaches to teaching in an absolute sense: the challenges of teaching include finding out what works best for pupils as individuals, or as teaching groups.

Undergraduates' view that they need training as instrumental teachers is supported also by other research. Working in the US, Fredrickson (in press) found that music performance postgraduates were not confident as instrumental teachers. He asked the postgraduates to keep journals related to their teaching of instrumental lessons for individual students, and found their 'anticipations of lessons upcoming' generally more negative than their 'recollections of lessons just past'. In other words, the postgraduates worried about giving instrumental lessons, planned them with care, and then found that their lessons were more successful than they had expected. There wasn't a sense of postgraduates being overconfident about their teaching, and then finding that it went less well than they had expected.

The students I would like to teach

The education undergraduates generally wanted to teach students less advanced than those sought by the performance undergraduates. However, preferences varied, and there were plenty of conservatoire undergraduates (notably females at the RCM) who were enthusiastic about teaching beginners and young children. The education undergraduates at the Australian university particularly relished the challenge of teaching students who find music difficult—although none of the other four groups strongly eschewed these students.

Why I would enjoy teaching

All the groups looked forward to seeing their students develop into better musicians, working out how to improve their teaching, and working out ways to help students understand a particular point. However, the US performance undergraduates were slightly less enthusiastic in respect of each of these points.

My responsibility for students' learning

None of the groups thought overall that it might be their fault, as teachers, if students did not practise as much as their teachers thought they should. Perhaps they expect their students to motivate themselves for practice, and do not see teaching students to practise autonomously as part of their role as teachers?[9] Having students give up tuition entirely concerned their teachers more, but not to a substantial extent.

---

[9] We return to practice, at greater length, in Chapter 9.

Teaching styles and curriculum[10]

All the groups strongly wanted the lessons they taught to be fun. Less substantially, but still positively, improvising and composing—not just performing—were welcomed as part of the performance curriculum. There was little enthusiasm for 'getting the notes right and adding the expression later'. The education undergraduates in the Australian conservatoire, and the American performance undergraduates, were most likely to favour repetitive drill as a route to improving a piece, and to consider that students should be introduced to staff notation from their very first lesson—but neither of these results were very strong.

The status of instrumental teaching as an occupation

There was some variation between groups, with (ironically) the university students training as class teachers in Australia rating the occupation of private instrumental teacher with highest status. (Is there something about school music teachers that leads them to do themselves down?) The Australian schoolteachers had also been the group that spoke most of doing instrumental teaching for the money. Perhaps these undergraduates see a close link between the status of particular fields of teaching, and the rates of pay that they believe are attracted.

It is clear, from these comparisons between groups of students in three countries, that the positive attitudes to work as an instrumental teacher which were found at the RCM are not confined to that institution.

Interestingly, the research did not show that aspiring performers who are taught alongside aspiring teachers develop more favourable attitudes to working as instrumental teachers. The attitudes of RCM undergraduates were, in general, less conservative than those of performance undergraduates at the institution in Australia with which it was compared. Training performers in an institution where they can socialize and study with classroom teachers does not necessarily further enlighten their approach to instrumental teaching.

---

[10] The question about examinations (Q22) did not translate well between countries, and so it is not included in this analysis.

Chapter 3

Instrumental teachers

Up the dark stairs we went . . . only to be driven down again by the dust and the decay, the old man's winy breath and the tobacco fumes at the top.

Yehudi Menuhin recalls the learning environment provided by one of his first violin teachers (Menuhin 1976)

Was the learning environment provided by one of Menuhin's earliest violin teachers really quite as bad as that? We will never know. But, however bad the air quality in this particular teaching studio, the young Menuhin and his mother were so enthused by the teaching that they went back for more.

Instrumental teachers today work in a range of teaching environments, and those who set up their own studios have more control than those who work in schools and students' homes over the conditions in which they will teach, and their students will learn.

While much of Chapter 2 related to the commonality of instrumental teaching and class teaching, the present chapter turns more to differences. The first section consists of two case studies of instrumental teachers. Next, there is a reprint of a section of *Music in the School* that is particularly relevant to instrumental teachers, because it focuses on the autonomy that they enjoy, when compared with class teachers. This relative autonomy brings additional responsibilities. Finally, there is a new section entitled 'On quality'.

Two case studies of instrumental teachers

This book contains observations, many of them brief, about the careers, work, and aspirations of many instrumental teachers. Here we consider more detailed case studies of two instrumental teachers. Both, as it happens, studied at the Royal College of Music, but at different times. One is at the beginning of her career, while the other is more experienced. The first instrumental teacher has discovered only recently that teaching is a joy, and a source of further learning for her as a musician: it is not only a route to earning money. The second instrumental teacher has deliberately continued to teach as he has worked his way upwards through the echelons of the music education profession. Neither of the teachers only works in instrumental teaching, or aspires to do so. Neither is necessarily typical of any group, either a peer group or an instrumental group, or instrumental teachers in general. But they both have an interesting, and encouraging, tale to tell.

A performance undergraduate who teaches: Louise Brown, viola

Louise Brown, viola, is an undergraduate RCM performance student who works part-time as an instrumental teacher alongside her studies. While she is not necessarily typical of students at the RCM (whatever 'typical' means in this context), her story as an instrumental teacher overlaps with that of other RCM undergraduates, and illustrates some points that have been made already in this book.

In March/April 2006, during the third year of her four-year B.Mus. (Bachelor of Music) course at the RCM she contributed three pieces of writing to this case study:

- completed teaching questionnaire (see Chapter 2, Table 1)
- statement entitled 'thoughts on teaching'
- evaluation report of a project in school

and agreed that I might draw on them in this case study, which I subsequently checked with her in draft.

Some readers may feel that they can detect some small elements of very slight contradiction between different sections of Louise's writing. I am not sure that these contradictions are real. But as we write reflectively we construct and summarize, and our reflective writing at any moment in time provides but a snapshot of our thinking at that instant, that we are free to review in the future. Louise and I have preferred to leave her writing virtually as it was first offered, rather than sanitize it. As her career progresses, Louise will continue her journey of performing, teaching, reflecting, and constructing, and she will be free to revise opinions that she has stated here (though I generally empathize with her views so much that I would be comfortable were this not the case).

The richness of Louise's writing provides me with much food for thought. She has caught the teaching 'bug': she has found that she does possess the patience needed, and has experienced the buzz that comes from realizing that she has helped to teach someone something that may help them in future. It is transparent that she is vesting immense effort in her work as an instrumental teacher, taking her responsibilities for her students' musical development very seriously, and preparing her lessons conscientiously. And given that I have met Louise, I feel confident that she is also inspiring students through the musical skills that she shares readily with them, and motivating them through her energy, social skills, and love of music. Further, we read that she is organizing her lessons so that her students learn to practise effectively earlier than she did, taking a balanced approach to playing by ear and from staff notation, and placing emphasis on making a good sound from the earliest stages of tuition. Finally, Louise's conversations with her own teacher about the benefits brought to their own performance by their own teaching indicate just one of the respects in which Louise has discovered expansive learning.

Yet Louise, like other music undergraduates also working in instrumental teaching, is labouring under disadvantages that are not experienced by musicians who are committing to a career in class music, through taking a statutory teacher training course. For example she:

- cannot discuss her ideas, and share her experience routinely, with lecturers and peers who are on a teacher training course. Most of her experience as a teacher appears to relate to students who have been learning for no more than three months. (So how does she formulate her view of where, in terms of learning, her lessons are leading?)

- feels that her teaching is limited through lack of knowledge of repertoire. As she develops, and casts around for, repertoire that meets her needs she makes some inspired choices—such as the James Bond theme and also the Lillian Fuchs study from her own repertoire—but also possibly one or two that are less happy. (Surely 'The Hall of the Mountain King' sounds better on an instrument lower than a viola and with other instruments involved too? And given that this piece features—rightly or wrongly—in many published and broadcast programmes for young children, was the initially hesitant response of some students at least partly because they felt patronized?)

- draws heavily on observations of just one experienced teacher of beginners to guide her approach to teaching. (This teacher provides Louise with valued advice that she makes her own and moves beyond—for example by using a broader range of materials—but what if this was not the case? Trainees on PGCE courses, for example, observe the teaching of a larger number of teachers.)

Neryl Jeanneret and I wrote (Mills and Jeanneret 2004: 29):

Conservatoires do not train performers simply by apprenticing them to an instrumentalist. While students' academic relationships with their main instrumental teachers are important, they also learn from a range of musicians.

The idea that one could learn to teach simply through apprenticeship to a single teacher is, we would argue, even more gross. Moreover, our research has shown that this approach rarely leads to professional fulfilment. While there are examples of stunning performer-teachers who started teaching young, they are outweighed by larger numbers of musicians who began teaching young, and gave it up young.

Louise's experiences in school bring her other opportunities to work with students who have been learning instruments for more than three months, work with many different teachers, and experiment with repertoire.

Other beginning instrumental teachers may not have such opportunities.

Case study of a performance undergraduate who teaches: Louise Brown, viola

Louise's teaching questionnaire

Background questions

Louise began working as an instrumental teacher (viola, violin, cello), alongside her studies, at the age of 19. A year later, in April 2006, she was teaching 15 students, aged 5–17, for a total of 5.5 hours each week. She taught 12 students at their schools, in some cases in groups, and three individually at their homes. She had taken on all 15 students within the last three months.

Attitudinal questions

Louise's responses were generally similar to those of her RCM peers, but she was:

- more[1] interested in teaching younger children
- more inclined to view it as a problem for her, as teacher, if students did not practise enough
- more eager to teach her students to improvise and compose, rather than just perform
- less wedded to 'getting the notes right and adding the expression later'
- more persuaded that experience as a teacher would help her improve her playing
- more used to hearing her own teacher explain 'how teaching helps her improve her own performing'.

---

[1] 'More' here reflects a difference of at least 1.5 points on the 7-point scale.

Supplementary text

Louise added that 'teaching is a huge challenge, but one that I enjoy very much', explained that—when teaching beginners—she particularly enjoyed teaching younger students because it was easier to find 'fun' repertoire for them, and observed that 'my teachers have influenced the way that I teach, although I aim to do things my own way'.

She also glossed her responses to two of the attitudinal questions:

The best way to solve a problem with a difficult passage is to keep on playing it again and again—until it is always right	3 (agree)

'Repetition is important in practice, as long as you stop and observe what needs improving after each time you play it, rather than just blindly repeating it over and over, otherwise you get used to playing the passage incorrectly. Slow practice is very important, gradually increasing the speed. With all my students, I take time to explain what and how I would like them to practise—I feel this was one area of my education that started quite late! No one explained to me how to practise properly until I got to about the age of 16 (nine years after starting!). I feel a little frustrated at how much sooner I could have grasped things had I have known.'

I think that it is important to start teaching students to read music from their very first lesson	3 (agree)

'I think that being able to read music is very useful. However, it is very easy to get carried away and put too much emphasis on notation, and in the process ignore even more important aural and memory skills. I try to introduce notation in little bits and often, although I usually don't use any in the first couple of lessons (or very little). At one school I teach at in particular, I really try to balance learning by ear with learning from written music, and in that order.'

Louise's statement entitled 'thoughts on teaching'

On how she entered teaching

'I stumbled into teaching by accident. I'd always thought that I wouldn't be a very patient teacher, and that it would frustrate me explaining things that seem obvious to me, but I realized at the same time that I would eventually need to teach a bit if I was serious about making a living as a musician. It wasn't something I thought I was looking forward to.' After a year at the RCM, a residency at a festival in America included giving some individual lessons: 'to my great surprise, I really liked it! I found that I had levels of patience that I didn't know were in me, and I managed to tap into them quite easily.'

On gaining experience of music in comprehensive schools

'The next year at college, I started to take part in the SA Scheme,[2] and found myself doing all kinds of things—initially helping out in classroom lessons, and then teaching composition to smaller groups of students, coaching chamber groups and giving short lessons on performing, as well as doing lots of playing myself. It was challenging and infinitely rewarding—the feeling you get when you help someone to learn something new or increase their confidence is wonderful.'

On taking on her first regular instrumental students

'In this past academic year, I finally started teaching regularly in London, at two schools: the first, a primary school in Clapham and the second, a secondary school in the East End. At the secondary school, I also take an after-school string ensemble, which is with all of my students at that school. To be honest, it's been financial need that ultimately pushed me to start now, but I love doing it. All of my current students are complete beginners, at the primary school between the ages of 5 and 7, and at the secondary school 11–14. I find it challenging, difficult at times but above all, fun. It's made me very aware of how I do things in my own playing, and I constantly have to find new ways to explain things to my students that engage them. At the moment I find the younger students easier to teach, although I think this is partly because I teach them individually, whereas the older students are always in groups. There is so much beginner material for younger students, but less which my older ones would enjoy so much. I find I write quite a bit of my own material for them at the moment, as well as adapting well-known tunes (such as the James Bond theme—very good for gaining control of the right arm!).'

On planning the structure of her instrumental lessons

'Every lesson starts with a set of physical warm-ups that relate to movements made while playing . . . and then involves some singing and usually clapping games as well as learning to play the violin or viola. I give weekly listening suggestions for music on the radio, or lend them CDs, as I think

---

[2] The Student Associates Scheme, funded by the Training and Development Agency, allows some RCM students to be paid a modest bursary while working alongside class teachers in secondary schools.

listening to [well-played] music of any genre is vitally important for instrumentalists (well, not just instrumentalists—anyone really!). From the beginning, I explain how the instrument works and how to get the best possible sound from it through the technique. I ask lots of questions as to why they think I'm asking them to do things in a particular way, and to get them to constantly evaluate their playing. Preparing lessons always takes longer than I think it will, but it's always worth taking the time to do it. I try to be as positive and encouraging as possible, as I know the effect that even just one harsh statement can have on young musicians. I know it's been a good lesson when my pupil has really enjoyed it, and that's my aim for every lesson. I find myself influenced especially by my first teacher, who I watched teaching this year, and her approach is fantastic, especially with younger students.'

Louise's evaluation report of a project in school

The project

This was a week-long 'creative partnership' between a comprehensive school in Worcester and the RCM, organized by Steve Tommey of Bishop Perowne CE High School and Performing Arts College,[3] that gave Louise a very varied and full experience of music education at that school.

On a music/drama session

'a drama lesson led by Steve was a fantastic idea. The students were working on *Mime* and their task was to devise movements to the music I played them. I used two melodies—the first, "The Hall of the Mountain King" from the *Peer Gynt* Suite by Grieg, and the second a study by Lillian Fuchs, which is made up of two very distinct sections. Although the children were a little inhibited initially, most of them warmed up very quickly, and came up with some lovely movements (and, more importantly, had fun!). It really made me aware of precisely what and how I played, and emphasized the importance of clarity in all aspects of playing.'

On a workshop that aimed to help six 15 and 16 year olds as performers

'The group I worked with . . . began to really open out with their playing. They were supportive of each other, and we finished off the day with an

---

[3] Steve Tommey is a Music Advanced Skills Teacher who works in Worcestershire Local Authority.

informal concert in the school's well set-out concert hall, complete with lighting. Students chose whether or not to perform, and I was very happy that one of the girls in particular from my . . . group (who earlier had been so shy!) volunteered to play. The concert was great, and I think the students all enjoyed simply having an opportunity to perform without being assessed in any way.'

On collaborative music/dance work with a class of 15 year olds

'[The dance teacher, Celia, and I] started with . . . a standard dance warm-up and then the warm-up that I use each day before playing, and then I introduced myself and my instrument, playing excerpts from Khachaturian's Viola Sonata to demonstrate some of the different ways the viola can be used. The students observed the different motions I made and made a few notes. From here, we did some movement, using 'call and response', where I would play something to them and they would reply with contrasting movements. From here, we went on to movements that were related to what and how I played. The students found this challenging, but with encouragement they grew more confident with their ideas. Celia proposed an overall structure for the piece, and then divided the class into groups to devise individual sections. Celia and I went round each group separately, in my case improvising music to accompany their dancing . . . It was a lot of fun improvising music to accompany the dance, and after the workshop I was able to use the school's excellent computer facilities to create a backing track on CD for the students to use for rehearsal in my absence (and eventually in performance [at a public concert a couple of weeks later], while I improvised live over it). I was so impressed [with the students] that I asked to work with two of the dancers to create a piece of dance to go with some movements of J. S. Bach's First Cello Suite (which I also performed at the public concert).'

On a visit to an in-service course for teachers

'I have used some of the songs we learnt in my instrumental teaching since, and they've been very well received!'

Overall

'The whole experience has been demanding and has stretched me creatively, and I feel I've learnt a lot from it . . . Steve allowed time each day to spend reflecting on the day's events together, and this was very useful. This seems to be characteristic of the school in general . . . The week gave me chance to consolidate a lot of things I've been working on in the past couple of years, and the opportunity to meet inspiring and experienced teachers, with whom I feel I've shared many views and have learnt from. The concert concluding the partnership was a lovely occasion, and it was great to give the young performers from the school a well-deserved opportunity to perform simply for enjoyment, not assessment.'

Case study of a performance graduate who teaches: Geoffrey Reed, clarinet

How I came to work in instrumental teaching

My own musical experience began in primary school when I started to learn the recorder, and later the clarinet. I was taught the recorder by the headteacher, whose influence and support continued way beyond primary school. Initial clarinet lessons with a private teacher were followed by a Local Authority music award which gave me free tuition with an excellent teacher and free access to the local youth orchestra. By the time I had been in the National Youth Orchestra for four years and arrived at the Royal College of Music as a Foundation Scholar I was all set to become a professional clarinet player.

It was in my second year at the RCM that a friend 'passed on' some clarinet teaching in a secondary school. Not long afterwards further opportunities arose, including some teaching at a privately run music centre. By this time I had realized two things: I was enjoying teaching young people and I was feeling less sure about my wish to live with the insecurities of a performing career for the rest of my life. My students seemed to respond positively to my teaching and it was both rewarding and exciting to watch their enjoyment and progress as they grew as young musicians. It seemed quite logical to follow up four years at RCM with a Cert Ed[4] course at Middlesex Polytechnic (now Middlesex University).

My first post was as a class music teacher in a high school, but within a year I had accepted the post of Head of Woodwind at Wells Cathedral School. The bulk of my career since then has been in Music Services, five years teaching woodwind as Assistant Area Director for West Berkshire and sixteen years as Head of Sefton Music Service.

The rewards and satisfaction of being an instrumental teacher have not diminished over the years. Although the progress of my career meant increased

---

[4] Certificate of Education. A teacher training course that led to qualified teacher status (QTS).

administration and management responsibilities, I was always able to teach young musicians and direct them in ensembles. Now, as Director of the RNCM Centre for Young Musicians,[5] I am helping to develop a new PGCE in Music with Specialist Instrumental Teaching in collaboration with Manchester Metropolitan University. I have the responsibility and opportunity to influence the next generation of instrumental teachers and I am confident that they will find their careers just as exciting and fulfilling.

Autonomy of instrumental teachers

As instrumental teachers in England do not have to teach the national curriculum they—or their managers if they do not work alone—have more autonomy than class teachers when it comes to devising and developing a programme of lessons.

How do instrumental teachers, with their greater autonomy than class teachers, shape their instrumental teaching? This section is from *Music in the School*, where it forms part of Chapter 6: 'Teaching instruments musically' (Mills 2005*b*: 82–91).

What should shape instrumental lessons? In 2001, 134 instrumental teachers working for eight local education authorities in England agreed to complete a questionnaire about instrumental teaching. These teachers mainly had several years' experience of teaching successfully in schools. Jan Smith and I wanted to know:

- what teachers believe makes instrumental teaching effective in schools
- what teachers believe makes instrumental teaching effective when students go on to study music in higher education
- how this all relates to factors including teachers' recollections of the instrumental lessons they received at school and in higher education, the courses that they have attended, and the lessons that they remember as 'special' from when they were students (Mills and Smith 2003).

Many of the teachers wrote at length, and gave us a great deal of very high-quality material when responding to our questions. First, we asked them to write about the 'hallmarks' of effective instrumental teaching in schools, and effective instrumental teaching in higher education. It soon became clear that many teachers consider that the hallmarks of effective teaching in schools are

---

[5] The Royal Northern College of Music Centre for Young Musicians provides musical opportunities, including instrumental teaching, for students of school age.

different from those in higher education. For example, three teachers' responses were as shown in Table 2.

Note, for example, how two teachers refer to students having 'fun' when writing about effective teaching in schools, but none use this word when referring to effective teaching in higher education. The images of instrumental teachers that come to mind when I read Teacher A, B, and C's writing about schools are quite different from those that result from their writing about higher education.

We found this difference more generally within the responses of the 134 teachers. We coded the hallmarks that 134 teachers had identified, and then ranked them according to the total number of teachers who mentioned them. The table shows the 'top ten' hallmarks of effective teaching in schools, and effective teaching in higher education. Teachers believe that effective teaching in schools and higher education shares six hallmarks:

- *the teacher is knowledgeable.* Clearly, a teacher needs to be able to play the instrument that they are teaching, play it well, know what they do to play it well, and know some other ways—that may be more suited to one or more of their students—in which the instrument can be played well. There are some rare examples of students who become successful performers despite initially having a teacher who is not a good player, perhaps because the teacher is caring and encouraging and provides an environment in which a child's musical talent may be developed (Kemp and Mills 2002). For example, a clarinet student at the Royal College of Music recently told me that his first clarinet teacher, from whom he learnt for several years, had 'failed Grade 3'. But it takes a rare commitment to music, and a considerable amount of luck, to survive teaching that is quite as unknowledgeable as that. It may be no coincidence that the clarinettist who is now at the RCM joined a band when he had been learning clarinet for only a few weeks, and played alongside young musicians with more technical accomplishment than his teacher.

- *the teacher is a good communicator.* The issues here include that teaching needs to be presented in a manner that is appropriate to students' age. Harald Jørgensen (2001) investigated whether starting to learn an instrument at a young age ultimately led students to achieve higher standards, and discovered that an early start was advantageous only if one was lucky enough to choose a teacher who is skilled socially and musically. Many teachers are effective at explaining material to younger students. They have learnt to build relationships between what they want to teach children, and what the children already know. They do not underestimate the enormous

Table 2 Three teachers' hallmarks of effective instrumental teaching at school and in higher education

	School	Higher Education
Teacher A	Trying to lay the foundations for good technique and habits, while trying to keep lessons fun and interesting. Pupils should enjoy playing but expect to work hard, practise regularly at home and be shown how to do it (Do we show pupils how to practise enough?). They should learn to play fluently and expressively and have opportunities to perform solos, play in small groups, and in larger orchestras.	The development of a good technique as a means to play musically and expressively. To encourage exploration and initiative but give clear guidance on how to work and what is expected. To play and perform as much as possible in different sorts of music—solo, ensemble, orchestra, other.
Teacher B	Enthusiasm. Able to relate to children. Sensitive to individual needs. Use of popular tunes. Encouragement.	Technique. Variety and breadth of styles. Encourage individual interpretation.
Teacher C	Being approachable, communicating well. Making lessons fun. Giving good descriptive teaching both for technical and musical ideas. Allowing the pupil some autonomy in the way their lesson goes—e.g. would you like to play top or bottom in the duet?—What do you feel needs most attention in this piece? Teaching with humour. Also, play and response work is brilliant for keeping people responsive and aurally switched on.	Giving good background to the style/character of a piece. Clear, easily understood technique teaching that enables the pupil to take off with their own musical ideas. Supporting the pupil and giving positive support when they experiment musically.

potential of children as learners, and so do not 'dumb down'—oversimplify—their teaching to the point that it makes little sense, and children feel patronized. They learn the routines through which children are accustomed to being managed by teachers at school, and so do not misinterpret children's uncertainty about what the teacher wants them to do as naughtiness, or inability to concentrate. When the instrumental teaching services run by local education authorities were first inspected, inspectors found that instrumental teachers who are qualified to work as class music teachers were more likely to communicate effectively in ways such as these (Mills 2000*a*).

◆ *the teaching is matched to what the students need.* This means that students are presented with challenges that build on their learning, are attainable, and feel worthwhile. In class lessons in all subjects, it is now very common for teachers to explain at the beginning of each lesson what students are intended to learn, and to review with students at the end of each lesson whether or not the 'learning objectives' have been achieved. Some instrumental teachers do this too, and this can help to build bridges between class music and instrumental music, and encourage students to focus on the progress that they are making. An example of one of the more mundane learning objectives for a lesson for some violinists might be 'to learn to play two octaves of the scale of G major, slurred, with two notes to a bow'.

In seeking to match their teaching to the musical needs of students, many teachers try to provide much more than instrumental skills through their instrumental lessons. Doris da Costa (1994) argues that it can be helpful to support instrumental lessons with classes for listening to music recordings. *A Common Approach 2002* (FMS et al. 2002*a*), includes 'out of lesson listening' in addition to composition and improvisation. Fred Seddon and Susan O'Neill (2001) found that, even when instrumental students had not composed as part of their instrumental lessons, their compositions had higher 'technical complexity' than those of students who had not taken instrumental lessons. In addition, the students who had taken instrumental lessons tended to give higher self-evaluations for 'how good their composition sounded'.

The teacher's learning strategies need to be matched to the students too. We do not all learn in the same way, or in the same way all the time. Siw Nielsen (1999) has investigated the learning strategies used by pipe organ students in higher education, and argues for 'strategies to direct attention to the task at hand' and 'strategies to secure efficient use of time' to be taught more extensively in instrumental music at school, in the same way as they are taught in other subjects including mathematics and reading.

Matched teaching is not the same as teaching that suggests that there is only one correct solution to a problem with technique or performance. Teachers who teach in this way may argue that students need to be able to 'control' a piece before they can 'shape' it. They often appear to be very knowledgeable, and are sometimes very popular with their students, and their students' parents. However, they do not help students to develop their autonomy as learners, or to understand the extensive range of approaches that may be used to interpret a piece of music, or solve the technical problems implied by particular interpretations. If the approach of 'first get the notes right and then add the expression' ever had its day, this has now passed.

◆ *the teacher is positive, and praises students.* Where the music provision in a school is weak, students may feel that their teachers do not praise them adequately for work done well. Being positive with students, and praising them when appropriate, is important at all stages of instrumental teaching, but perhaps particularly when students are going through periods of potentially disruptive transition, such as moving from primary school to secondary school. While secondary schools can provide students with wonderful educational opportunities that could not possibly be available in primary schools, because of their smaller size, the sheer fact of changing school can lead students to reappraise their commitment to instrumental lessons. There is more homework at secondary school, the journey to school often takes longer, there are new friendships to be built, it may take a few weeks for the secondary school to set up a timetable for instrumental teaching, and the instrumental teacher available at secondary school may be someone whom students have not met previously. The *Young People and Music Participation Project*, which included 1,209 students in their last year at 36 primary schools (O'Neill 2002), and which tracked many of them through to the end of their first year at secondary school, reported that the students who continued instrumental lessons often had greater confidence in their ability, and an instrumental teacher who communicated belief in the students' potential to do well at music.

◆ *the teacher provides plenty of opportunities for students to perform.* Students opt for instrumental lessons because they want to play an instrument. The teachers who answered the questionnaire recognized this by endorsing lessons where students have plenty of time to make music—and where issues, including some technical problems that need to be resolved through talk, or away from the instrument, are dealt with very efficiently. The teachers also approved of lessons where students are allowed to play whole sections—or even whole pieces—for detailed appraisal: students are not stopped routinely every time that something goes wrong.

- *the teacher gives plenty of attention to the development of instrumental technique.* Teachers felt strongly that there was no place for teaching that overlooks the development of a good technique. Technique needs to be considered dynamically, with students and teachers routinely diagnosing the student's technical problems and working out ways of solving them in a manner that is appropriate to students' physique. Part of this is the adjustment of technique as students grow. A right arm position that works well for a violinist who has just acquired a full-size bow, for example, may work less well when they have grown another six inches taller.

Interestingly, there are four hallmarks of effective teaching in schools that teachers mention less frequently in respect of higher education—see Table 3:

- *the teacher is enthusiastic.* Enthusiasm is infectious: enthusiastic teaching helps to sustain the enthusiasm that students brought to their first instrumental lesson, even at stages when they feel that progress is hard won.

- *the teacher is inspiring.* Teachers wrote of trying to inspire students through their own playing, and their own love of playing, and music in general.

- *the teacher is patient.* Teachers wrote of needing to be able to draw on a range of learning strategies, in order to help students make progress—to try different ways of helping students to learn if they are not successful initially.

- *lessons are fun for students.* The role of fun in instrumental lessons has sometimes been underestimated in the past—but the teachers who completed our questionnaire were clear that fun is essential. Fun lessons build on students' interest and enthusiasm. They are worth attending. It is interesting that the teachers mentioned 'fun' much less frequently in respect of higher education. Perhaps this was because they assume that students in higher education will bring their own 'fun' to instrumental lessons even if the teacher does not, or that instrumental lessons in higher education are always fun? The need to inject fun—as well as plenty of music—into lessons for students of school age forms part of the training as instrumental teachers that many students at music college receive. For example, fun is a central theme of *Spelrum*, a textbook used widely in Sweden and also in some other countries. The author, Robert Schenck,[6] draws a parallel between what he

---

[6] Robert Schenck is an instrumental teacher whose book *Spelrum: en metodikbok för sång- och instrumentalpedagoger* (2000*b*) has influenced instrumental teaching, and the training of instrumental teachers, particularly in Sweden. *Spelrum* is available in English as a manuscript entitled *At play: teaching musical instruments and the voice* (2000*a*). The idea that learning an instrument is about being 'at play' [personally], rather than solely 'playing' [music], is central to Schenck's book.

wanted his 13-year-old daughter to gain from her hobby of horse riding, and what he would want her to gain from learning an instrument:

Naturally I hoped that my daughter would learn to ride well, make friends, experience the trials and tribulations of dealing with live and powerful animals, and get fresh air and exercise. But what was it all worth, what would she learn, and how long would she keep it up, if she wasn't enjoying herself? Above all, I wanted her to have fun! (Schenck 2000*a*: 4)

It is difficult to see why these four hallmarks would not also be advantageous in instrumental lessons that take place in higher education.

There are also four hallmarks of effective teaching in higher education that teachers mention less frequently in respect of schools:

- the teacher develops students' individual voices
- the teacher teaches a wide repertoire of music
- the teacher has high expectations of students
- the teacher offers students advice about the development of their careers.

It would be wrong, however, to suggest that the first three of these, in particular, are not relevant to instrumental lessons in schools. A teacher with low musical expectations of students may assume that they will give up—with the result that they probably will! Or they may be unaware how much application even young students are expected to show in other subjects at school, for example in English and mathematics, and consequently not challenge them in their instrumental lessons. A wide repertoire of music is as important in school as in higher education, and built into the schemes of work used by several of the local education authority music services where the teachers work, with students learning to play popular melodies, songs from the shows, melodies from around the world, and specially composed music as well as arrangements of the classics. The development of musical autonomy, which encompasses the development of students' individual voices, is a theme throughout *A Common Approach 2002*, to which some of the teachers who took part in our survey contributed.

One explanation is that the teachers listed these three qualities less frequently because they are so widespread that they do not differentiate effective teaching from less effective teaching.

Another explanation relates to the different levels of experience from which instrumental teachers write about effective instrumental teaching in schools, and effective instrumental teaching in higher education. The teachers have all been trained to give instrumental lessons in schools. They have all been trained by the music services for which they work, and many of them also have Qualified Teacher Status (QTS), usually gained via a Postgraduate

Table 3 The 'top ten' hallmarks of effective teaching at school and in higher education

Ranking at school level	Hallmark	Ranking at HE level
1	Enthusiastic teacher*	(11)
2	Knowledgeable teacher	1
3.5	Communicative teacher	9.5
3.5	Fun for students*	(21.5)
5.5	Teaching matched to students	9.5
5.5	Praise/positive teacher	3
7	Performance opportunities	6
8	Technical focus	2
9.5	Inspirational teacher*	(15.5)
9.5	Patient teacher*	(29.5)
—	Development of individual voice	4
(11.5)	Wide repertoire	5
—	Teacher gives career advice	7
(21)	Teacher has high expectations	8

* Hallmarks that are in the 'top ten' for schools, but not HE

Certificate of Education, taken over a year on completion of a degree in music. However, training to teach instruments in higher education is much less widely spread, and so teachers must draw more heavily on their own experiences of being taught.

We asked teachers to write about the strengths and weaknesses of the instrumental teaching that they received at school and in higher education, and to comment on whether they thought that their approach to teaching had been influenced by the ways in which they were taught. Most thought that it had. Some teachers wrote only about trying to emulate the strengths of the teaching they had received, while others wrote only about trying to avoid the weaknesses, and a third group wrote on both of these subjects. Many teachers were keen to point out that they did not blindly teach students as they had been taught.

But one finding was that many teachers are still influenced, now, by the 'special' music lessons that they had when they were students. These lessons often had a sense of 'revelation' as teachers (when students) suddenly learnt something that helped them to move their playing into a new gear.

One teacher's special lesson was a 'masterclass' where she realized how much she could learn from watching her peers play, and analysing what they did well and what they could do even better, and noticing how the 'master' taking the session helped each student to make progress. This teacher now encourages children to comment on each other's playing, and suggest improvements, in many of her group lessons. What she found out about learning from one's peers is related to the observations of Janet Ritterman (2000) that former students of the Royal College of Music, describing their time there, frequently refer unprompted to what they have learnt about performance from contact with other students. This led Janet Ritterman to consider whether:

- the types of peer learning to which these students refer could be formalized, and if so how?
- the attitudes and approaches that students develop in relation to peer learning and performance might help to inform their studies in other areas of the curriculum.

Another teacher's special lesson taught her to listen more closely to her playing. Until then, she had not listened to her own playing much, because she was so busy trying to play the right notes at the right time. Her tutor played to her, one note at a time, and did not move on until he was told all about that one note: whether it was in tune, whether it was too loud, whether it sounded warm enough, and so on. When the teacher applied this to her own playing, she soon learnt to play with a much better sound, and much better tuning, than she had ever done before. So this teacher often includes short activities—or games—based on close listening in her lessons.

This close relationship between the special lessons that teachers recalled and their hallmarks may be related to what psychologists refer to as 'peak experience'. Although this term was initially used (e.g. Maslow 1954) in the 1950s to refer to the most wonderful experience of someone's life, it has more recently been used, for example by John Sloboda (2002) in reference to specific fields. Thus one might speak of a peak experience in music or, as here, a peak experience of being taught music.

One sometimes hears the anecdotal assertion that instrumental teachers simply teach as they were taught. Clearly, this is a myth, at least in the context of local education authority music services. Teachers appear to analyse the strengths and weaknesses of their various teachers and create their own teaching method that draws heavily also on other influences, including any initial training that they have received, and the in-service training provided formally by their employer and informally—for example through conversation with other teachers. However if, as it appears, a teacher's peak experience of being taught has a strong influence on their teaching style, it may be helpful for teachers to work on recalling their peak experience and analysing what made it so significant to them as learners. It may also be helpful for teachers to have the opportunity to recapture or update their peak experience, by getting involved in musical activities where they are taught, as well as teach.

One teacher's special lesson was rather different from the positive experiences described above. She was studying three instruments at music college—let us say that they were flute, violin, and piano—and her flute teacher complained that the student had not done enough flute practice since her previous lesson, and tried to order her to give up the violin. The student took umbrage at this, stormed out of the lesson, gave up the flute immediately, and says that she has never regretted this decision. Clearly, however, 'special' lessons of such negativity would rarely have such seemingly positive outcomes (Mills 2005*b*: 82–91).

On quality

> I firmly believe that it is really impossible to speak really deeply about music. All we can do then is speak about our reaction to the music.
>
> Daniel Barenboim, pianist and conductor, introduces the 2006 Reith Lectures (2006*a*)

Some might argue that it is as difficult to speak about music lessons as about music. But there are many professional circumstances in which we have no option but to try. In their quest for perfection, instrumental teachers continually ask themselves questions such as: 'What is the quality of my teaching? Was that last lesson any good? How could I make my teaching (even) better?'

Here, we consider what the results of inspections of music services can tell us about the quality of instrumental teaching, particularly in schools. We then consider some further issues relating to quality.

During 1999–2000, HM Inspectors of Schools (HMI), who work as part of Ofsted, carried out inspections of the instrumental teaching in a sample of over 20 LEA music services.[7] The first 11 of these inspections, alone, included

---

[7] Local Education Authorities (LEAs) subsequently became part of Local Authorities. Ofsted also inspected some music services in subsequent years, but these were 'good practice' inspections for which services were asked to select their best teaching, so that the work inspected was not intended to be, and cannot be taken to be, representative.

evaluation of 501 instrumental lessons (Mills 2000*a*). When a lesson is inspected, the inspector makes a series of judgements, including one that relates to the 'quality of teaching'. While the precise words that Ofsted, and earlier inspection systems, have used to define 'quality of teaching' have varied over time, the definitions have all shared the same principle, namely that teaching is judged by the extent to which it enables learning. Often, inspectors have been required to write a few words about, and make a numerical judgement on, the teaching in every lesson that they observed. In 1999–2000, Ofsted graded the quality of teaching on a 7-point scale running from outstanding (1), through good (3), to satisfactory (4), and very poor (7). While the grade given to the teaching of an individual lesson is important information, it does not give us the whole story of teachers' influence on students' learning. Each lesson is but a segment of a curriculum: the cumulative effect of lessons is crucial.

Fig. 2(a)(p. 54) shows that the proportion of lessons that were graded 'satisfactory or better' or 'good or better' varied quite widely between the first 16 music services that were inspected. Given that lessons were selected for inspection within each LEA to be as 'random' as possible, this suggests that the quality of instrumental lessons that students received varied widely around the country. For every 'satisfactory or better' lesson in LEA *P* there was 1.5 in LEA *A*. For every 'good or better' lesson in LEA *F* there were 4 in LEA *B*.

In fact, the quality of instrumental teaching can vary widely even within a single school. A teaching approach that meets the needs of one group of students can fail to meet the needs of a second group. Further, the quality of the work of two or more instrumental teachers who visit the same school can vary widely. And this can be the case even in schools where the instrumental teaching takes place in areas, such as a school hall, that senior teachers walk through routinely, so that it is difficult to countenance that they are not aware of any problems.

I visited a village primary school where a violin teacher and a drums teacher worked, one after the other, on the same day of the week, in the school hall. This was a high-achieving school in terms of mathematics and English, and also in other respects, and the headteacher had a reputation for insisting on high standards from his class teachers. He appeared to be less demanding of the quality expected from the work of at least one of the instrumental teachers who visited his school from the LEA music service, and who taught groups much smaller than those taught by his class teachers. He seemed reluctant to challenge the practice of a music teacher who he saw as possessing musical skills (but not pedagogical skills) that he lacked.

I observed two lessons: a violin lesson followed by one on drums.

The violin lesson was of magically high quality. A boy and a girl had been learning for only a few weeks. The boy had started first and the girl, who was two years younger, had joined him a couple of weeks later. Both of the students were playing with a lovely tone, beautifully in tune, and with a relaxed and free bowing arm. They really were playing violin. They had learnt some pieces, and scales, by ear, and had been shown how to relate some of them to staff notation. The teacher had asked them each to prepare a composition for homework. These drew upon the scales and pieces that had already been learnt, but also included new rhythms and phrase patterns. The teacher was enthusiastic about the compositions, and made one or two suggestions about how they could be developed, or notated in part, if the students wished. Indeed, the teacher was enthusiastic, and developmental in her approach, throughout the lesson. She had brought her violin with her, and was a role model of an enthusiastic, talented, and self-critical violinist. She used her time well, and divided it seamlessly between working with the students together, working with them individually (while the other student observed and commented), and supporting the students as they worked as a pair.

The drums lesson was rather different. Given that drum kits are large and heavy, it was reasonable that there was only one kit there for everyone—three students and the teacher—to share. It was less reasonable that only the teacher and one of the students got to play it. (The teacher volunteered that the student who played was the 'most able'—this was no wonder, given the preferential support he was receiving!) The other two boys had practice pads, and were only allowed to play these occasionally. No wonder that one of the boys became frustrated, started to play rather more frequently than the teacher wanted, and was reprimanded. I would not have been surprised had they both acted in this way.

Fig. 2(b)–(e) relate to just the first 11 music services that were inspected. Fig. 2(d) shows that the quality of the teaching generally became higher as students became older. For every satisfactory or better lesson for students aged 7–11, there were (proportionately) 1.2 such lessons for students aged 16–18. For every good or better lesson for students aged 7–11, there were 1.5 such lessons for students aged 16–18. At the time, inspectors suggested that one of the main factors here was that some instrumental teachers had low expectations of younger students. Instrumental teachers had often not had opportunity to take part in the general training—for example in numeracy and literacy—that schoolteachers had received, and were sometimes unaware of younger students' capabilities in all fields.

Fig. 2(b) shows that the lessons taught by teachers with QTS were, on average, of higher quality although there were, of course, exceptions to this general rule: teachers who taught exceptionally well despite not being qualified, and some teachers with QTS who were very weak. The differences were stronger in

(a) The quality of instrumental teaching in 16 LEAs

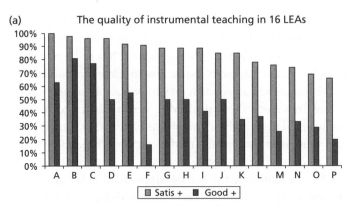

(b) Quality of teaching by those with, and without, QTS (qualified teacher status)

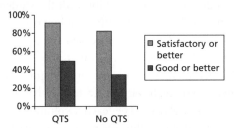

(c) A closer look at instrumental teaching in the 7–11 and 11–14 age groups

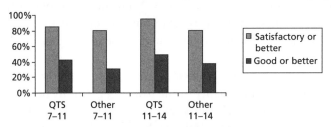

(d) Quality of instrumental teaching in different age groups

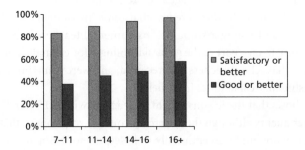

Continued

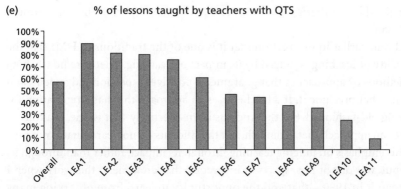

Fig. 2(a)–(e) Ofsted inspection of the instrumental teaching in a sample of over 20 LEA music services

the case of lessons that were good or better. For every 14 good or better lessons taught by an instrumental teacher with QTS there were, proportionately, only 10 such lessons taught by teachers without qualifications. For every 11 satisfactory or better lessons taught by a teacher with QTS, there were 10 lessons taught by a teacher without QTS.

Fig. 2(c) unpacks this for students aged 7–11, and students aged 11–14.[8] Lessons for students aged 7–11 were 28 per cent less likely to be good or better if they were taught by a teacher without QTS (24 per cent for students aged 11–14). Lessons for students aged 7–11 were 5 per cent less likely to be satisfactory or better if they were taught by a teacher without QTS (15 per cent for students aged 11–14). At the time, inspectors suggested that these differences often showed through particularly in instrumental teachers' approach to managing students, and students' time. Teachers without QTS, who may not have received training in managing students, often related well—on a social level—to younger students, but sometimes found it difficult to convert this into 'good' teaching and learning. The same teachers were sometimes over-controlling of their older students, as though they expected the volunteer students who attend instrumental lessons suddenly to start misbehaving wildly without provocation. I explained earlier (p. 45) some further respects in which teachers with QTS generally communicated more effectively with students.

Fig. 2(e) simply shows that the proportion of lessons taught by teachers without QTS varies widely between music services. The 150 music services in

---

[8] We were able to carry out this analysis more robustly in these age ranges, as these were where most lessons were observed.

England have differing traditions and policies in respect of the appointment of staff.

I said earlier in this section that it is one of the traditions of HMI that the quality of teaching is judged by its impact on learning. There are no teaching methods or approaches that guarantee a positive inspection judgement, and none that preclude it. If a teacher uses an approach that has a reputation for being old-fashioned, but the students learn effectively, that is fine. If a teacher uses an approach that is modish, but the students do not learn, that is not fine. This emphasis on judging teaching through its impact, rather than through its input, was one of the aspects of inspection that drew me to this work when I began it in 1990—that and the opportunity to learn from observing many other teachers at work.

But I digress.

I have said that inspectors judge teaching through its impact on learning. But surely there are some teaching approaches that could never work? Clearly, lessons have to provide environments for students that are safe. But, once they have assured the safety of their students and themselves, teachers have much latitude about how they proceed. Take, for example, this fragment from a lesson that Yehudi Menuhin reported that he received from one of his earlier violin teachers, when learning to play with vibrato: '[My teacher shouted] "Vibrate! Vibrate!" with never a clue given how to do it' (Menuhin 1976).

My guess is that most of the readers of this book would not advocate simply shouting 'do X' as the most efficacious approach to teaching a new skill, X, to a student. I do not feel that I, personally, would have learned well from such teaching. And in his autobiography, *Unfinished Journey*, Menuhin wrote of this approach to teaching vibrato as though he disapproved of it. But while I would agree that this approach is unlikely to prove satisfactory in the case of most violin students, it appears to have worked well for Menuhin, and so a notional inspector in the room for Menuhin's vibrato 'lesson' might have given it a favourable inspection grade.

Following observation of a large number of instrumental lessons, I have come to the conclusion that many instrumental teachers who are particularly expert performers, including a high proportion of those who work in conservatoires, sell themselves short when talking about their instrumental teaching. Because they communicate through music so effectively, they have not needed to develop the verbal language about teaching that the rest of us take for granted. When pressed to talk about how they teach, they may overlook features that are striking to an observer. In order to find out about the quality of instrumental lessons, we need to visit some and take a look. When coming to conclusions about the quality of instrumental teaching, we cannot rely entirely upon what teachers say about their teaching. We can rely even less upon (usually derogatory) anecdotal views that instrumental teachers 'teach as they were taught', and so forth. (And, for what it is worth, my experience is that, in general, they don't.)

The quality of music education is not always as it might first seem. In particular, views of whether specific schools are 'musical' or not (whatever this means) cannot always be relied upon. Susan O'Neill and I (Mills and O'Neill 2002) investigated the 'quality of provision' in music for 11 year olds in ten primary schools, and found that this was highest in some schools that were not necessarily perceived as 'musical' in their local community, but where teachers with a range of roles in music—class teachers, subject leaders, instrumental teachers—were working together effectively. At the heart of this group of teachers were class teachers who may or may not have been music graduates, but who certainly knew the students in their class very well indeed:

primary students can sometimes be served better by a teacher who knows them well, rather than a teacher who knows music well, but does not know them at all. Even outstanding primary music teachers tend to become a little less effective when they work with a class other than their own. (Mills 2005b: 28)

This integration of instrumental and class music can also be generated in secondary schools. There are countless examples of schools where the instrumental and class music teachers work together effectively to this end. When I worked as a full-time head of music in a secondary school and (voluntary) instrumental teacher there, it was easy for me to integrate my instrumental teaching with other work at school. At the first secondary school, all my violin and viola students (along with everyone who I was also teaching percussion, recorder, singing) took part in performances of Britten's *Noye's Fludde*. At the second school, there were more ensembles and a greater choice of groups that students could join. None of the students who took instrumental lessons from me took them in isolation from other instrumental activities.

This degree of integration is harder to emulate for teachers who visit schools only to give instrumental lessons, or who teach students in studios or in the students' homes. When students at the RCM were asked to rank 12 careers in music according to how much they would like to do them, they chose 'instrumental teacher working at home' ahead of 'instrumental teacher working in schools'. As well as limiting their ability to build links between their students' instrumental lessons and their students' other experience of music, this also may decrease their chances of taking up the work (teacher in a university or music college) where many of them seek to spend most time beyond their first choice of 'performer or composer'. RCM alumni who have returned to the college as teachers mainly built up their early teaching experience in institutions, such as schools or local music services, rather than at home. They report that the advantages of working in institutions included the fact that administrative demands were reduced (for example because there was often an administrator who organized timetables and payment), and there were chances to consult with more experienced teachers who were a ready source of advice about matters including repertoire or approaches to teaching (Mills 2003; 2004b; 2005a).

Perceptions that quality in education has changed over time are not always real. In contemporary anecdotal writing, and also on television, it is common to find the 1950s being cited as a time of educational excellence—frequently on the somewhat questionable grounds that some students were taught in selective schools (from which it follows that others were not). Yet there was actually so much criticism of education in the 1950s that James Petch was moved to write: 'Education is one of the professions in which pessimism tends to be an occupational risk, and there is no sure factual antidote which can be prescribed' (Joint Matriculation Board 1956: 6). I have argued elsewhere that, at any point in time: 'it seems likely that there are facets of education which *are* improving, and facets which *are* deteriorating, and facets which only appear to be moving in one of the two directions, [and that] many find improvement harder to recognise than decline' (Mills 1996: 37).

Until a few years ago, I might have argued that instrumental tuition was a rare educational area in which some practitioners were perhaps inclined to be a little complacent. Ironically, as professional development has become a more common feature of instrumental tuition in all contexts, so that instrumental teaching has become more open to view, it has, perhaps, joined the many areas of education that are now more likely to be subject to over-criticism. There is much to commend in respect of the instrumental teaching that takes place in many educational contexts. There is also scope to disseminate this effective teaching more widely, so that more instrumental teachers know of it, know that they are part of it, learn from it, and contribute to the debate about what makes instrumental teaching effective.

Chapter 4

Why take instrumental lessons?

On Tuesday I have a cool piano lesson that's the best thing of the day.

Anthony, age 9

I have guitar lessons which are good and fun, and I have just learnt how to play Jail House Rock!

Steven, age 14

I know I'm not a freak anymore, that there are people who feel like I do.

We wake up to music, we listen to music all day and we fall asleep to music. It makes you happy, it makes you sad, it reminds you of old boyfriends. We've had the chance to do stuff we never would otherwise. Without this I'd be so bored, I just look forward to Wednesdays.

Participant in Youth Music project

My life would be empty without music because I would have nothing. I listen to it all the time and I play three instruments; guitar, piano and bass guitar. I really enjoy working on them and perfecting songs, writing my own material.

Participant in Youth Music project, aged 15

The usual sad stories of being first made to sing, and then made not to sing, at school . . .

John Holt writes of children who are judged 'unmusical' at school
(Holt 1978: 100)

Anthony and Steven, students at Christ Church Cathedral School in Oxford, had written diaries for researchers of the shape of their Tuesdays. Music shone through the day of both boys. The pleasure that they derive from their instrumental lessons comes through clearly beyond the factual diaries—or lists—that were all they were asked to provide, and Steven is also fired up by a particular new addition to his repertoire.

Two participants in Youth Music, quoted above, are striking examples of students for whom music pervades their lives. Some, possibly all, of their musical engagement is being nurtured by activities outside school.

The John Holt fragment is less happy, and reminds us of how young people's interest in the music that we want to offer them can be destroyed through procedures that are insensitive. Students have been made to sing in a compulsory audition for a singing group that they may, or may not, have wished to join—and then are made not to sing as their singing was deemed to be inadequate. Just imagine how good that makes them feel!

Of course, students can be discouraged as readily outside, as inside, school.

In this chapter we consider the question 'why take instrumental lessons?' under several (loosely organized) headings:

- Why take instrumental lessons rather than teach yourself?
- A teacherly view
- The learners' and carers' view
- The advanced western classical learner's view

Finally, we reflect on the emphasis on performance that is often provided by instrumental lessons, and consider some of the challenges, and not only opportunities, that this provides.

Why take instrumental lessons rather than teach yourself?

The question 'why take instrumental lessons?' is not the same as 'why learn an instrument?' Many people learn to play instruments without taking lessons from teachers.

Larry Adler, legendary mouth organ soloist, worked out for himself what mouth organs could do, got on with ensuring that he could cause them to do this reliably, and built an extraordinary repertoire about his, and the mouth organ's, capabilities. Some years later, the mouth organ—or harmonica—is becoming better established as an instrument on which one might take lessons. In 2006 Philip Achille—Youth World Champion of chromatic harmonica—made it through to the quarter final of the 2006 BBC Young Musician of the Year Competition, which has traditionally been the province of western orchestral instruments and piano.

Countless children of the 1950s and beyond have learnt to strum on guitar from tutor books including Bert Weedon's *Play in a Day* (Weedon 1957). John

Holt is an example of an adult who learnt in this way. He acquired his first instrument, a guitar, in 1951, at the age of 28:

All of a sudden I wanted a guitar. For a while the idea seemed extravagant, as I still had very little money. Finally one day I walked into Schirmer's music store and asked what guitars cost. The man in the store said I could get one very cheap, but that it would not be much fun to play and might give trouble. He recommended a Martin, for one hundred dollars. He showed to me. It looked lovely, sounded even better. I'll take it, I said, bought some little instruction and a book of Burl Ives songs, gave him a check, and took the guitar home.

I loved that instrument. From the instruction book I learned how to make a few of the simpler chords. I spent much time just slowly strumming these chords, enjoying their rich, mellow sound, and the feeling of the guitar vibrating against me. Sometimes I would come home late at night from a committee or board meeting or a lecture, keyed up and agitated, in no mood for sleep. I would take out the guitar, look at it, admire the pretty, different-coloured woods, hold it up to the light to make sure that the finish was unblemished, wipe off a finger-print here and there, enjoy the look and smell and feel of it. Then I would play the few chords I knew, and the sound and vibrations were immensely relaxing and soothing. (Holt 1978: 88)

Lucy Green (2001: 86, 84) has written of an acclaimed popular drummer who says that he developed his undoubtedly fine technique by 'just [doing] what came naturally', and of a popular guitarist who began his technical development on his own, but who took advice from a friend who plays classical guitar before turning professional. Lynne Buckley (Mills 2005a: 11) (see p. 11) has written of how the gospel singers among the students at her school honed and developed their techniques and performances collectively. NIAS (1997: 11) has written of Cheryl, aged 13, who sings, and has learnt to play the accordion, guitar, whistle, and harp by sitting alongside her father in a folk band where she has already become the best player. We can probably all think of examples of people who have 'taught themselves' to play instruments, whether or not this might be thought to be the 'authentic' way of learning the instrument and style or genre in question. For what it is worth, I took lessons on violin—in the conventional classical way—from the age of 11 to 21, and singing lessons from the age of 19 to 21, but learnt to play the other instruments that I play essentially on my own, having developed a habit of seeking advice from experts, initially my mother, from an early age. For example, I 'taught myself' descant recorder when I was 7, and French horn in my late twenties. Perhaps I did miss out on some nuances of technique by operating in this way. Perhaps not. But I became able to play the repertoire that I really wanted to play, and make the quality of sound that I wanted to make, rather earlier than was usual if one had a teacher and weekly lessons. This was motivating for me. And I learnt a lot about how I learn that I continue to apply in other contexts.

Different ways of learning an instrument bring different advantages and disadvantages, and there are different ways of learning on one's own, just as different experiences flow from working with different teachers. I would be foolish to pretend that my piano playing, for example, has the technical facility or security that it might have developed had I learnt from a teacher who worked me progressively through a systematic sequence of scales, studies, and pieces. But the advantages of learning as I have include being able to sight-read (because I have never done much 'practice'), and to work out quickly which notes to leave out of a badly transcribed piano accompaniment (because I simply would not be able to play them). I also value the musical pleasure that flows from being confident to buy the music of almost anything that I want to play from a music shop, work out how to play the easier bits, and then join them up with the more challenging bits. And it is perhaps telling that I can often 'improvise' on the violin—for which I had lessons and teachers—only through working out the staff notation of what I am going to play in my mind's eye, and then playing it. And, importantly, I still love playing piano, including learning new pieces. Perhaps the piano lessons that could have made a much better technician of me would have turned me into a concert pianist . . . Or perhaps they might have dispirited me and led to me 'giving up'.

Methods of learning instruments other than through attending regular lessons with a teacher are not necessarily 'easier', or fraught with lower 'standards' (whatever we mean by either of these). Trevor Wiggins (1996: 24) has written frankly of the challenges that he found in learning Ghanaian drumming while in Ghana:

My version of knowing is that I have a complete mental image (wrong word!) of how it should sound and I consider this to be separate from the skills needed to perform it. For my teacher, the two are totally integrated. The internalising of the music, by its nature, implies the skills.

I found that 'teaching myself' instruments including French horn, trombone, folk guitar, classical guitar, piano, harpsichord, viol, viola, and electric bass required me to develop skills in evaluation, self-analysis, and problem-solving that I simply did not have on violin or as a singer, where, for several years, there had been an authoritative teacher on hand telling me what to 'do'. This sense of authority was particularly strong with violin, where my 'technique' was remodelled from scratch by each of the three teachers whom I was assigned successively in each of my three undergraduate years. I began each October with the bowing-arm, and so forth, that looked quite like those of my previous teacher, and ended each June with a technique that looked quite like that of the teacher whom I was about to lose—but that oddly never had quite the same aural effect. On all these other instruments, it was up to me to listen closely to the sounds that I was making, analyse carefully and improve how I was using my body, and seek to integrate sound and action in some sustainable and profitable way. I found this most instructive and satisfying and, in due course, it led me to question aspects of my violin technique that I wished that I had questioned much earlier. I have written elsewhere (Mills 1986) of my realization, at the sadly late age of 28, that I found it difficult to produce an even vibrato throughout the fingers of my left hand because my index finger is longer than usual, so that the hand position that had worked well for my teachers—who may well all have had index fingers of more usual length[1]—did not work well for me. Devising a new hand position for myself, and learning how to use it whatever I was playing, took only a few months.

Some learners prefer to learn on their own because the teaching they receive does not work out:

Matt, age 13, plays guitar. Yes, he used to take guitar lessons, but they cost £160 a year, and were a waste of money, because he feels that he did not learn anything. He refers to his former guitar teacher as 'the man with the book'.

Matt's guitar lessons seem to have been shaped by the tutor book that his teacher chose for them to work through. Matt clearly had very little respect for this approach. It was probably a notation-centred tutor book, whereas Matt was interested in playing MUSIC. Matt feels that he made progress more rapidly once his lessons ended, since when he has learnt by playing alone, or with his friends. (Mills 2005b: 82)

Turning to a musician who is better known than Matt, Larry Adler has also provided a graphic account of instrumental lessons going wrong. After several years of taking piano lessons he progressed, at the age of 11, to the Peabody Conservatoire of Music in Baltimore. After two terms, he was required to give a student recital. He prepared a Grieg Waltz, based on a recording by Rachmaninov:

The supervisor . . . eyed me sternly through her pince-nez as I sat down at the piano, and said: 'And what are we going to play, my little man?' I know I was pint-sized, but

---

[1] The anatomist Frederick Wood Jones (1941) coined the term 'digital formula' to refer to the relative length of an individual's fingers (or toes) on either hand (or foot). Most people are thought to have an I < R (index finger less than ring finger) on both of their hands, and I replicated this result in a sample of 100 medical students at the University of Oxford (Mills 1983). However, I also found that the less usual left hand 'formula' of I > R was more prevalent among a sample of instrumentalists at specialist music schools or in professional orchestras—unless they were violinists or viola players. I do not believe that anyone needs a particular 'digital formula' in order to succeed (whatever we mean by this) on an instrument that they particularly want to play. But where we are learning from instrumental teachers, we need them to analyse our technique in terms of how it works for us, rather than how it might have worked for them with their doubtless differing shape.

goddammit, *we* weren't going to play anything. *I* was, and I didn't like being patronized. To hell with the Grieg waltz . . . I changed into a rip-roaring version of 'Yes, We Have No Bananas' . . . She stopped me after twelve bars. 'Thank you. That will do. We have heard *quite* enough!' She sent me home, and followed it up next morning with a letter to my parents telling them to keep me there. I was expelled. (Adler 1994: 22–3)

This is anecdotal writing, to which the supervisor may not have had the opportunity to contribute her side of the story . . . Nevertheless, it provides food for thought.

Of course, learning without a teacher is not always free of problems. John Holt writes of how he did not spot the so-called *accidentals*—in this case just a few sharps and flats—written in the staff notation of the tutor book from which he taught himself guitar:

By playing all the songs as if they were in C, I must have changed a few of them in slight but interesting ways. One of my favourites was The Colorado Trail. Some time later I heard a recording of Burl Ives singing it, and thought, 'that's funny, he doesn't sing it the way it's written in his song book.' It did not occur to me that *I* had sung it wrong. Actually, I liked my rather melancholy minor or modal version better than his (correct) version on the record. 'Why did he change it?', I wondered. (Holt 1978: 88–9)

My husband, David Acheson, was taught mistakenly by his father to tune the Spanish guitar that he received at the age of 12 rather like a mandolin: in perfect fourths throughout and not with the customary major third between the second and third strings. I say 'mistakenly' with some reservations because guitars may, of course, be tuned in many different ways, but the issue here was that the 'fourths' guitar was not aligned with the guitar tutor book that had also been provided. When David placed his left-hand fingers in position for his first ever chord (C major), as shown in the guitar tutor book, and strummed down through the strings, the result sounded ghastly. (In addition to the expected notes of C, E, and G, the chord will have contained the notes C# and F!) David had a lot of respect for his father, assumed that the tutor book was in error, and threw it away. He gave up on chords, and became fluent in picking out the melodies of popular songs by ear on his (idiosyncratically tuned) guitar.

Both of these stories—one relating to an adult beginner and the other to a child beginner—have happy endings. John Holt sorted out his problem with sharps and flats, and in due course moved on also to flute and cello. David Acheson learnt to tune his guitar more conventionally from a friend at university, and still draws on his melodic facility in arrangements and compositions that now also include chords.

Of course, for every one of these success stories, there may be several examples of people attempting to teach themselves an instrument, and giving up, despondent, through lack of progress. But the same, sadly, is true also of those who begin their instrumental learning by taking lessons from a teacher.

And it is possible for learners who begin self-taught, to continue effectively with a sensitive teacher. Lucy Green (2001) has written of a guitarist who sought specific advice from a classical player before 'going professional'. John Holt, on moving to Boston, sought out a flute teacher at the New England Conservatory of Music:

[Bill] was (still is) a very friendly, pleasant, easygoing, good natured man, just the person I needed to help start me on this journey of exploration and adventure. We introduced ourselves, he asked a few questions about myself and musical background, and we talked a bit. Soon I felt at ease. He asked me to play a scale. I played it as I had been playing it by myself, as a collection of notes, none having anything to do with any other. Bill said, more or less, 'Well, that's all right, you can lay the notes. But there are big holes between the notes. Now try to make the notes longer, make each note join into the next, make them sound like a piece of music.' This idea of legato playing, of making everything, even scales, sound like music (which they are) was one of the first things Bill had me work on.

Another good thing about his teaching was that from the beginning he had me work on real music, good music. He did have me get an exercise book, by Taffanel and Gaubert, with the impressive title, *Grands Exercises Journaliers de Mécanisme*, rather lamely translated 'Big Daily Finger Exercises'. The first piece we worked on was a Handel sonata, first the slow movement, then the quicker last movement. Soon after that he had me start on a much bigger piece, the Suite for Flute and Strings in A minor by Telemann, a famous and very lovely work. (Holt 1978: 121–2)

Here we have an instrumental teacher who does not shirk his responsibilities to guide his student's technique, and builds on it with a repertoire that motivates and challenges their musical development.

A teacherly view

In *Music in the School* I wrote of children who were leading active musical lives, but who were not taking instrumental lessons. Here I focus on just three of these children—Alan, Amber, and Amy—and consider speculatively how taking instrumental lessons might, or might not, add to their musical lives. What might these particular children hope to gain from instrumental lessons should they take them in the future? First the children:

Alan, aged six, moves stealthily across the classroom. He is the Wolf creeping out of the deep, dark forest. As he creeps, he makes music: a pattern of mysterious taps and scraping sounds which tell us that the Wolf and the forest are sinister and fearful. No-one has instructed him: Alan chose the drum himself and decided for himself how the Wolf's music should go. As he creeps slowly across the room, he is lost in the world of his imagination, intensified by the music he is making. (Paynter and Aston 1970: 1)

Alan touched the hearts of music educators around the world when John Paynter and Peter Aston opened their groundbreaking book, *Sound and Silence* (1970), with this account of his Wolf. Alan also opened some minds, and pricked some consciences because, actually, he is not unusual. I would guess that we have all—for example as parent or teacher—observed children working with confidence, imagination, and autonomy to produce their equivalent of his Wolf. We will also have seen much younger children working imaginatively with simple music-making materials—cardboard boxes, whatever, it does not matter—to produce musical structures that they develop and, in many cases, revise . . . Every one of us is born with the potential to make our own music.

In a Reith lecture given in 2006 Daniel Barenboim (2006*b*) observed that the human foetus has aural acuity from 45 days of gestation, and argued that this acuity was wasted as children are born into a musically impoverished environment. Sandra Trehub, experimental psychologist at the University of Toronto, countered what she saw as the simplicity of his message:

I would say that infants are intensely engaged by music, and when their mothers . . . mothers all over the world, informally sing to them, and they sing expressively . . . often without training and so on but the expressiveness and sincerity of those performances is absolutely captivating for infants. And what you see really is that as children enter whatever you want to call it, the public music machine or the music lesson industry, some of that starts fading away. But you have intense passion for music early in life.

and Barenboim largely accepted her point.

Some of us have our enthusiasm for music stamped out of us. A music education that is too heavily structured can be as damaging as no music education at all in this respect.

In *Music in the School* I speculated on what Alan might have gone on to do:

He will, I guess, turn 40 soon. Did he receive a school music education that built on his Wolf experience at the age of 6? Or was his creative and holistic approach to music curtailed by a teacher who taught him as though he was an empty bucket to be filled, either when he was at primary or secondary school? Or did he have some of those narrow sort of instrumental lessons that discourage you from doing anything except playing the notes on a printed page for years on end? Is he a fulfilled musician—not necessarily a professional one—who still loves making music, or a narrowly trained instrumentalist who wishes that someone had taught him to play by ear and improvise? Or did he give it all up years ago, and now consider himself to be 'tone-deaf' or 'unmusical'? (Mills 2005*b*: 26–7)

In other words, did Alan become one of John Holt's students who were 'made to sing, and then made not to sing' (see beginning of this chapter). I do hope not.

I guess that we will never know what really happened to Alan. But were he 6 now, and had I some sort of responsibility for his music education, I have to say that I would not presently be rushing out to initiate instrumental lessons for him. If Alan somehow came up with a related idea for himself—perhaps by saying that he wanted to join in activities offered optionally at school, such as a singing club or chance to learn violin or recorder—then fine. I would be content for him to give them a try, but would want to monitor these experiences, and check that they were not closing in the wonderfully open approach to music that Alan has at present. There is still plenty of time left for Alan to take instrumental lessons, if he wishes, as he grows older. Nobody needs to start lessons on any instrument by the age of 6 if they are to 'succeed', whatever we mean by this.

Thinking more broadly, in the short term I would want Alan to continue developing his musicianship much as he is organizing this for himself now. Perhaps Alan will create further pieces of music theatre. Or do the Wolf again. Or do the Wolf differently. Or even do the Wolf again in a way that we do not think is quite as good as the first time. Or perhaps he will decide, for himself, to move on to a song, or an instrumental piece without movement. Yes, I will make sure that he has the time, space, and materials (including instruments and other sound makers) needed for this work. Yes, I will encourage him if he says that he wants to try developing some music with other children. Yes, I may even encourage him to listen to some extracts from recordings, or even entire pieces, that remind me of his own music—and see what he says about them, or how he responds in other ways. (I am thinking here of picking up on Alan's structural or timbral ideas, for example, not music nominally about Wolves such as Prokofiev's *Peter and the Wolf*). But I would try hard not to force any of this. To draw a somewhat primitive analogy with the sweet corn seedlings that I am presently growing on my windowsill, I would risk stunting his musical root growth, and threaten his entire musical future, were I to transplant him into my vegetable plot just yet. In the meantime he needs the musical equivalents of water, sunlight, and someone who is taking an interest.

I would be seeking—in so far as this is ever possible—to facilitate, rather than guide, steer, or direct, Alan's progress. This he is already organizing effectively for himself. Let us leave him to continue to do this for a while, and take stock (with apologies for the pun) later.

Amber [aged 5] was reading a book on *Peter Rabbit*. She delivered the story in an animated voice with speech inflections noticeably different from the ones she used in her normal conversations. At the point in the story where Peter Rabbit met Winnie-the-Pooh, Amber shifted abruptly to sing a song, *Winnie the Pooh*. After singing several phrases, Amber continued to tell the story. To build up climax and anticipation, Amber slowed down her speech and whispered 'a . . . big . . . black . . . wolf' in long sounds; to keep the intensity, Amber continued to whisper as she described how the big black wolf chased Peter Rabbit. When she described how Peter Rabbit climbed a tree to escape, she raised her voice gradually to the peak of her vocal register. Amber slowed down her speech to convey a gloomy mood as she described how the wolf cried because he could not climb the tree. She rounded off the story by stating 'The End', and switched to look for songs in her folder.

Thereafter, Amber sang two verses of *The Wheels on the Bus*, as she was going through her music scores collection. In the second verse, she sang in a high, piercing sound to imitate baby cries. However, without a pause, Amber suddenly switched back to the 'story-telling' mode and introduced the character of a bumble bee into her story. Again without a pause, she inserted a *learned song* fragment about bees in the story-telling. This *spontaneous song* then emerged into a *pot-pourri* song, which included some fragments of a song about fishing. The singing sequence was sung slower and slower until it gradually integrated seamlessly with another section of story-telling. Amber again returned to the excerpt describing how the big black wolf ate up other animals. This and the earlier segment on a big black wolf were not from the story book which Amber was reading. Since Amber was familiar with Prokofiev's *Peter and the Wolf*, she might have been trying to incorporate the story of this instrumental work into her *nursery musical*. (Mang 2001: 118–19)

Just think of the waste were Amber to be sent now for instrumental lessons from an instrumental teacher who thought that they should 'start her in music from the beginning'. Given Amber's energy and intelligence, she would probably absorb and run with whatever tasks she was asked to complete in her first lesson, and subsequent lessons. Perhaps she might initially be taught the layout of staff notation, and the fingering of two or three notes on an instrument that she had never played before, and then asked to play a simple melody using these notes read from a score. As Amber would have only just started to develop a technique on her new instrument, this exercise would not allow her to demonstrate the expressive capability that she had shown when singing. Perhaps Amber might also be sent home with an amorphous instruction to 'practise' some musically narrow fragments on her instrument for a set number of minutes each week before her next lesson.

It is easy to see how Amber's teacher might never find out what she could already do when she started her instrumental lessons. As well as narrowing the range of her musical activity, Amber's notional instrumental teacher risks expecting too little of her.

Amber has already acquired so much musical development that could be left behind—even eradicated—through the distraction, and seeming importance, of her new lessons. Amber already knows many songs and stories that she develops into further songs and longer pieces, and this reflects some understanding of form. She works confidently—when there are others listening and not only when she is on her own. She sings well. She draws on timbre, tempo, and pitch in ways that adults recognize, and uses her singing and speaking voice securely, and in novel ways, to convey them. She makes use of her formidable memory and imagination as she does so. She adapts musical ideas to fit new circumstances. I could carry on . . .

How would all this pre-existing musical development feature in Amber's—probable—piano or violin lessons? If her instrumental teacher ever learnt that Amber could do all these things, might they suggest that Amber put them all on hold for now, and 'come back to them later'? If so, would she, or could all the skills that Amber has built up be left behind, inadvertently, for ever? Might Amber emerge, chrysalis-like, at the age of 18, as one of those undoubtedly very able instrumentalists who claim not to have a musical idea in their heads that has not been injected intravenously via somebody else's staff notation? One who feels unable to improvise, and who perhaps feels unduly dependent on her teachers in respect of communication, interpretation, and expression? And, along the way, might Amber have dropped a few marks in the aural tests of the graded performance examinations that she will have taken at a dazzlingly young age, through fear of not being able to sing her responses 'properly'?

Back to Amber aged 5. As with Alan, but for some different reasons, I do not feel that Amber is ready for instrumental lessons as yet. She manages her own musical development effectively at present. She is busy creating music herself, based partly on material that she already has in her head. She is provided with resources in the form of songs and books, and imaginatively combines ideas from different sources in ways that are reminiscent of the spontaneous songs, frequently influenced by known songs, that Coral Davies (1986) captured in her classic article 'Say It Till a Song Comes (Reflections on Songs Invented by Children 3–13)'. As educators, we might wish to place a wider range of resources in Amber's path—perhaps musical instruments and other sound makers, or recordings of music without words in the form of either lyrics or sound tracks—and see what, if anything, she makes of them. But, beyond this, let us (notionally) leave Amber, like Alan, to continue her own musical development for a while, observe what happens, and review this a little later.

Finally, Amy:

Amy [aged 32 months] is not one to 'plink-plonk' on the piano, but loves to watch her father play. He shows her how to play E-D-C: she copies him and says 'That's *Three blind mice*.' She works out how to continue *Three blind mice*, playing E-D-C E-D-C G-F-E G-F-E. She then stops abruptly, and goes off to play with some toys. (Mills 2005*b*: 164)

In *Music in the School*, I commented on this as follows:

What can we tell from this about Amy's musical development? Clearly, Amy knows the song *Three blind mice*, and furthermore recognizes it when just the beginning is played using the 'wrong' timbre—the piano instead of the voice—and without words. To put it another way, she has internalized the melody. The way that she continues it—repeating E-D-C without stumbling, and later G-F-E—suggests that she has spotted the pattern formed by the simple repetition of motifs. We do not know how she knew that the note after the second C was a G. It is possible that she was just lucky. We do not know if she has spotted that E-D-C and G-F-E is a sequence: she may just work out G-F-E note by note. The sudden breaking off of playing at the end of the extract may mean that she has anticipated the greater challenge of the next phrase, and decided not to attempt it—at least while she has an audience—or it may just mean that Amy fancies doing something else. Either way, it is clear that formal piano lessons of half an hour or more might not be the best way of meeting Amy's current needs as a learner. Indeed, a regular routine of lessons might constrain Amy's development by stopping her learning through play—like she does in the other aspects of her very exciting life. There is plenty of time for Amy to have piano lessons later. (Mills 2005*b*: 164)

But this was not the end of the story . . .

Two days later, Amy's grandmother asks if Amy would play *Three blind mice* on the piano, and shows her the first note: E. Straight away, Amy plays E-D-C E-D-C G-F-F-E G-F-F-(D)-E. (The D was a slip that Amy instantly corrected.) Granny encourages Amy to play this again. 'No thanks', says Amy, and goes off to do something else. (Mills 2005*b*: 165)

And I commented as follows:

Consciously or subconsciously, Amy has been doing some mental rehearsal of *Three blind mice* since she played it two days previously. The repetition of the Fs, which reflect the syllables of the lyrics, suggests that she has been thinking about playing piano while singing the song, either out loud, or in her head. Amy is learning rapidly, but not in a way that could be bottled in a piano lesson. She has access to expert musicians who set her challenges that the national curriculum would suggest are well beyond her, but which she meets with room to spare. And she adds to her own learning in between the times when adults are intervening to help her, just as she does with all the other aspects of moving on and growing up. (Mills 2005*b*: 165)

Two years after writing these commentaries, I remain of the view that Amy—at 32 months—was not ready for piano lessons, or lessons on any other instrument. Amy already has some skills that will be of use to her should she learn piano—or another instrument—in future. For example, she appears to be able to 'internalize' music so that she can work on it in her head, and spot and enact patterns including sequences. She also appears to have physical memory for what she has played previously. But Amy is not yet 3, is busy learning all manner of all-important skills through play—and also has not shown us that she has the concentration needed to sit down at a piano for the entire duration of her piano lesson, or allotted periods of 'practice'.

I said at the start of this section that I would consider speculatively how taking instrumental lessons might, or might not, add to the musical lives of Alan, Amber, and Amy. I have now suggested that none of them is ready to take instrumental lessons just yet. However, I am clear that taking instrumental lessons in the future could be a wonderful opportunity for each of them, if that is what they would like to do, just as instrumental lessons can be wonderful experience for many learners of any age. But the lessons—as for everyone—should be the sort that acknowledge, build upon, and continue to sustain learners' broader musical interests, skills, wishes, and needs.

Robert Schenck has offered some advice on this, originally written with parents and carers of prospective instrumental students in mind, but that also contains some thoughts that are relevant to instrumental teachers:

Questions relevant to parents with [young] children who are about to start [instrumental] lessons

◆ Are the available instrumental lessons for very small children suited to their special needs in that there is room for both establishing a natural, relaxed way of playing the instrument and for general musical activities and games which promote creativity and a playful approach to music making?

◆ Is the foremost objective of the lessons to give the students a positive and rewarding first contact with formal music training?

◆ Are there advantages in beginning to play the instrument at such an early age, or are children who begin the same instrument around the age of [say] ten, and who have previously participated in general music groups, going to catch up quickly with, or pass, those who started earlier? Or will there be more obstacles in the way of instrumental development if the child waits until 10 years of age as compared to beginning as a pre-schooler?

◆ Is there a possibility that starting too early on the instrument might create unnecessary obstacles?

◆ Might it be wiser to offer the child as much playful general music training as possible and avoid 'narrowing down' musicality, motor skills and expressiveness to a specific instrument?

◆ Are the available instrumental lessons for children around 10 adapted to their age group, and to their creative needs and overall musical development, besides offering them a sound instrumental platform to build upon?

Instrumental teachers should also ask themselves these questions with regard to their own teaching

(Schenck 2000a: 85)

We now turn more specifically to the thoughts of learners and carers.

The learners' and carers' view

While it seems safe to assume that the purposes of taking instrumental lessons will nearly always include learning to play the instrument in question, learners—and their carers or parents in the case of children—may also have some other purposes in mind. These might include:

A chance for a learner to engage with the timbre of an instrument with which they have fallen in love. This sounds a sensible reason for choosing a particular instrument to learn, doesn't it? But loving the sound of an instrument is an aspect of choosing what instrument to play that is sometimes totally overlooked. Students may start lessons on particular instruments for reasons that are entirely a-musical (e.g. there was an unused clarinet in the cupboard at home!), or because of some probably ill-founded view that a particular instrument should be learnt 'first', when students have an expressed and burning musical desire to play something else. (For example some people think that the piano should necessarily be learnt before any other classical instrument, or recorder before flute, or violin before viola. I could continue . . .) Insisting that students play an instrument other than the one they want to play is no way to encourage people into music.

We return to the subject of choosing instruments that are thought to be 'suitable' in Chapter 5.

A chance for a learner to develop some particular interest in, or affinity with, music. I am thinking here about interest in, and affinity for, music in 'general'—rather than just in relation to a particular instrument that is a focus of study. The opportunity for learners of any age to develop their interests in, or affinity with, music through taking instrumental lessons is all to the good.

In saying this, I am not interested here in only students who are thought (by someone) to have particular 'talents' for music. Perhaps people do indeed have different talents (whatever we mean by this), in which case these individual talents should clearly be developed. But while it may be thought that some people have talents (of some sort or other), it does not follow that some other people do not have them too, or that the needs of a group who are thought to be relatively highly talented should necessarily be privileged over those who are thought (rightly or wrongly) to be less talented.

Instrumental lessons are for everyone, and can develop the musical interests and affinities of everyone too. Everybody, including the most highly achieving musicians in the world (whatever we mean by this too) has musical capacities that they fail to develop fully. Great instrumentalists, for example, readily volunteer, or agree, that this is the case for them.

Enhancing a learner's insight into music. All students who attend maintained schools in England follow a national curriculum in music: taking instrumental lessons either at school or separately could provide a means of enhancing this experience. Instrumental lessons can provide a particular context for 'engag[ing] students in high-quality making of, and response to, music. In music one learns by doing the activities that musicians do—making and responding to music—performing, composing, and listening. In other words, one learns through, not about, music' (Mills 2005*b*: 13). This should be an insight into music that:

- provides plenty of opportunity for the use of students' creativity and imagination. Even within western classical music, the supposed distinctions between 'performers' and 'composers' are often overplayed. When asked about the role of imagination in musical performance, the cellist Pablo Casals observed: 'Every year the leaves of the trees reappear with the spring, but they are different every time' (Corredor 1956). Kathy Primos (2001) has observed that, in sub-Saharan Africa, musicians search for the correct re-creation, rather than reproduction, of music.

- really is music. Instrumental lessons give students a concentrated experience of creating, interpreting, and responding to music. While they may also have some further benefits, they provide a concentrated experience of 'music for music's sake'.

The opportunity to gain some further qualifications. In countries including the UK, the experience of taking instrumental lessons on western classical instruments is often coupled with an opportunity to take graded performance examinations. Where well used by teachers and students, these examinations can add to the educational experience of instrumental lessons, help to motivate learners and focus their efforts, and also enhance learners' qualifications. Where examinations start to drive, rather than enhance, teaching and learning, their role becomes questionable.

To gain experience of learning in smaller groups. While a wish for children to have the opportunity of learning in a small group may be driven in the first instance by carers or parents, the make-up of a group can soon become very important to the learners. Robert Schenck refers to a group of five girls to whom he taught recorder early in his career. They were an enthusiastic group whom he greatly enjoyed teaching, but they had widely differing levels of skill and, as a teacher, he was keen to give each of them a better experience of playing by regrouping them with students of more similar ability as soon as he had the opportunity at the beginning of the next academic year. However, the girls had anticipated his unspoken intention, and had other ideas. At the end of the academic year, they all completed forms stating that they wanted to continue recorder the following year, but then all added: 'I only want to play the recorder next year if I get to play with [the names of the other four students].'

Robert Schenck complied with the girls' wishes, and everyone continued to make progress together happily.

To have fun. Teachers can often choose whether or not to make their lessons fun. John Holt writes in a volume on his own instrumental learning as an adult: 'Most of all, I want to combat the idea that any disciplined and demanding activity, above all music, can never grow out of love, joy and free choice, but must be rooted in forced exposure, coercion, and threat' (Holt 1978: 4–5). He observes further:

> People who know of my love for music today often say to me, 'Don't you wish that your parents had made you take music lessons when you were little?' The answer is, No, I don't. I think that such forced exposure would probably have turned me away from music, as it has so many others. (Holt 1978: 65)

Here, Richard Pepper, a woodwind teacher, explains how he seeks to make scales fun:

> My lessons often start with my playing a short phrase to the class. All I tell them is the starting note . . . This technique can be useful as an introduction to a new scale. The scale builds up in short manageable sections and employs a variety of fun rhythms. This can be continued the following week until the whole scale is learnt. The scale is learnt as an aural exercise combined with a tactile memory. The whole process is wordless, has a constant sense of pulse and can experiment with dynamic levels and a variety of articulation. The scale sheet is a memory jogger rather than a most uninviting challenge. (ABRSM 2004: 16)

It goes without saying that learners' reasons for taking instrumental lessons can vary. Even Steven and Anthony, quoted at the head of this chapter, and students at the same school, may have quite different reasons for taking instrumental lessons.

Susan O'Neill (2002) investigated, as part of a substantial research project—the Young People and Music Participation Project (YPMPP)[2]—the rankings that 317 students aged 11 gave for 14 statements about why they played their instruments. The students were asked to rate each of the statements on a 7-point scale from (1) not at all to (7) a lot. These results are shown in Fig. 3. O'Neill commented as follows:

---

[2] YPMPP (1998–2001) was funded by the Economic and Social Research Council (ESRC).

The results show that the main reasons children give for playing instruments are they enjoy the challenge and opportunity to learn something new. Children also rated being creative, relieving boredom, playing with others, and pleasing parents and teachers as strong reasons for playing instruments. Having an image as trendy/cool and pleasing friends were the least likely reasons for playing an instrument. This suggests that the social pressures children might expect from peers are not yet an important influence on children in this age group in terms of their involvement in playing an instrument.

Robert Schenck (2000a; 2000b) has suggested that the hopes of parents, when their children begin instrumental lessons, are not dissimilar from those when their children join a sports team (see Table 4).

He points out that the goals of the students are also important: 'Their objectives may be conscious or unconscious, explicit or vague, but in any case they are extremely important' (Schenck 2000a: 22), and observes that these goals may be quite surprising.

Sometimes the interest of carers and learners may be stimulated by the enthusiasm of someone else, such as a headteacher. In *Music in the School* I wrote of a primary school, with no tradition of instrumental teaching, where the headteacher persuaded his governors and the local authority to invest in instrumental tuition and instruments for the school, for an initial period of a year. Sixty of the older students volunteered to take part, and all were given places. At the end of the year, the school orchestra gave its first performance, and 58 of the students remained, and wanted—and were given—the opportunity to continue playing the following year. There were no charges to parents, and the students played a full range of orchestral instruments, including the frequently less popular instruments of oboe, bassoon, and viola. Instrumental lessons had been integrated

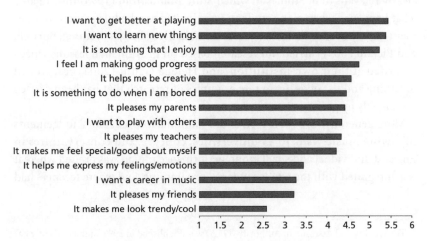

Fig. 3 Reasons for playing instruments (O'Neill 2002: 11)

Table 4   Some typical parental hopes

Sports team	Instrumental lessons
Enjoyment	Enjoyment
Make friends and feel like part of the group	Make friends and feel like part of the group or ensemble
Get exercise, fresh air and a feel of the ball	Experience music
Develop coordination	Develop coordination
Grow and develop as a person	Grow and develop as a person
Feel pride in the ability to play the game and improve	Feel pride in the ability to make music and improve
Learn the technique of the sport	Learn the technique of the instrument

Source: Schenck 2000a: 21

thoroughly into the culture of the school, and the parents and carers had become so keen that many of them wanted to take up instruments themselves.

The advanced western classical learner's view

This brief section turns to advanced learners, and considers what they hope to gain from continuing instrumental lessons. It is based on a study, in one conservatoire, of the characteristics of the individual instrumental, including vocal, tuition that undergraduates say that they find effective (Mills 2002).

Prior to this study, there had been very little recent research that focused directly on teaching and learning in higher education in England, or was clearly relevant to it. Studies in which Sture Brändström (1995) investigated what happened when piano students were invited to schedule piano lessons as they felt they needed them, Vanessa Young and her colleagues (Young, Burwell, and Pickup 2003) carried out research based on instrumental lessons video-recorded at their own institution, and Helena Gaunt (2004) researched breathing and the oboe, form rare examples of research that has been carried out directly by performer-teachers.

More generally, QAA (HEFCE 2000)[3] summarized assessors' judgements following music visits to 44 universities, colleges, and conservatoires in England. Individual and small group performance tuition was praised where it was integrated with the whole students' programme, and where teachers had

---

[3] The Quality and Assessment Authority (QAA) was established in 1992, and it currently has a remit to safeguard and help to improve the academic standards and quality of higher education in the UK.

the expertise and experience required to respond to a student's needs. The published reports on individual conservatoires in England, Wales, and Scotland provide some insights into the teaching styles that assessors judged effective. Teaching which was 'authoritative without being intimidating and which [was] often inspiring and imaginative', 'well focused, with clear and understood objectives, often highly stimulating and imaginative', or 'stimulating with a nice balance between technical considerations and those of interpretation and creativity' was praised. That which was 'excessively dogmatic or overbearing with the student in a reactive rather than a creative role', or which 'engaged only superficially with the problems confronting the student' was criticized.

The study on which this section is based (Mills 2002) relates to one conservatoire. It utilizes the course evaluation questionnaires that undergraduates completing Years 1 or 2 of their four-year course filled out at the end of the 2000–1 academic year. Students had been asked two questions about their individual tuition that related particularly to the research:

1. What are the ingredients of instrumental teaching that are effective for you?
2. Think about an instrumental lesson/class that went well for you. What was its focus, and what made it particularly effective?

The return rates were high. A total of 102 Year 1 students (99 per cent) and 80 Year 2 students (86 per cent) filled out the questionnaires.

There was an obvious common thread to students' responses to Question 1:

Students want to feel that they have made good progress with their technique, musicality, practising skill and confidence, and they want inspiring teachers who love teaching, show interest in students' musical and personal development, are firm when necessary, and who present detailed criticism constructively. They want their lessons to take place regularly, and to feel planned and purposeful. They appreciate the conservatoire's policy of employing only teachers who are, or were, at the top of their profession as performers.

Moving beyond this common thread, the syntax that the students used to write about these ingredients betrays a range of received teaching styles that may be loosely categorized as follows:

1. Transmission
   My teacher tells/shows me what to do.
   '[I like my teacher to] give just praise and criticism and to [teach] a balanced repertoire, to be strict with deadlines and to expect much output from the student.' (Year 1)
   '[I value] the ability of my teacher to see a technical problem and show me himself how to solve it.' (Year 2)

2. Collaboration
   My teacher and I work out together what and how I should improve.

'We have begun to recognize common goals for my musical future, based on his experience.' (Year 1)

'We have successfully identified the causes of problems and devised ways of overcoming them and becoming a better player.' (Year 2)

3. Induction

My teacher teaches me to how to learn to be a musician.

'[I value] talking about music, even sometimes disagreeing about some things and the learning process.' (Year 1)

'[I value] being given ideas from the teacher to bounce my ideas off . . .' (Year 1)

'he teaches me to think on my own, and never imposes anything.' (Year 1)

'[I value my teacher] asking me how I think any problems I am having may be tackled rather than just giving a solution, therefore helping me to develop my own problem solving skills.' (Year 2)

Nearly all the students answered Question 2 with examples that reinforced their responses to Question 1, for example:

'When a recurring problem was finally realized by me and I was able to address it through specialized practice and relevant studies' (Year 1—induction)

'I was learning a piece that I enjoyed playing and we were trying to find a way of creating different colours. It was interesting to learn how to create a sound by doing two simple things when before I'd imagined the sound I wanted and hoped it would happen!' (Year 1—induction)

'The focus was on a particularly technically challenging passage—we identified tension in the embouchure and fingers as the cause of difficulty and worked on relaxing my approach to playing to succeed.' (Year 2—collaboration)

'When I had just started the 2nd movement of [X] concerto, and we underlined *all* areas of interpretation and direction required, which helped me develop my understanding and playing confidence of the piece in my own practice time. (Year 2—collaboration)

'[When] my [teacher] eliminated a problem in playing that I'd had for years, in a matter of minutes.' (Year 1—transmission)

'It has been when my professor has been extremely strict, not letting one note go, extremely detailed, that I have benefited most . . . The more intense the lesson, the more I have come away with.' (Year 1—transmission)

However, a few students, typically those who usually appear to have been taught through transmission, identified an experience other than an individual lesson that was special because it provided a different point of view on their work, for example:

'People who were listening (other students) were asked to speak openly about what was good or bad. This was very worthwhile and a new thing for me.' (Year 1)

'It is interesting to hear everyone's responses and we are always asked a lot of questions.' (Year 1)

'When the principal of [X] orchestra sat in on my lesson, every comment made was justified and the lesson was very focused on details and very constructive. Although it was hard work and picked up on my faults, it was in a positive constructive way, that was justified and inspiring rather than running me down!' (Year 2)

In essence:

- the students' prime concern is that their lessons enable them to make progress as instrumentalists
- they vary in their views of the teaching strategies that would work best for them, not least the extent to which they should be trained to improve their playing autonomously in the future
- they actively seek detailed and fundamental advice, but want it to be provided by musicians who are outstanding, inspiring and constructive.

(Mills 2002)

Since this research was completed, a Special Issue of the *British Journal of Music Education*, entitled *Instrumental Teaching in Higher Education* (Mills and Moore 2005), has added a further seven articles, each with at least one author who is a performer-teacher, to the higher education instrumental teaching literature.

Kim Burwell (2005) uses the lesson conversations between teacher and student as a lens for considering the extent to which instrumental lessons do—or on occasion do not—prepare higher education students to learn independently in future. Carole Presland's (2005) research also turned to the independent learning of students as she discovered that they did not feel cheated of support when assigned to tutors who could not, because of location, attend all their public performances: students valued the opportunity to take risks, and even make mistakes, without simultaneously wondering about the reaction of their tutor. Interviews of experienced performers strengthen Patricia Holmes's (2005) belief that practice should be taught as a creative and imaginative process. David Corkhill (2005) addresses the content of instrumental lessons, and suggests that they should prepare students more effectively for the orchestral profession. Also within the field of lesson content, Hilary Moore and Fiona Hibbert (2005) consider whether a controversial approach to learning—brain gym—can be used to enhance instrumental progress, report some potentially encouraging results in an initial investigation, and recommend further research. David Purser (2005) found variation in the educational philosophies of wind players who work as conservatoire instrumental teachers, and this led him to ask whether 'accumulated wisdom' could be pooled and questioned more effectively were training to be provided for new conservatoire teachers. Elisabeth Barratt and Hilary Moore (2005) turn to assessment, and propose a means through which the assessment of jazz could be carried out more authentically within the jazz bands where students work.

An emphasis on performance

This section is from Mills 2005*b*: 66–70.

'Why do people go to recitals? Partly to be amazed by the pole vaulting, but also because they hope the performer will break their heart.' (A concert pianist, London: December 2001)

'But if my children were encouraged to use their imagination and intellect, surely it would take them longer to get through their music grades?' (A parent, Oxford: December 2001)

A problem

Performance can be wonderful. But it is also much misunderstood. The pianist reminds us of the impact—magic even—of live musical performance. He speaks of western classical music that is played at recitals, but what he says could apply to almost any music. He is talking about aspects of performance that come partly from what a composer has written, and partly from what a performer has done to bring the writing alive, but his message could apply also where the performer is the composer as well, where the music has never been written down, or where music is improvised by one or more musicians. A performance can amaze us and move us. How better to give this to children than by teaching them to be performers? And students who opt to take instrumental lessons are saying that they want a taste of this, a chance to do more performing of a particular type than they would do otherwise.

The parent reminds us of what can go wrong when the matter of 'teaching children to be performers' is misunderstood. He sees examination certificates, rather than performances, as the goal of performance training, and limits his view of the process that his offspring should go through accordingly. He sees the instrumental lesson as something that should help his children assemble what they need to the standard required by examiners, and the use of their imagination or intellect as fripperies that would slow this down. I think that it would also be safe to say that he sees performance as something that relates only to western classical music.

My conversation with this parent followed the broad drift of many conversations with other parents over the years. On learning that I work in music, the parent had told me that one of his children was not hurtling through her grades at quite the dizzying speed of the others because she spends some of her practice time on improvisation. What could he, as a parent who is interested in music but, in his view, *not musical*, do about this? The piano teacher had suggested that his daughter was not as musical as his, more focused, other children—and had hinted that she should give up lessons—but the parent would like her to carry on, at least for a while, even if she was not going to reach the high standards of her brothers.

As usual in such conversations, I observed that it is healthy and musical to want to apply one's new musical skills imaginatively and intelligently, and that perhaps the piano teacher could be urged to capitalize on these strengths of his daughter's approach. Perhaps the parent raised this thought with the piano teacher and she took some action; perhaps he didn't or she didn't. Whatever the outcome, at the time of our conversation, the parent—and possibly also the piano teacher—shared some misconceptions about performance and how it is made. Even within the realm of western classical music, the re-creation that is performance requires much more than the ability to play the right notes in the right order. Performances that are not quite note-perfect may occasionally be preferred to ones that are, if the trade-off is a higher degree of expression and communication. Performers find ways of playing pieces that make sense, and which communicate much more than a string of notes to their audience. To do this, they draw on resources that are not found on the printed score, and which they develop through intellectual and imaginative engagement with music, and through experience.

It is never too early to start to develop and build upon a student's intellectual and imaginative engagement with music. When we watch a young child at play with musical—or sound-making—materials, we can see that this engagement comes naturally. Children frequently focus intently as they experiment with different ways of making sounds, different ways of making different sounds, different ways of assembling sounds into patterns or motifs, and as they try to repeat or re-create sounds, patterns, or motifs that they made earlier. This natural engagement can be drawn into education, and developed through composing, listening, and musical approaches to performing. Instrumental teaching that is no more than repetitive drill or that consists, in effect, of a list of instructions to follow, switches it off.

We should not worry that thinking about expression while learning to play accurately is too difficult for children. They have formidable musical potential that remains untapped. Children in Japan work within the western and Japanese tonal schemes in their class musical lessons, without confusing them, and sometimes fuse the tonal schemes when devising playground games (Murao and Wilkins 2001). Surely, this is much more difficult.

Clearly, there is no single 'right' way of performing, or interpreting, any piece of music, although there may be limits, or 'bounds' to what is acceptable in particular cultural circumstances. A professional performer's unusually mournful and slow performance of the first movement of Beethoven's so-called 'Moonlight' Sonata, say, might be deemed 'tedious' in a recital at a country house, 'daring' in the Purcell Room, 'well-judged' at a memorial service, 'innovative' on a CD, and not really noticed as part of a film score. Examinations and competitions are occasions when performers—and their teachers—worry particularly about what their audience wants, rather than what they would like to give them. And yet examiners and adjudicators, as performers themselves, may be open to a wide range of interpretations and styles. The cellist Lowri Blake, who also works widely as an examiner, explains:

A so-called romanticising of Bach cannot be dismissed: it may be superlatively good technically, and wonderfully communicated, but not 'authentic'. How far is that the student's own choice, his teacher's, or a complete lack of awareness of twenty-first-century baroque practice? Or, perhaps this is a truly innovative student developing a whole new concept of fashion and stylistic practice—it must be considered on all its merits![4]

Lowri Blake is speaking of students at a conservatoire. We need to set younger students on this path of playing expressively, and not only accurately. Expression is not the same as licence: we can encourage—teach—children to play expressively without reducing our expectations of their technique, listening skills, or ability to vary their timbre, play strictly in time, or follow a conductor's beat. In fact, playing expressively requires greater control of all these than playing robotically. Mick Jagger made this point informally: 'It's alright letting yourself go, as long as you can let yourself back' (Green 1982). If we do not facilitate expressive playing through our teaching, then the only students who become expressive players will be survivors, rather than successes, of our teaching.

A piano teacher once spoke to me of one of the many higher education students who she had taken on after they had been learning with other teachers for several years: 'Alice is so musical. Whatever she plays—even scales—there is always something special about how it sounds.' Perhaps playing expressively and communicatively did come easier to Alice than to her, equally technically competent, peers. But perhaps it was more that Alice's musicality had somehow survived some regimented and potentially stifling piano teaching that she had received from her previous teachers. Alice was a singer. She loved singing, particularly musicals and Gilbert and Sullivan, and she put her all into it. She carried this over into her piano playing. I sometimes heard her humming as she practised piano, and perhaps she sang in her head for much of the time that she played. She carried the phrasing that came naturally to her as a singer into her piano playing. It seemed that everything that she played on

---

[4] Conference for instrumental teachers (known as professors) at the Royal College of Music, London, in 2002.

piano was a *Song Without Words* to her. In Tânia Lisboa's terms (2002)[5] she was working multi-modally. I feel sure that her peers could have been taught to work multi-modally too or, better still, could have been taught piano in a way that kept alive the musicality that they had brought to their very first piano lesson.

How can we keep this musicality alive when giving lessons on piano, or on other instruments? In lots of ways. We can draw students' attention to the high-quality performances that they produce from their very first lesson, even if we suspect that their quality may have arisen partly fortuitously, or if students find it difficult to repeat them. We can organize special projects, perhaps related to *New Ears*[6] or *Fingers are Great Inspirers* from [John Paynter's] *Sound and Structure* (1992), that challenge students to listen to, and use, the sounds that they can already make in different ways. We can make improvising a routine part of lessons, and a routine part of practice. We can sing as we teach, and encourage students to join us. Above all, we can organize instrumental lessons so as to destroy the myth that students have to spend years getting things 'right' before starting to 'express themselves'. *Leave your imagination and initiative at the door, all ye who enter here . . .* We may want to focus on accuracy and control in instrumental lessons, but they are not our only concern. We can organize instrumental lessons so that students make music as they develop their technique.

This approach can start with the very first instrumental lesson. It simply is not the case that students need to spend whole lessons on a-musical preliminary activities such as learning how to assemble their instrument, clapping rhythms, or learning to read music before they start to make music, of some carefully chosen sort, on their instrument.

I recently observed a 7 year old's first ever keyboard lesson. This was scheduled to last a mere 15 minutes, and the teacher had to use some of that time to collect the student from her very distant classroom. He used the time well. When the teacher and student arrived at the keyboard teaching room they already had a professional relationship, and the teacher knew what sort of keyboard the student had at home, and that she had 'just being playing around on it' so far. The student sat down at the keyboard immediately, ready to play. The teacher taught her a right-hand five-note eight-bar melody by ear, then showed her how it fitted with a three-chord autochord accompaniment and taught her that, and finally taught her to also add an autorhythm. The student

---

5 See also p. 170.

6 See pp. 122–3 for further information about these projects.

left her first lesson with a worthwhile memorized piece that she could work on, including by playing it to her friends and family, during the week.

The teacher showed me this memorized piece written out at the beginning of a tutor book that he has prepared, for use with his own students. He planned to give a copy to the student I saw, and show her the memorized piece written down, two or three weeks later: 'when this will no longer get in the way'. Playing a piece that she already knew, while following it written down, would form her introduction to staff notation.

This student is being introduced to staff notation musically, in a way that shows that staff notation can be used to record a piece of music that is complete in someone's head, whether or not it has ever been played to an audience. The strengths of this approach also include its similarity with the way that young children learn the relationship between writing and oral language. Children often learn to spot words that are important to them—such as their name in birthday cards or on birthday cakes—long before anyone has taught them how to work out what a written word says from its individual letters. (Mills 2005*b*: 66–70)

Chapter 5

What instrument?

The fact is that if I had stayed with the piano I could never have been in the same league as Rachmaninov or Horowitz. But with the mouth organ . . . Nobody existed before me. I was the world's first soloist.

Larry Adler, mouth organ (Adler 1994: 26)

We were arranged in height order. The taller ones got big instruments.

James Gourlay, tuba player and Director of the School of Music at the Royal Scottish Academy of Music and Drama (RSAMD), reflects on how he came to take up tuba, rather than—say—cornet, when at school (Wojtas 2006)

I wrote [to a man] who knew many skilled musicians, told him I wanted to learn to play one of the instruments of the classical orchestra, and asked which he thought would be best. He wrote back that he was glad to hear it, and would ask his musical [*sic*] friends. After a while he wrote again to say that most of the people he asked recommended the flute; it was easy to carry, easier to play than most of the others, made a pretty sound, had much good music written for it, and could play violin parts on string quartet music.

John Holt, author of *How Children Fail*, decides on an instrument to play at the age of 40 (Holt 1978: 117)

'Choosing' an instrument

Larry Adler took up piano, and James Gourlay tuba, when children on the strength of some decisions that were made for them by adults. John Holt, a fierce critic of primary education that does not centre on children's needs, took up flute as an adult, but nevertheless turned to others to guide him when choosing an instrument to play. In fact, as is often the case, some of the information provided by the 'expert' who advised him was inaccurate—there are many violin parts that a flute cannot play, either because notes outside its range are needed, or because particular techniques (such as double stopping) are required.

So far as we know, not one out of Larry Adler, James Gourlay, or John Holt were asked as part of their assignment to instruments whether there was one that they wanted to play—for example because they loved the sound that it makes.

This chapter relates to the pseudoscience of 'suitability for individual instruments'.

James Gourlay and Larry Adler—each an acclaimed performer—arrived at the instruments on which they made their names through quite different routes. Larry Adler took up mouth organ on his own initiative—initially alongside the piano lessons that had been chosen for him—and then focused on mouth organ as this instrument went 'right' for him and (as we have already read on pp. 63–4) piano went 'wrong'. In James Gourlay's case, a school decided what, if anything, he would play. For him, the choice proved to be 'right' (though we will never know whether another instrument might have suited him even better). But what about the other students who took up instruments at his school? Were the instruments that they were assigned 'right' for them too? Or did some of the students give up lessons after a while because they—or someone else—felt that they were hopeless? Did anyone ask any of these children what instrument they wanted to learn—for example because they were attracted particularly to the sounds that it makes when played well? Did they even ever hear it played well?

Advising students about which instrument to play

Why do we end up playing some instrument(s) rather than others? What makes an ideal flute—or singing—student? What is the instrument on which a particular student is likely to make most progress (whatever we mean by this)? As we address these questions, how can we also protect the interests and self-esteem of students—particularly children—who 'give up' instruments each year in the probably entirely mistaken belief that they lacked aptitude for the instrument in question, so that their prospect of progress was always doomed?

For many instrumental teachers, working in many situations, the issues of whether a notional Belinda, Betty, or Boris would make the best trombonist, or whether Belinda might be better suited to electric bass than trombone, barely arises. We are contacted by a third party—perhaps Belinda's parent or schoolteacher—who knows that we teach trombone, and who tells us that

Belinda would like trombone lessons. We look at our diaries or timetables and, possibly after the preliminary of a 'consultation lesson' if Belinda will be a private student, or after organizing a space in a group if she will be a school student, we take her on. If there is any conversation at all about whether Belinda might try some instrument other than trombone, or whether there might be a potentially more promising trombonist among Belinda's peers at school, we are left entirely out of the loop.

Actually, 'out of the loop' may be the best place to be for any such conversation, as those commonly heard stories about what makes a good player of a particular instrument are, to be frank, so much phooey. To take just one instrument, I guess that we have all heard the stories about trombonists needing long arms and thick lips, and we have probably also heard the stories about trombonists being advantaged by being male and (as they reach an appropriate age) enjoying drinking alcoholic beverages—notably beer—with other males. There is no provable truth to any of this. The arm stretch required by trombonists, in due course as they need to play particular low notes, is nothing out of the ordinary—and there are plenty of other notes to be played, and there is much musical fun to be had, in the meantime. Orchestras, brass bands, and jazz bands are full of trombonists—many of them female—with lots of different sorts of lips. The stuff about social drinking stems from anecdotal understanding—little more than gossip—of the lives of professional musicians, to which some musicians have sometimes contributed their own pennyworth. For example, a professional orchestral clarinettist, when contributing to some research, volunteered that 'the brass are the drinkers, the wind are the thinkers, and the strings are the stinkers' (Davies 1978: 203). Material of this ilk can add a spice to what one reads in the Sunday newspapers. Clearly, however, it has no place whatsoever in sensible educational discussion about whether or not to take up an instrument.

Perhaps the teachers at the school attended by James Gourlay (see beginning of the chapter) were being cynical when they assigned their instruments in height order? Perhaps they were after a particular (aesthetically pleasing?) sloping visual effect, reminiscent of Escher's (1960) *Ascending and Descending* when the school band appeared on stage at concerts? But if they thought that students actually need to be big to play big instruments (or small to play small ones) they were sadly mistaken. And, even were this to be the case, children do grow . . .

Larry Adler was, I feel sure, right to say that he made much more of mouth organ than he could ever have made of piano. But this was for the reasons that he suggests above—because he developed and established mouth organ as a solo instrument. No expert visited Larry Adler as a child, gave him some tests as to what instrument he should play, and pronounced him suited to mouth organ. But this was, perhaps, mainly because the mouth organ did not figure on the musical antennae of experts in the time. (When Larry Adler first toured the UK, having already established a formidable reputation in the US, *The Times* reported that he was a trombonist! (Adler 1994: 112).) Larry Adler had, however, been tested as suited to the piano—and as we have already read, this did not turn out too well.

The best test of whether somebody—of any age, shape, demeanour, disposition, or musical background—will make a good player of any instrument that they really want to play, be it bassoon, banjo, or Scottish bagpipes, is to give them some lessons and see how they get on.

And if they do not get on too well this may, of course, be because the teaching, rather than the learning, is 'at fault'. People can generally learn anything they want to learn provided that they are taught sufficiently well. Some people learn some things more easily than other people, of course. Some instrumental teachers and students have to work together very hard to analyse the problems, challenges, or obstacles that students are facing, and work out ways of solving them. But this is surely what teaching is mainly about? Whoever went into teaching expecting it to be easy, or money for old rope?[1] The pleasure that teachers derive from succeeding with students who find it more difficult to learn is enormous. This is a reward that is sought actively by many teachers. A particular teacher who works mainly in a conservatoire speaks of an external student whom he took on because he wanted the challenge: 'There was a lad who really wanted to play in the Royal Artillery Band, and he really did not seem to have the ability. He could not play at all. But he was so determined that he made it. This was eye-opening' (Mills 2004*d*: 192). The extent to which this teacher credits the student, rather than himself, for the student's success is typical of many teachers of students who find learning difficult. I have little doubt that this teacher contributed significantly to this student's progress. I would have loved to be a fly on the wall for some of the lessons!

Another instrumental teacher writes to *Libretto*, a professional magazine published by the ABRSM,[2] about a tricky situation when taking on a student who has been taught by someone else (ABRSM 2006):

---

[1] The UK expression 'money for old rope' is said to originate 'from the days of public hangings. It was a perquisite of the hangman to keep the rope used to hang his 'customer'. The rope, however, was popular with the macabre crowds, so the hangman used to cut the rope up and sell it' (Rabun 2001).

[2] The Associated Board of the Royal Schools of Music (ABRSM) is the largest of the UK based international boards that offer graded performance examinations for a range of instruments.

Problems with reading

I have a nine-year-old pupil who came to me having passed Grades 1 and 2.

She is bright, keen and a joy to teach. However, she passed the exams not being able to read a note of music and learns by rote and by watching my every move. Her parents are wondering why I've gone back to the very beginning and am not starting on Grade 3. I don't want to dampen this pupil's enthusiasm but am having great difficulty in getting her to read music. I would value your comments.

And receives the following helpful published advice from Clara Taylor, Chief Examiner:

This is a very specific situation but similar things will have happened to many teachers. There are two elements to tackle: the level of understanding shown by her parents and the pupil's motivation and enjoyment in her playing.

Do the parents appreciate what is involved in an all-round musical education? It may be worth showing them by looking at books or demonstrations of what their daughter will have to master to make the most of her potential. It is likely that they are unaware of the discipline and continued effort that doing the job properly entails. If they show complete disinterest [*sic*] in this thorough approach, it's probably a losing battle as their attitude will rub off on their daughter.

Let's assume that they do want to pursue the full coverage of skills necessary to progress. In this case, you can explain carefully to your pupil that every one understands she has been learning in a slightly different way but that your way is going to enable her to have her playing much better. Lots of appreciation for efforts made will be necessary to keep her motivation high. I would suggest that she has a parallel path of fun pieces, perhaps including duets with you, once you are certain where her musical tastes lie and which styles give her most pleasure. Children will make enormous efforts if they feel that work is appreciated and that praise is likely to come as a result. (ABRSM 2006: 22)

While I agree with every word that Clara Taylor writes here, her advice to the teacher overall is slightly gentler than I might have offered. Yes, learning to read staff notation is crucial for anyone who wants to get fully to grips with the western classical piano repertoire, because staff notation is the main way in which it has been documented. But learning to copy music by ear is valuable too. Indeed skills similar to these are tested in the 'aural' section of the ABRSM graded examinations for individual instruments.

The teacher's expression 'back to the very beginning' is an ominous one. What a shame if the student, ten years hence, found herself needing to learn anew how to play by ear, because she had not maintained the skills that she had at the age of 9. Is the teacher really thinking of taking the student back to the very first page of the very first tutor book (or whatever) that the teacher likes to use, and insisting that only staff notation is used as they do so? Perhaps the teacher could be encouraged to allow the student to keep her aural skills alive while she learnt to read music? Perhaps the duets suggested by Clara Taylor, or some improvisation or composition, could be ways forward here?

On every occasion when a student stops learning an instrument—be it flute, drums, or singing—at least partly because they have come to the conclusion that this instrument is 'not for them', their teacher doubtless introspects at length, and considers whether there is anything that they could, possibly, have done better.

Is there an instrument that I could play?

The notion that some instruments require particular characteristics of physique, personality, or so forth, has a long and international history. It has served to discourage learners from taking up instruments that they would greatly have liked to learn, and has been used to justify instances of lack of progress, for many years.

More than 70 years ago, Charles Lamp and Noel Keys, two researchers who worked on the west coast of America, became concerned that children were being discouraged from playing instruments that they greatly wanted to play solely on the strength of: 'a priori reasoning and uncontrolled observation' (Lamp and Keys 1935: 587). They designed an experiment to test theories that:

- stringed instruments require slender fingers
- brass instruments require lips of a thickness that is proportionate to the size of mouthpiece
- woodwind and brass instruments require even teeth.

This was careful research. The researchers moved well beyond the *a priori* reasoning and imprecise observation of which they complained. They recruited 150 students who were about to begin lessons on an instrument, and used the 'state of the art' technology of the time to make their measurements, and test their observations, as rigorously as possible. Thickness of lips was gauged with micrometer callipers of the type then used by dentists for oral measurements. The slenderness of students' fingers was also based on measurements made with micrometer callipers, and defined precisely as the ratio of the length of the middle finger to its width at the first joint. The evenness of students' teeth was gauged using a scale that was devised with a professor of orthodontics, and based on three photographs taken of every student. Just think how long it must have taken to collect and process the 450 photographs alone, using the technology available in 1935!

After a year, the researchers reviewed the progress of the students, and related this to the measurements that had been taken of them.

None of the theories behaved as expected. The slenderness of students' fingers bore hardly any relation to their success on violin. Indeed, one could predict a violinist's success just as readily by considering the evenness of their teeth! The evenness of students' teeth made no measurable difference to their achievement on woodwind or brass instruments. The student with the thinnest lips, and the student with the thickest lips, both went on to become successful French horn players.

Lamp and Keys' painstaking research did have some impact on instrumental learning in the school system of San Francisco where, at least for a time, students were allowed to learn the instrument that they most wanted to play—rather than the instrument to which teachers thought they should be assigned. But the practice of assigning students to instruments—using the types of theories based on untested observation that Lamp and Keys eschewed—remains persistently alive. Books that purport to help parents select the most suitable instrument for their child without consulting a teacher (possibly also without even asking the child what they would like to play!) are readily available through internet and high street booksellers. In some schools and music services, instrumental teachers who find themselves oversubscribed choose who to teach by considering characteristics such as how long their arms are, which hand they use when writing, their ease in singing some particular songs in tune within a particular range, and so forth. None of this matters provided that the student wants to learn the instrument, and the teacher teaches them in a way that is observant of, and builds upon, their personal, physical, and psychological strengths, including motivation, and areas for development. Larry Adler felt that he was not taught in such a way:

When I started the first hesitant steps in learning the piano, I found I could pick out tunes by ear, and even harmonise them. Two years of piano lessons did me little good. Scales bored me, and I always held my hands low, actually below the keyboard, so that only my fingers came over the top like spiders' legs.

Years later Artur Rubinstein, the Polish-born prodigy who was playing Chopin in public at the age of eleven, stared at my hands as I played and proclaimed loudly: '*Impossible!*' Well, I did it. (Adler 1994: 22)

I certainly would not wish to be arbiter, particularly at this late date, of whether Larry Adler should, or should not, have been taught to play with his hands higher, in order to develop his keyboard facility! But, in either case, he still managed to play the piano well by most people's standards, and had his achievements on mouth organ as an outlet for his further creative ability. Other students who fail on an instrument can find themselves, in effect, marooned.

Fifty years after Lamp and Keys had completed their research, I asked 50 instrumental teachers in England about the factors that they thought promoted success on various instruments, and whether—and if so how—they used them when deciding which students to 'select' for instrumental tuition that had become oversubscribed (Mills 1983). The instrumental teachers proposed a very wide range of 'factors' that fell loosely under the headings of physical, personality, psychological, and musical.

With respect to physical features, theories very similar to those that Lamp and Keys had were still in widespread use. There were also many other theories:

Some cello teachers refused to teach anyone who wrote with their left hand. Some teachers of violin and viola rejected children whose arms seemed to be longer than usual. Children with short necks were likely to be rejected by some flute teachers, as were children with long necks who wanted to play violin or viola. The lip-thickness theory had been extended from brass to woodwind, with thin lips considered necessary for the flute, and thicker lips for clarinet, oboe, and bassoon. Students who lisped were considered unsuited to any brass instrument. Students who had an awkward gait were considered unsuited to percussion instruments, because of the danger of them knocking instruments over when they moved to a different instrument in a symphony orchestra. Asthma or hay fever was considered to be a problem on any wind instrument. Almost without exception, these theories had not been tested beyond the teacher's personal experience as a student and as a teacher. There was little evidence of teachers talking even to their immediate colleagues about their experience, and no evidence that the derivation, questioning, or testing of theories about physical characteristics had formed a significant part of any professional training that they had received. (Mills 2005*b*: 117)

The theories of some teachers were contradicted by those of others. For example, the cello teachers who declined to teach students who are left-handed were contradicted by other cello teachers who considered that left-handedness was advantageous.

The 50 instrumental teachers also had some theories about characteristics of personality that are shared with some anecdotal writing. *The Right Instrument for Your Child* (Ben-Tovim and Boyd 1985), includes diagnostic tests for parents to carry out with their children, and bases its personality theories on a simplified version of the role of different instruments (rather than instrumentalists) in a western classical orchestra:

The observation that several string players play the same music in many orchestral pieces, that the horns tend to sit separately from the rest of the brass, and that trumpets sometimes make a lot of noise, has led to suggestions that the violin is suitable for 'quietly behaved children' with 'no outlet for boisterousness or exuberance'; the horn is the best instrument for children who 'prefer to relate to small groups and usually have just one or two close friends'; and the trumpet is suited to the 'individualist' with 'prima donna temperament' . . . Beliefs such as these have, over the years, denied countless children and older learners the opportunity to take up an instrument of which they might have made a great success. (Mills 2005*b*: 119)

Students, including children, who take up instruments do not all do so with a view to making a living in a western classical orchestra! And such orchestras are much more than the printed scores of Mozart or Brahms in human form. But even were both of these the case, it would be nice to think that young people who are starting to learn instruments now, and who will still be playing professionally at the midpoint of this century, will have the opportunity to reinvent the orchestra, and the nature of orchestral musicians. Orchestras now are about much more than converting paper scores into sound, even when they are playing classical works composed in the distant past. The orchestra of the future in some—at present unknown—contemporary way or ways, will surely help to shape the further development of music.

Anthony Kemp (1996) has carried out sustained and comprehensive research into the personality of musicians. He has conducted this through using questionnaires, notably *Sixteen Personality Factor Questionnaire* (16PF) of Raymond Cattell (Cattell et al. 1970), which has been used widely throughout the world to investigate personality in a wide range of contexts. Kemp has found that professional musicians, in general, have some personality traits that differ from those of other people, and that the personality traits of those who are specialists in different instruments vary. For example, professional musicians are more introverted than other people, and oboists are often the most anxious of musicians. However, the implications of these findings do not include the recommendation that we should be picking out particularly quiet students to learn instruments, and then assigning the most anxious of them to oboe. The 'introversion' that Cattell measures is an umbrella for a host of traits—including 'aloofness', 'desurgency', 'shyness', and 'self-sufficiency'—for which individuals who gain the same overall 'score' may have quite different results, and be quite different to be with. And the same is true of other dimensions of personality, such as anxiety. Moreover, we do not know whether musicians have developed particular personality traits through training as musicians, or always had them. For example, were oboists always anxious, or did they become so because they found oboe reeds so unreliable to work with? In Kemp's words:

Those who have received instrumental lessons from an early age, who have frequently been perceived as special by parents and somewhat different by peers at school, who have endured long hours spent in solitary practice, and who have applied themselves to hard work at college are likely to emerge with a fairly unique combination of personality traits . . . they are likely to be essentially introverted, reflecting the demands, not only of an internalized saturation with music, but also the effects that the acquisition of instrumental skills have over an extended period of years on a developing personality.' (Kemp 1996: 139; quoted in Mills 2005b: 120–1)

To put this in other words, while musicians may, indeed, have some personality traits that differ from those of other people, it is impossible to say whether they have always had them, or developed them as a by-product of their musical training.

In *Music in the School* I wrote:

> There is nothing, of which I am aware, in personality research that could fairly or reasonably be used to prevent a student who is eager to learn a particular instrument from undergoing the best test of potential: having some lessons from a flexible and sympathetic teacher, and seeing how he or she gets on. (Mills 2005*b*: 120)

Some of the 50 instrumental teachers also considered that successful students of their instrument required some particular musical, usually aural, skills. These tie in with another publication of the time—*You Can Make Music!* (Ben-Tovim and Boyd 1986). As part of a diagnostic system intended to guide potential students, mainly of adult age, towards an instrument on which they might make progress, Atarah Ben-Tovim and Douglas Boyd devised and published a set of three preliminary tests intended for all instruments, with follow-up tests for individual instruments. The individual tests are a Right Time Test that addresses whether 'now' is a good time in a person's life to begin learning an instrument, a Musicality Test, and a Skill and Motivation Test. The Musicality Test is shown in Table 5.

After completing the three preliminary tests, potential learners could fill out the specific tests for some (or all) instruments that the book stated fell within the range of difficulty that was appropriate to them. Collation of the tables shown in *You Can Make Music!* shows that the difficulty of the instruments[3] that were considered in the book was classified as shown in Table 6.

For me, at least, Table 6 raises as many questions as it yields answers. Why does the piano require less 'musicality' than the harpsichord? Why does it not matter if you take up the orchestral double bass at a time that is right for you, when this is important for violin, viola, and cello? Why do most of the brass instruments, and orchestral percussion, not require high levels of 'skill and motivation', and what might be James Gourlay's view on this? Why can the electronic organ and recorder (which the book acknowledges has a significant early music and baroque repertoire) be learnt at the wrong time, and without musicality or skill and motivation? Why can the drum kit, saxophone, flute, and clarinet—like the piano—be learnt without musicality?

---

[3] Readers who feel that the list of instruments chosen for research is quaint may wish to bear in mind that *You Can Make Music!* was written more than 20 years ago. Nevertheless, my recollection of 1986 is that there were more students, including adult students, learning rock guitar or folk guitar, say, than harpsichord.

Table 5 The musicality test

	Score nil	Score 10 each
1 Can you quickly recognize the National Anthem, a favourite piece of music, or a popular television theme tune?	No	Yes
2 If you hummed or whistled 'God Save the Queen', could someone else recognize it?	No	Yes
3 When listening, do you ever move to the music: tap a foot, drum your fingers, 'conduct' to yourself or dance?	No	Yes
4 Can you name three professional musicians?	No	Yes
5 Is listening to music an important part of your life?	No	Yes
6 Do you often sing, whistle, hum to yourself when alone, or sing along with radio, cassettes?	No	Yes
7 Do you find it impossible to sing hee-haw with the hee very high and the haw very low?	Yes	No
8 Do you find it difficult to march in step, or dance in time, to music?	Yes	No
9 Each instrument has a characteristic sound. Some are easy to recognize; others more difficult. Can you identify the sound of eight or more of the following? FLUTE/PIANO/ELECTRIC GUITAR/TRUMPET/VIOLIN/ELECTRIC ORGAN/DRUM/HARP/ SAXOPHONE/TROMBONE (Give yourself five marks if you could identify between five and seven of the instruments.)	No	Yes
10 If you heard a short rhythm tapped on a drum or a table top, could you play it back aloud?	No	Yes

SCORE:

To score, multiply by ten the number of times you circled a YES or NO in the right hand column.

If you score 70 or above, you are certainly musical (*sic*)* enough to learn an instrument. It does not matter whether you have previously achieved anything musical in your life or not, for you have the potential to do it now. You should find a wide choice of instruments on which you could succeed.

A score of between 50 and 70 also means that you are musical enough to learn an instrument. Why the lower score? Think back to your childhood or early life. Did you—like so many adults—suffer a musical accident from which you still bear the scars? If so, it is a great pity but not a reason to stop you beginning to make music now. However, you may need to take a little more care in your selection than someone with a higher score, in order to give yourself the best chance of success.

* I have argued that everyone is 'musical'.

Source: Ben-Tovim and Boyd 1986: 19–20

Table 6 Difficulty of instruments considered after the completion of the three tests

	Right time test	Musicality test	Skill and motivation test
Harpsichord, classical guitar, oboe, bassoon, French horn, violin, viola, cello	✓	✓	✓
Piano	✓	—	✓
Orchestral double bass	—	✓	✓
Trombone, trumpet, baritone, cornet, euphonium, tenor horn, tuba, orchestral percussion	—	✓	—
Drum kit, saxophone, flute, clarinet	—	—	✓
Electronic organ, recorder	—	—	—

The content of the Musicality Test also allows some room for debate. Clearly, it would not be right to criticize this test for its use of particular songs 20 years down the line. But why should skills such as humming or whistling a well-known melody 'in tune', or being able to sing hee-haw with the pitch contour of a donkey, be at all relevant to a person's potential on oboe, orchestral double bass, or trumpet, for example, given that oboists, bass players, and trumpeters are only very rarely asked to sing as they play? The answer is that they have no proven relevance whatsoever. However, tests not unlike these are still to be found in some current education practice. In *Music in the School* I wrote:

Ask a teacher how they would find out whether or not a student they have not taught before is 'musical', and while many—rightly in my view—will ask you what you mean by 'musical', some will reply that they would use aural tests. Perhaps they will ask a student to sing back notes played on the piano, or say how many notes there are in some chords played on the piano, or say which of two notes played on a piano was the higher, or clap back some rhythms and say how many beats there are in a bar. These tests are almost invariably used to 'weed out' students who want to learn to play a musical instrument, or to sing in a choir, when 'too many' have volunteered. The tests are hardly ever used to offer some particular encouragement to students who had not thought of learning a musical instrument, or singing in the choir, but who might give it a try were their self-esteem boosted through the knowledge that they had done rather well in an aural test. (There is sadly so much about many approaches to selection for instrumental tuition that is about leaving some students out, rather than encouraging them to join in.)

The tradition of giving these sorts of tests is so long that adults sometimes set them automatically, without thinking clearly what the tests are intended to achieve, and then planning items accordingly. It can be almost like one of those 'word association' games:

say the word 'music' and someone thinks 'aural test' and sets one. This can lead to some bizarre uses of aural tests. For example, I recall a secondary headteacher who insisted on giving the aural tests listed above, individually in a practice room, to each of the music graduates whom he had short-listed for a class teaching post at his school! Why? What was he hoping to achieve through this? If he wanted to know how well the applicants could play an instrument, why not ask them to bring their instruments to the interview and play them? If he wanted to know how well they could sing, why not ask them to teach a song to a class of students? In fact, the headteacher's achievement was that the candidates were angered by what they saw as his arrogance in setting them aural tests, several of them went home, and he was left without a music teacher!

But where teachers do give a reason for setting aural tests for students, they often speak of wanting to know what is going on 'in students' heads'. Probe further, and teachers may explain that they want to know whether students can hear that notes have differing pitch, even though they cannot play them yet, and so forth. But we do not know whether students who have the 'right' things going on in their heads will necessarily make 'better' instrumentalists, or if they will receive more social, educational, or musical benefit from receiving instrumental lessons. And it is, of course, possible that 'what goes on in students' heads' might be improved through experience of learning to play an instrument.

But setting these points aside, it is not even clear that such aural tests could help ascertain what is going on 'in students' heads'. Unless they have already had some musical training, students simply may not know what to do in the tests. Why should a student know automatically what we mean when we say that one note is 'higher' than another, when 'higher' is being used in a way that does not relate to the more usual, spatial, sense of the word? Students may not know what they are expected to copy about notes on a piano or clapping unless this is explained, or they have seen it done before. Counting the number of notes in a chord will not make sense to a student who has not been told what a 'chord' is.

In addition, three of the tests are easier for students who have experience of playing, or playing around on, a piano, for example because they have one at home. Because the timbres of a piano and a singing voice are so different, it can be difficult to match the pitch of a piano note with your voice—even if you can hear the note in your head, and remember the sound of it being played. A student who has learnt how to apply the concept of high/low to the timbre of instruments they play, for example their own singing voice and a descant recorder, may not, yet, be able to apply this to the less familiar timbre of the piano. And a student who has experimented on a piano, building up notes into 'chords' (whether or not they were called chords) will find it easier to reverse the process, and say how many notes are being played at once. But, actually, the 'face validity' of the chord dismantling test seems very low. Why, for example, might it help a beginning trumpeter to be able to work out how many notes there are in a piano chord?

In fact, children's ability to tell the differences between (i.e. discriminate) pitches is typically much finer than is often supposed. Everyone's ability in pitch discrimination depends on the frequency range used, and is often finest within their vocal range for singing. Working within this range, as long ago as 1893, J. A. Gilbert (Shuter-Dyson and Gabriel 1981) found that children aged 7 could, on average, assess the direction of some intervals as small as two-thirds of a semitone. In the early 1960s, Arnold Bentley (1966) found that they could assess one-third of a semitone. In the early 1980s, I found that:

- the average 7-year-old could assess the direction of an interval as small as one-sixth of a semitone, i.e. a 1 per cent difference in frequency
- the average 11-year-old could assess the direction of an interval of about a 0.85 per cent difference in frequency
- some children as young as 9 could judge the direction of an interval as small as one-tenth of a semitone; that is about a 0.6 per cent difference in frequency.

The discrepancies between the three sets of findings are probably due to the differing quality of the recording and replay equipment available at the time. There is no reason to suppose that the children of the 1980s necessarily had pitch discrimination any finer than those of the 1890s. Researchers of pitch discrimination have often reported the results of work with children aged at least 6, because younger children may have difficulty coping with a test that requires them to write their responses. But there is no evidence that younger children do not perceive fine differences in pitch. Bridger (1961) observed that some babies under five days notice pitch differences of about four semitones, and they may be able to perceive much smaller intervals. Indeed it is difficult to understand how children could acquire language, and particularly accent, without pitch discrimination.

It is likely that an investigation of children's pitch discrimination using contemporary digital technology would lead to the finding that their discrimination is even finer than it appeared using the technology of the early 1980s. All this suggests that, if a student is not able to assess the direction of intervals as large as the smallest intervals to be found on a piano, there is something wrong with the test, or the way that it has been explained, rather than the student.

Students' ability to sing in tune is a highly dubious predictor of any sort of musical ability. The assessor may be interested in whether the student can 'hear in tune', yet a student who can hear fine differences in pitch may stil lack the vocal control needed to sing a simple song, or isolated notes, in tune. Or they may just have been asked to sing in a pitch range that is too high or too low for them. In other words, a student who sings well in tune probably has fine pitch discrimination, but the converse is not true.

Students who do not sing well in tune at some point in time frequently learn to do so subsequently. Some even teach themselves. Back in the 1980s, I met Andrew, a 6-year-old who had been rejected from a neighbourhood choir because of his poor pitching. According to my tests his pitch discrimination was better than that of any of the other 250 children up to the age of 9 that I had tested (Mills 1988). Andrew was an unusually determined boy. He wanted to get into that choir, and his parents had overheard him trying to teach himself to sing in tune by matching his voice with piano notes. By the time he was 9, he was one of the stars of the choir, and also a promising trumpeter. But not all children have Andrew's persistence or opportunity. It is so easy for teachers to accidentally write off developing singers as unmusical. (Mills 2005*b*: 121–4)

In 1983, I tested out some popular theories about physical, personality, and musical suitability for particular western classical orchestral instruments on a sample of 299 students aged 7–18 years (Mills 1983). For each student I had two sources of data: their scores on some aural tests that I had devised (Mills 1988),[4] and the response of their teacher to a form that I had devised for each instrument. The forms asked teachers to indicate whether students had, or did not have, characteristics associated with prevalent theories about potential on the instrument in question, and to make predictions about students' achievement on the instrument. I converted these predictions of achievement (which I called 'G') into a scale with a minimum of 1, and a maximum of 9.

The form that I devised for trumpet is shown in the first two columns of Table 7, and the final column comments on the form. When I analysed the completed forms, I did not find a single strong positive correlation between a characteristic and a prediction. In other words, there was no evidence that any of the theories were valid! And when I studied the forms that had been completed for individual students, I found:

high-flying instrumentalists with all sorts of supposedly undesirable features: short-armed trombonists, thick-lipped trumpeters, left-handed cellists, thin-lipped asthmatic oboists, buck-teethed bassoonists, clumsy percussionists, and so on. These students had been given a chance to play a particular instrument, despite their physical characteristics not fitting in with the theories, and were making very good progress.

This ties in with my present-day experiences at the Royal College of Music in London, where my work includes a course on 'how to teach your instrument' for undergraduates who are talented performers. A group of 60 students to whom I recently explained that some instrumental teachers select students by size and shape just looked at each other and laughed. One student spoke for others when she suggested that 'there are students of all shapes and sizes playing most instruments here, but it does not make any difference to how good we are.' A student who plays double bass, and who has already started to give bass lessons to children, admitted that she had spent some time explaining to parents that children do not need to be a particular size before starting to learn to play bass: 'If they are small, they can begin on an instrument that is not much bigger than a violin.' A very short woman and a very tall man, both cellists, offered the view that most physical characteristics bring both advantages and disadvantages. The woman envies the man's ability to stretch larger intervals with his left hand; the man wishes that he did not need to 'overlap' his fingers when playing a long way down the fingerboard, close to the bridge.

Observant teachers notice the individual physical differences of their students, and draw their students into the conversation about how to develop technical ways of achieving

---

[4] I later published these aural tests so that school teachers could use them to help spot students with unusual potential for music but who had not previously had much experience of playing instruments. In other words, they were intended to be used positively. However, most of the reports that I received of the use of these tests related to them being used negatively—to provide evidence, typically for parents, of why their child was purportedly not suitable for tuition on some instrument, or should be encouraged to 'give it up'. This was a travesty of their original purpose.

Table 7 Trumpet—current student

ORIGINAL FORM		COMMENTARY	
TRUMPET Teacher	School/centre		
————	—————————		
Student	Student's age at aural test		
————	————		
1. Please mark each statement below with a tick or a cross to indicate whether or not it is true of this student		*Statement type: source*	*Response predicted for successful trumpeters*
	Please tick or cross		
Usually writes with the left hand		*Physical: teachers*	*Right hand*
Sings in tune		*Musical: teachers*	*Sings in tune*
Has an awkward gait		*Physical: teachers*	*Does not have awkward gait*
Attends instrumental lessons punctually		*Personal: teachers*	*Attends punctually*
When the right hand is placed palm down on a table, with the fingers together, the index finger is closer in length to the middle digit than is the ring finger*		*Physical: digital formula research*	*Could be either. Left hand (6) more important*
When the left hand is placed palm down on a table, with the fingers together, the index finger is closer in length to the middle digit than is the ring finger*		*Physical: digital formula research*	*I > R*
Displays double-jointedness in any left-hand digit		*Physical: teachers*	*Does not display double-jointedness*
Displays double-jointedness in any right-hand digit		*Physical: teachers*	*Does not display double-jointedness*
Has tapering finger tips		*Physical: teachers*	*Does not have tapering fingers*
Concentrates during instrumental lessons		*Physical: teachers*	*Concentrates during instrumental lessons*
Suffers from one or more of the following: hayfever, bronchitis, asthma, tonsillitis		*Physical: teachers*	*Does not suffer from any of these*
Is currently undergoing orthodontic treatment		*Physical: teachers*	*Not currently undergoing orthodontic treatment*
Is able to tuck the upper lip inside the upper teeth		*Physical: teachers*	*Can tuck the upper lip inside the upper teeth*
Has a reversed bite (i.e. underbite—lower teeth naturally closing outside upper teeth)		*Physical: teachers*	*Does not have a reversed bite*

Continued

Table 7 Cont.

ORIGINAL FORM		COMMENTARY	
	Please tick or cross		
Has no protruding upper teeth		*Physical: teachers*	*Does not have protruding upper teeth*
Has thin lips		*Physical: teachers*	*Has thin lips*
Has no gaps between any of the front six teeth on either jaw		*Physical: teachers*	*Does not have gaps between teeth*
Does not lisp		*Physical: teachers*	*Does not lisp*

2. The student has reported the following successes in practical trumpet examinations. Please alter the table if it is incorrect.

Board	Grade	Class/Mark	Student's age at examination

If trumpet lessons were to continue throughout the student's school career, what Associated Board practical grade do you anticipate the student would reach by the following age(s)?	
11 16 18	
3. Please add any comments about the particular case here.	
4. Please add any comments about this form here.	

* These two questions relate to research on relative finger lengths that was motivated by my reading of anatomy textbooks, rather than teachers' views (Mills 1983). Please see also Chapter 4 n. 1 about digital formula. While the general population is thought to have a 'digital formula' of I < R on their left hand (index finger shorter than ring finger when resting against the middle finger), empirical evidence that I had collected indicated that successful performers on most western classical instruments except violin and viola were more likely to have a 'digital formula' of I > R. I am firmly of the view that 'digital formula' does not predict success in any sense that is inevitable. Trumpet students with the 'wrong' formula of I < R can, and do, still succeed! The point is that they are more likely to succeed where they have teachers who are observant of their physical skills, and help them find ways of improving them, rather than expecting them to mirror the physical skills of their teacher who, as a successful trumpeter, is likely to have an I > R formula on their left hand.

Source: Mills 1983: 411

musical ends that are consonant with the shape, size, flexibility, and so forth of their bodies. This is what the teaching of technique is all about. Whatever instrument a student plays, their body is part of it. This is obvious in the case of singing, but also true of every other instrument. An oboe is more than the pieces of hardware that one puts back in the case at the end of a rehearsal. A piano cannot function without a pianist. In the past, teachers have sometimes not been adept at noticing physical differences between themselves and their students, and have tried to teach young people to play exactly like them, regardless of their shape. Students' physical differences need to be worked with, and on occasion worked around, just like temperamental oboes, wolf notes on cellos, and the idiosyncrasies of pipe organs and the buildings that they play in. (Mills 2005b: 117–18)

The forms that I used to collect data from individual teachers looked very similar for all instruments, but were personalized to reflect the main theories about what makes a good player of a particular instrument. The form for trumpet is shown in Table 7.

The table is not presented here as an example of a particularly effective 'research instrument'. Rather, it is offered as an example of a 'research instrument'—in this case a form—that was developed in good faith by many teachers, and me, following much discussion and reading of books, but that nevertheless verged on useless. This was even though it appeared to be 'sensible' to those of us who assembled it. Not one of the items in the list of supposed predictors of trumpet potential proved useful. To put it another way, none of the correlations between any of the items on the list and teachers' prediction of the future achievement of students (G) was statistically significant. While it may, or may not, be the case that writing with one's right hand, for example, makes playing the trumpet easier, the effect of factors such as these—if indeed this is a factor—is obscured by all the other things that are happening. Perhaps writing with one's left hand really is a disadvantage for a trumpeter, but the effects of this disadvantage were offset, in the case of the left-handed trumpeter in my sample, through them having a better instrument, or a more imaginative and inspiring teacher, or ready access to a band to play in. We will never know. But I would not be at all surprised were having a good instrument and an effective teacher to prove more useful to an aspiring trumpeter than an ability to write with their right hand. You don't often have to write at the same time as playing a trumpet. But the superior sound you get from your better instrument, the excitement you get from playing in your band, and the buzz that comes from having an inspirational teacher are with you from the moment that you take your trumpet out of its case, and return whenever you think of taking your trumpet out of its case again. Perhaps it is worth working to improve your (literal) dexterity with the trumpet valves just to experience all that . . .

Returning to the numbers, the 'regression equation' that predicted G most effectively from the listed items proved to be:

G (trumpet) = 6.48 + 0.83 (sings in tune) − 0.68 (thin lips) + 0.24 (current orthodontic treatment)

Thus, to get the most accurate measure of a student's likely achievement on trumpet (range from 1 to 9) we:

- write down 6.48
- add on 0.83 if their teacher said they sing in tune
- *subtract* 0.68 if their teacher said they had thin lips (although the theory is that thin lips are advantageous on trumpet!)
- *add* 0.24 if the teacher says that they are currently taking orthodontic treatment (although the theory is that current orthodontic treatment limits trumpeters' achievement!)

The observant reader may also have noted that nobody can gain G (trumpet) that is lower than 5.8, or higher than 7.6.

Regression equations do have their uses, when handled carefully. But my experience of working with these instrument lists in 1983 makes me very cautious about the usefulness of other lists, such as those that appear in *You Can Make Music!*, in which scores for diverse characteristics are added up to give a measure of potential for a particular instrument. A scale constructed by adding up scores on items cannot possibly be any more use in predicting anything than a regression scale constructed from the same items.

1985 revisited

After my work with the lists, I wrote some guidance for schools on offering instrumental tuition to students (Mills 1985). The five headings below are drawn from that publication: the text below the headings updates the comments that I added in 1985:

1. *Do not offer children tuition on an instrument until they have become familiar with several instruments.* Students can sometimes end up learning one instrument at school, rather than another, for no good reason. I have already said that, in particular, they may not have chosen the instrument for its sound, and may even be unaware what their 'chosen' instrument sounds or looks like! (James Gourlay is certainly not the only person who was assigned to an instrument for reasons that were random.)

   In 1985 I suggested that schools organize programmes whereby students experienced high-quality performances on several instruments before choosing what they would like to play. I suggested also that these performances be given, where possible, by young performers at the same school.

Many schools organize these sorts of programmes very effectively. For example, in 1998 I wrote of Highfields School, Wolverhampton, where performances by Highfields students are reinforced through high-quality photographic displays of high-achieving Highfields students playing their instruments (Rose et al. 1998).

Over the last few years, local authorities—and more recently schools—in England have been provided with some additional funding in order to run introductory programmes of instrumental teaching for students in primary schools. Sometimes known as 'tasters' these schemes can serve a very useful purpose. However, they need to consist of worthwhile musical experience, and lead seamlessly to something that builds comprehensively upon the skills that students have gained. It is counter-productive to give students a whistle stop tour of learning several instruments, and leave any-one with the erroneous impression that there was even one instrument that they were incapable of learning to play well, if that is what they wanted to do. (I recall a taster course, run by a local authority in a primary school, that provided students with four group lessons on each of flute, trumpet, violin, and keyboard, and that gave some students the incorrect impression that they would always be unable to produce any sound from a trumpet or flute, or a pleasant sound from a violin.) It is counter-productive also to give students a series of dynamic instrumental lessons on, say, clarinet, but then turn off the supply when the 'taster' ends. Finally, it is counter-productive to offer 'taster' courses that are musically vacuous. I recall a taster course in Indian music, run by a local authority in a Saturday music centre, that gave students several weeks' experience of playing freely on some very nice new Indian instruments—harmonium, sitar, tamboura and tabla—but where nobody present, teacher or students, knew anything about Indian music, or how the instruments were usually played. When observing a lesson on this course, I struggled to think of anything positive that I could say about it. There was no observable growth in students' musical skills, and they did not learn to work more effectively in groups, as they worked entirely as individuals, with their individual work sometimes drowned by that of their peers. There was no use of any of the verbal language of Indian music, such as raga. The stu-dents looked bored, and were starting to become fractious. One of them wandered around the room, disrupting the free play of his peers. The teacher knew that she was out of her depth musically, and had retreated behind a desk, from which she barked only admonitions about behaviour.

When the young Yehudi Menuhin was given a toy violin, after saying that he wanted to play violin, he broke it, and was rewarded with a genuine violin and genuine lessons (Menuhin 1976). Students who are similarly unful-filled by their taster experiences in school may receive shorter shrift. The providers of instrumental taster courses should take care that they are suffi-ciently long to allow students to develop confidence; consist of worthwhile musical activity; and lead seamlessly to the chance to continue learning an instrument for all students who want this. This means that students who have been learning trumpet, say, should have the opportunity to continue to learn trumpet immediately. (And if more than an occasional student wants to drop out of playing trumpet, or any other instrument, serious questions should be asked about the quality of its 'taster' provision.)

2. *Do not let children become discouraged from taking lessons if, at first, they cannot make a pleasant sound on any instrument.* Wind and brass teachers, in particular, sometimes used to select potential students by giving them an instrument to play, and seeing whether they could produce a note from it. This begs the question of what the lessons are for! It is far more important that students should love the sound of their chosen instrument played well, and be keen to work at emulating this.

   Of course, children will often want to try blowing their instrument before their first lesson. Teachers take care to ensure that they do not become despondent if they cannot produce a note at this stage. There are many examples of such young people who need help with producing any note from a wind or brass instrument, but who go on to be successful players. Anecdotally, my mother, who took up French horn at the age of 17, and who went on to play for her living, reports that she was unable to make any sound from the horn for several lessons. Her story is similar to that of other musicians.

3. *When considering the potential of a normal healthy child for an instrument, give more weight to their motivation to play the instrument than their appar-ent physical suitability for it.* In the light of what I have already written in this chapter, there is little more to be said on this subject, at this stage.

4. *Do not discourage children who cannot make up their mind which instru-ment to play from playing any instrument at all.* Such children can be encouraged to consider which instrument they most like the sound of, and reassured that deciding which instrument to play is not an irrevocable decision.

   This is different from assigning students to particular instruments on the grounds that these are what are available. In 2002, Susan O'Neill reported substantial mismatch between the instruments that students in their last year of primary school (aged 10) and their first year of secondary school (aged 11) wanted to play, and the instruments that they were, in fact, learning to play. No wonder that some of them discontinued their lessons when they moved from primary to secondary school (O'Neill 2002: 5).

The differences in the instruments that boys and girls play, and also that boys and girls want to play, are reflected by gender stereotyping of instruments that begins before children have entered school (see Abeles and Porter 1978; Griswold and Chroback 1981). It is well known that, when asked to choose between western classical orchestral instruments, boys tend to favour the louder and lower ones, and Susan O'Neill's table adds popular instruments into this picture. There are no reasons why musicians of either gender should not play any instrument, and plenty of examples of them doing so successfully. Gender stereotyping of instruments by students, families, and schools needs to be addressed head on, because it limits the progress of students, and the enjoyment that they could ultimately obtain from music. Arranging for students aged 7–8 to attend 'counter gender-stereotypic' performances in which they hear and see instruments played well by musicians of the 'wrong' gender can be of help (Harrison and O'Neill 2000). Teachers continue to develop further approaches in an attempt to resolve this problem (see Table 8).

5. *Do not assume that children who do not make a success of the first instrument on which they have lessons would not make a success of another instrument.* Not everyone aspires to work in music but there are many examples of individuals who took up a second—or third—instrument at a relatively old age, and then went on to play it for their living. For example, within western classical music, these include musicians who entered a conservatoire as a specialist in one instrument, and left it with an orchestral or teaching post in an only distantly related instrument that they took up during their conservatoire studies. Examples include musicians who transferred from flute to clarinet, violin to trombone, trombone to tuba in the case of teaching posts, and piano/oboe to percussion, piano to viola, and trombone to percussion in the case of orchestral or ensemble posts. (Mills 1985; 2004*d*)

Table 8 Percentage of girls and boys who most want to play and actually play specific instruments

	Girls %			Boys %		
	Most want to play (age 10)	**Actually play (age 10)**	**Actually play (age 11)**	**Most want to play (age 10)**	**Actually play (age 10)**	**Actually play (age 11)**
1	Piano 17.7	Recorder 31.9	Recorder 24.6	Drums 25.1	Recorder 20.2	Recorder 23.1
2	Flute 16.9	Flute 13.2	Clarinet 13.9	Electric Guitar 23.9	Piano 13.5	Keyboard 17.6
3	Keyboard 11.3	Violin 11.7	Flute 13.4	Keyboard 11.0	Keyboard 12.9	Guitar 8.3
4	Saxophone 11.0	Clarinet 10.5	Keyboard 11.8	Saxophone 9.8	Guitar 12.9	Drums 6.5
5	Drums 8.6	Piano 9.7	Violin 9.6	Piano 5.5	Drums 9.2	Piano 6.5
6	Violin 8.6	Keyboard 9.7	Piano 8.6	Guitar 4.9	Clarinet 3.1	Clarinet 5.6
7	Clarinet 7.3	Cello 4.7	Cello 4.3	Electric Bass 4.0	Electric Guitar 3.1	Cornet 4.6
8	Electric Guitar 3.5	Guitar 2.3	Guitar 4.3	Bagpipes 2.0	Cello 3.1	Electric Guitar 4.6
9	Guitar 3.0	Cornet 0.8	Cornet 2.7	Trumpet 1.7	Violin 3.1	Violin 3.7
10	Harp 2.7	Organ 0.8	Viola 1.6	Flute 1.7	Trumpet 2.5	Trombone 2.8

Chapter 6

Instrumental lessons, music, and life

It is an acknowledged fact that, when properly carried out, class-work in music . . . has most certainly the effect of stimulating the mental faculties of those who take part in it, and, as a result, of improving the standard of work in other departments.

Stewart MacPherson in *The Musical Education of the Child: Some Thoughts and Suggestions for Teachers, Parents and Schools* (MacPherson 1922: 13)

Linda, aged 16, is principal cornet in the youth brass band of an internationally famous adult band. But she dreams of playing French horn in an orchestra for her living, and has acquired one and started lessons. I knew nothing of this until one day she arrived at a school orchestra rehearsal with a horn instead of her cornet, and asked if she could play the horn part. She then proceeded to play it superbly at sight. She has not told the band that she has taken up French horn, because she feels certain they will try to stop her. She tells me that her bandmaster has no respect for any music other than brass band music, and also that he would assert that the embouchures of the two instruments would conflict—so that playing French horn would wreck her cornet playing.

Edited extract from author's teaching notes: 1981

Spider is a brilliant drummer who plays in a bhangra group. He has long hair, always wears a hat and can appear to be sullen. He asked about drum lessons at school but failed the audition given by the drum teacher. The audition was decided by the teacher talking to the students and deciding who he thought would have the best attitude. Spider had a neighbour with a drum kit and used to go round to 'have a go'. After school he had no qualifications and became unemployed. He has recently started community workshops and young people love his music. He asked about giving some lessons in his local school but when he appeared in 'ripped' jeans was asked not to return.

(NIAS 1997: 11)

European classical music that we have today will not survive unless we make a radical effort to change our attitude to it and unless we take it away from a specialized niche that it has become, unrelated to the rest of the world, and make it something that is essential to our lives ... Some of us are more fanatic about music, more interested than others, but I think we should all have the opportunity to learn not only it but to learn from it.

Daniel Barenboim: 'The Magic of Music': third Reith Lecture 2006
(Barenboim 2006c)

These four quotations, arranged in chronological order, are all about some aspect of making music relevant to, and part of, everyday life.

Stewart MacPherson, writing in 1922, provides us with an early published assertion that studying music has educational benefits that extend beyond music. Note the carefulness of his language: 'acknowledged fact' (rather than 'proven fact'); 'when properly carried out' (random or ill-considered musical activity will not do); the proposal of a mechanism for the link—'stimulation of mental faculties'.

Linda, who I taught long before the (in this case) closed brass-band world was opened to wider public scrutiny by the film *Brassed Off* (1996), reminds us how, probably, any form of music can be viewed as the only music worth doing by some of its protagonists. And how difficult it can be for someone who wants to carry on doing that music really well, but also to spread their wings. The bandmaster's view of expertise in brass-band cornet playing as an 'answer-filled expert' (see p. 25) conflicts with Linda's view as an 'accomplished novice'. (I wonder that happened to Linda. Did she achieve her goal of playing French horn for her living? Is she still active as a musician?)

Spider, a fine bhangra drummer, was initially excluded from receiving drum lessons, and subsequently excluded from passing on the drum skills that he, against the odds, had nevertheless managed to accumulate. This was although young people wanted to learn from him, and although he was not welcome in school only because of some irrelevant matters of dress and speech. As a potential student, he battled against problems a little like those who want to start playing a western classical instrument—say piano—but who are prevented because their singing is not too good. As a potential teacher, he has been 'banned' from school for much the same reason that caused him to feel excluded as a student.

Daniel Barenboim argues that western classical music needs to be made less precious, more essential to life, if it is to survive.

In this chapter we take the view that an ambition to relate the music that students do in instrumental music to other aspects of their lives is at least arguably 'good'. We can think back to the thoughts and experiences of Stewart MacPherson, Linda, Spider, and Daniel Barenboim, and perhaps also to our individual experiences, and those of others who we know, as this chapter considers instrumental lessons, music, and life from four main angles:

- Systems
- A broad approach to music[1]
- Learning that broadens
- Music helping other learning

Systems

Schools have plenty of systems and so, particularly in the case of lessons that take place in schools, there are many ways in which instrumental lessons can be linked constructively with the systems that already govern much of students' lives. Does the school have a 'merit' system that rewards special achievement or behaviour that 'goes the extra mile'? If so, how can instrumental teachers tap into this? Does the school have assemblies that are given by particular year groups or particular classes? If so, are there some ways in which instrumental students can (if they wish) feed into these? Does the school run leadership schemes such as the Duke of Edinburgh's Award? If so, do the members of staff organizing these schemes know of the leadership achievements of instrumental students, for example when working in bands, chamber ensembles, and youth orchestras? I could go on . . .

Taking time to make links with school is virtually always worth the effort. Students generally spend more time each week in class music lessons, rather than instrumental lessons, and there are usually further activities, such as ensembles, that students can access. Instrumental teachers take care not to underestimate the musical potential and achievements of schools, most usually primary schools, where there may be no music graduate in charge of the music curriculum. These teachers often lack confidence rather than competence, primary children often benefit from having a teacher who knows them

---

[1] This section includes two essays drawn from *Music in the School*, chapter 6: 'the instrumental curriculum and the school' and 'the optional instrumental curriculum'.

rather than one who only knows music, and primary schools that are modest about their music educational achievements sometimes actually provide a more effective music education (Mills 1989b; 1997).

Just occasionally, I suppose, students—of any age—may want their instrumental lessons to take place in a world that is entirely separate from the rest of their lives. While this view should be respected it should also be questioned; one reason is that the lack of 'grounding' of instrumental teaching leaves it vulnerable should there be a change in students' circumstances. If the instrumental tuition is not needed for anything else in a student's life except instrumental tuition, then it is easy for a student to decide to dispense with it entirely.

Separation of instrumental tuition from the rest of students' school lives would be particularly questionable where the lessons take place in school, so that facilities including a teaching room, and possibly also administrative support and the interaction with other instrumental teachers, are provided. Why, to be frank, should the school provide any of this if it has no idea what—if anything—is being achieved, and no opportunity to link with it?

It is, of course, harder for teachers to draw upon the school systems of students who they teach away from school—but not impossible and very worthwhile—as many instrumental teachers have already shown.

A broad approach to music

It goes without saying that students' musical interests typically extend well beyond their instrumental lessons. Indeed, had they no other prior musical interests, they probably would not have thought of taking up instrumental lessons.

Susan O'Neill has prepared a wide range of tables[2] that show school students' involvement in various musical activities during their last year at primary school, and their first year at secondary school. Here I include just two of them. Table 9, prepared by Susan O'Neill, shows that many school students in their last year at primary school, and first year at secondary school, are involved in a range of singing activities, although it seems that the extent of these may diminish, to some extent, as students enter secondary school.

Table 10 shows the same school students involved in a range of listening activities which, in some cases, seem to increase on entry to secondary school.

Recent data (Ward 2006: 4) has suggested that students have acquired further listening equipment in their bedrooms since 2002, so that the popularity

---

[2] The tables are based on the responses of 1,209 students in their last year at primary school (age 10, Wave 1) and 832 of the same students who were followed through into the first year of their secondary school (age 11, Wave 2).

Table 9 Percentage of children's responses for singing, aged 10 to 11

How often do you . . .?	Never %		Not very often %		Sometimes %		Very often %	
	age 10	age 11	age 10	age 11	age 10	age 11	age 10	age 11
Sing by yourself when there isn't any music playing?	17.0	11.6	17.9	21.8	30.1	32.5	35.0	34.1
Sing by yourself to music on the radio, tape or CD?	6.0	5.4	8.7	12.1	23.4	23.6	61.9	58.9
Sing a song you have made up?	26.5	27.2	24.6	25.0	23.3	26.9	25.4	20.8
Sing with a friend?	27.1	25.4	20.6	25.8	28.3	26.8	23.8	22.0
Sing with someone in your family?	31.2	28.6	26.2	31.5	23.6	25.3	19.0	14.6
Sing in music class at school?	18.9	16.4	17.3	20.2	28.3	40.6	35.5	22.8
Sing in the school choir?	58.4	69.5	9.5	13.3	9.3	7.6	22.6	9.6
Sing in front of people (in a school concert, church choir, a band, etc.)?	32.4	52.4	19.7	20.9	25.3	16.6	22.5	10.1

Table 10 Percentage of children's responses for listening to music, aged 10 to 11

How often do you . . .?	Never %		Not very often %		Sometimes %		Very often %	
	age 10	age 11	age 10	age 11	age 10	age 11	age 10	age 11
Listen to music by yourself	2.4	1.6	5.8	4.1	30.6	31.7	61.2	62.6
Listen to music with a friend?	10.9	6.5	21.7	17.6	46.7	47.9	20.5	27.9
Listen to music with someone in your family?	8.7	6.5	20.9	20.3	33.0	41.5	37.5	31.7
Go to a concert to listen to music?	47.2	35.6	31.9	37.2	15.4	22.2	5.0	4.9
Listen to music at school?	8.9	6.1	24.6	27.8	39.6	51.6	26.9	14.6
Listen to music at home?	0.8	0.5	4.1	2.7	16.4	15.9	78.7	80.8
Listen to music at a friend's house?	16.1	8.4	24.4	19.0	35.1	41.0	24.3	31.6
Listen to music on the radio?	10.3	4.2	16.2	14.0	30.1	30.4	43.4	51.4
Listen to music on tapes or CDs?	1.4	0.1	2.3	2.8	10.2	13.9	85.7	83.1
Watch music videos?	24.7	19.5	24.2	25.2	29.2	28.4	21.9	26.9

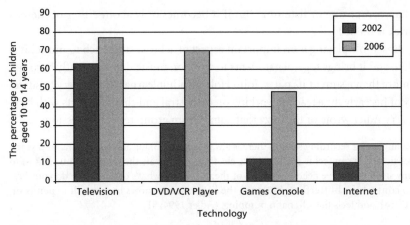

Fig. 4 What is in your child's bedroom? (*Times Educational Supplement* survey of 500 parents)

of listening activities may have further increased. However, it is also worth bearing in mind that students' greater access to computers may have led them to spend more time making, and not only responding to, music (see Fig. 4).

It is unwise ever to make assumptions about the range of music that students will be engaged in outside school. I recently visited an English choir school, a school where boys from the age of 7 or 8 to 13 spend much of their time outside school lessons singing, or learning to sing, the Anglican liturgy in a cathedral or university college choir. Many of the choristers also learn one or more western classical instrument. But one of the choristers also takes weekly tabla lessons at home. I wonder whether the school knows this, and draws on his skills and knowledge during their class music lessons? And does the student see his experience of three instruments: piano, singing, and tabla, as entirely separate, or linked in some way?

I wrote in *Music in the School* (Mills 2005*b*: 149) of a secondary school that was teaching a class music course on Indian music in total musical silence, by working through a textbook, although there was a boy in the class who had been learning tabla for several years. The teacher did not know that the boy played tabla, and so had not asked him whether he was willing to share his expertise.

How sad if the same is happening in the choir school. And how sad, too, if the tabla teacher does not know about the piano lessons and liturgical singing, the piano teacher does not know about the tabla lessons, and also if the singer/tabla player/pianist has not thought of making links between any of his wide range of musical activities. Instrumental tuition provides an opportunity for students who wish to focus on one instrument, and on performing rather than composing or listening. But if it becomes only about either of these, a trick is missed.

Ensemble playing is an important aspect of 'a broad approach to music'. It is fun, and it brings together students to work on music that frequently becomes 'more than a sum of its parts'. John Holt, an adult learner, speaks very positively of his early flute teacher working on orchestral and chamber parts with him. Larry Adler wrote of the buzz that comes from group recording sessions:

At any major recording session there is always a lot of joking and leg-pulling to ease the tension. You can feel it crackling like electricity in the air the moment you walk in to any studio, and I've been in enough of them to know what's coming. You do your best to control the butterflies, but even the biggest star knows how much depends on [them], and feels the adrenalin pumping. (Adler 1994: 5)

The instrumental curriculum and the school

Keith Swanwick (Swanwick 1999: 106) writes of the need for instrumental teachers in schools to avoid becoming 'a string of individuals passing through, as if visiting the dentist'. An extract from *Music in the School* (Mills 2005*b*: 75–80) continues this theme:

It is easy, but dangerous, to think of the music curriculum, in the broadest sense of the word, as divided into separate 'boxes'. Instrumental tuition forms one box, school music forms another, and the informal music-making that students carry out on their own at home or with their friends is a third box, and so on. An instrumental teacher might feel that their box contains all the constituent parts of a graded performance examination—perhaps scales, pieces, and studies, sight-reading and ear tests, and so forth. A schoolteacher might think just in terms of the requirements of the national curriculum, GCSE or A level. Trying to divide music into boxes can make things appear easier for teachers, because they only have to concern themselves with their own box. But it is rarely in students' interests for their learning to be so compartmentalized. It typically leads to diminished expectations of what they are able to achieve. Teachers may entirely overlook the skills and understanding that students have developed in another box, and either teach them again or assume that students are not capable of developing them. Students quickly learn the bounds of what particular teachers expect, or do not expect, them to do—this is part of induction into an educational system—and may not show a teacher that they have a musical life that lies outside the box that surrounds the ambit of the teacher.

A particular conversation with eight children aged 8 and 9 comes to mind here. It was one of those schools that propels itself to the forefront of my mind when I bristle with anger on reading (yet again) in a newspaper that children today do not want to learn, or that school teaching is an easy job because of the long holidays. The school is a maze of dark steep stairs and dark narrow corridors under leaky roofs. It is set in a derelict industrial landscape intersected by several busy roads of speeding 'through traffic'. It does not have a supply of money from its community that it can use to help improve its buildings or environment: nearly all its students are entitled to take free school meals, and many of them are refugees. The school had fallen on hard times educationally, and was working phenomenally hard to try to improve itself. It was making a good shot at teaching the children everything that it should be teaching them, including numeracy, literacy, and the national curriculum in music—including composing.

The children had just had a cornet lesson from a visiting instrumental teacher. In many respects, it was a very good cornet lesson: the children had worked hard, had fun, and emerged from the lesson playing their cornets better than when they arrived. The teacher had told the children at the start of the lesson what he intended they should achieve by the end of it, this was ambitious, they had achieved it, and he had ensured that they knew that they had achieved it. But it was one of those box-bound cornet lessons. There were no obvious links with the music that the children do in their class lessons, at home, or in the community. The teacher operated as though the children only did music during their cornet lessons, and when they were at home practising the cornet pieces that he had given them.

The children had rumbled this. When I asked whether they ever composed on their cornets, they explained—somewhat sheepishly in the first instance—that during cornet lessons they played the music that they had been given, but that when they were at home practising they made up their own cornet tunes. In a sense, they had brought together composing from school music, and cornet playing from their instrumental lessons, in their private musical lives. I asked them whether they ever played their cornet compositions to their cornet teacher, or to their schoolteacher. Of course not. The children clearly thought that I must have come from another planet to be even asking this question. They patiently explained again about only playing the music that one is given during cornet lessons, and then added that one does not bring compositions to class music lessons either—the composing that one does there has to be in response to ideas from the teacher. All this was said without a trace of cynicism.

Just think how much more progress the children could make, musically, if the education system in which they found themselves helped them to bring together their music education in class music, in their cornet lessons, when they are playing their cornets at home, and so on. No teacher can know everything about the richness of children's individual musical lives. But teachers can give children opportunities to talk about, and to show, the music that they do out of school, and try to build on this. Instrumental teachers can liaise with schoolteachers about the content of their curriculum. And they can give children some composing tasks to carry out during their practice time at home, and listen to the compositions that they have made at home on their own, from time to time.

In some local education authority music services, composing is a routine part of the instrumental curriculum. Teachers may set students practice tasks such as composing a melody based on a scale that they are learning, or composing a study or exercise that will help them to consolidate a new technique, and then make time in the next lesson to listen to the students' compositions, and work with them on improving them. Students may be encouraged to share their instrumental compositions with class teachers, and to keep any notes on their compositions, or any scores that they write, in the folders where they store the work completed during class music lessons.

Pat Gane (1996) developed ways of helping instrumental teachers to integrate their curriculum with the national curriculum, even though students may start instrumental lessons at widely differing ages, and show different rates of progress in becoming instrumentalists. She suggested ten 'instrumental levels' based on a notional student who starts instrumental lessons at age 7–8, achieves level 4 (roughly equivalent to Grade 2–3 in a performance examination but broader in scope) on leaving primary school at age 11, and who achieves level 7 (roughly equivalent to Grade 4) on completing the national curriculum in music at the age of 14. She defines five 'areas of learning' for the instrumental curriculum:

- performing/playing
- composing/improvising
- listening/aural
- appraising understanding
- personal development

and offers sample programmes of study and linked assessment profiles for a notional student, Warren Black, who began the violin aged 7 in September 1995, and who reached level 6 by July 2001. Warren and his teacher, Mantovani, completed an assessment profile each July, and two of the sections (the general section and the section relating to composing/improvising) from July 1998, when Warren was level 3 and aged 10, are shown in Table 11 (Gane 1996: 59).

Pat Gane's work relates, of course, to the 1995 version of the national curriculum for England (DfE 1995), but the ideas that it contains have the flexibility to

Table 11 Extracts from the assessment form of a 10 year old

Composing/Improvising	Teacher's comments
Makes up simple Question and Answer phrases in keys G, D, A, C, e, a;* devises simple accompanying ostinati and riffs; makes up simple musical ideas e.g. on a given mood or idea; uses symbols to achieve a planned effect; can use some musical elements expressively: melody/rhythm/ dynamics and simple texture; uses simple structural ideas e.g. repetition, contrast, question and answer.	Improvising is good, some excellent, for instance the jazz riffs you made up for our blues arrangement; composing is hampered by your tendency to accept your first go; try and refine ideas a bit more.
	Student's comments
	I liked the jazz piece; I don't like writing music down much because it takes too long.

General notes
Well done, Warren: I am really pleased with your progress this year; you deserved your merit in the Grade 2 examination; you are much more comfortable with your work now; you have been a good member of the string club and played in class composition projects too I believe; you seem a lot happier with the change of group this year; next term you are ready to begin level 4 work; I will keep you in the same group for one term and then perhaps move you to another one.

* G, D, A, C major; E, A minor.

be applied to any version of a national curriculum that encompasses composing, performing, and listening, including the current curriculum in England.

A Common Approach (FMS et al. 2002*a*), a published instrumental/vocal curriculum framework that reflects the distilled thoughts of hundreds of instrumental teachers in the UK, has taken even further ideas that are similar to Pat Gane's. 'Creating, developing, and interpreting musical ideas' is one of six interrelated areas of musical experience that teachers are encouraged to integrate into their day-to-day and longer-term planning. From their earliest lessons, students learning string instruments, for example, are taught to improvise and compose on their instrument, as shown in Table 12:

By the time that string students have reached the most advanced stage of *A Common Approach 2002*, the possibilities for teaching activities include those shown in Table 13.

It is possible to think of many music projects which involve the creative use of instrumental skills, have potential benefits for instrumentalists as performers and creators of music, and that could be led either by instrumental teachers or by school teachers. *Fingers are great inspirers*, Project 4 from John Paynter's *Sound and Structure*, in which musical instruments themselves inspire musical ideas by the ways in which they seem to be asking to be played,

Table 12 Extracts from Programme Study 1 of *A Common Approach 2002: Strings* (FMS et al. 2002c: 9)

Possible teaching activities*	Points to note
Ask students to explore different ways of making musical sounds on the instrument in response to an imaginative or pictorial idea	The teacher can promote pupils' confidence by: ♦ demonstrating how to experiment with musical ideas ♦ providing step-by-step assistance with models, patterns, and procedures ♦ emphasizing the open-ended nature of the activity—all outcomes are valued and enjoyed.
Help pupils to make up short and simple rhythmic/melodic patterns from suggested musical starting points, e.g. two or three selected notes, ostinati. Abstract or pictorial ideas could also be used.	
Repeat the process, selecting and discarding musical ideas for musical coherence.	
Lead pupils in a discussion about the musical effect of their improvisations.	
Play 'Follow my Leader': a pupil plays three or four notes, then the next pupil plays three or four more, starting on the last note of the first player, and so on.	
Ask pupils to compose short pieces from a given starting point, e.g. a story, poem, theme, picture, or one of the musical techniques suggested above. Discuss the outcomes. Initially, this could consist of asking pupils to write down their improvisations as an aid to memory, perhaps using their own forms of shorthand as a precursor to staff notation.	Through composing, pupils are able to explore the music from the inside. Composing is valid in its own right, but it can also be used to develop performing skills, knowledge, and understanding. Productive links with general classroom work should be made wherever possible. It may be necessary to store pupils' ideas for them since their creative imagination may run ahead of their ability to write down their ideas, at least where staff notation is concerned.
Provide opportunities for pupils to perform their compositions to others.	
Encourage pupils to use their instruments in creative activities in the classroom, applying technical skills already acquired.	

* Instrumental teachers should harness the composing interests of pupils whenever it is appropriate. This may be as an integral part of the instrumental curriculum, or to support the pupils in other areas of the national curriculum.

Table 13 Extracts from Programme Study 5 of *A Common Approach 2002: Strings*
(FMS et al. 2002c: 57, 59)

Possible teaching activities	Points to note
Continue to link improvisations to repertoire being studied, e.g. pupils improvise a short piece in the baroque or romantic styles.	Improvisation provides an obvious and enjoyable way of exploring musical devices and conventions. It often provides the groundwork for more extended compositions. These advanced improvisations can be as challenging for the teacher as the pupil!
Teach a well-known jazz standard, e.g. 'I Got Rhythm': • play pupils a recording of the piece • familiarize them with the 32-bar AABA form and teach them the chords and melody. Play it with them as a pupil/teacher duo, swapping roles • demonstrate how to embellish the melody freely and encourage pupils to do the same when their turn comes • finally, ask them to improvise over the chords, making fewer references to the original melody.	
Ask pupils to compose pieces for more than one instrument, e.g. string quartet, solo string instrument and piano . . .	Pupils can use techniques associated with pieces being learnt. These may include contrapuntal textures and more complex structures, and can involve a higher level of technical difficulty for the performer . . . Encourage pupils to exploit the idiomatic potential of instruments.

is a case in point. Pieces of music for individual instruments can be built from *glissandi* on a harp or trombone, by moving chord shapes up and down the neck of a guitar, or by hitting a suspended cymbal in different places, with different strokes or mallets, and with different methods of damping sounds. There is scope to build these ideas into pieces for mixed instruments that begin, perhaps, with each instrument stating its ideas, and move, via combination of these ideas, to the development of one instrument's ideas by another instrument

New ears, Project 9 from *Sound and Structure*, challenges instrumentalists to identify their preconceptions about music—for example that music is melodic, or that specific instruments usually use only a small, prescribed, range of all the sounds that they are capable of producing—and deliberately try to override these preconceptions as they compose music that is new in some way (Fig. 5).

Project 9: New ears

Tradition can be something of a liability. So much that is valuable and stimulating has been received from the past that just to be aware of those achievements can be daunting, and may hinder new ways of thinking about things. Then again, familiarity can breed contempt, but it also tends to confirm assumptions. We have all heard so many good tunes that we may take it for granted that music, to be called music at all, has to be tuneful—or, at least, melodic.

Similarly, it is very easy to associate particular instruments with certain kinds of music, and that strengthens our convictions about what is or is not 'beautiful' and 'musical' sound. It is easy to imagine a harpist playing calm, unruffled music with lots of gentle sweeps across the strings; even when harp music is fast and energetic it still has that same 'beautiful' quality. Could this instrument ever produce an ugly sound?

Yet, if we had never heard the familiar instruments being played—if we came upon them unexpectedly and with no preconceptions—we might discover many unusual ways of playing them; and we'd listen to their sounds with new ears.

Assignment 1

For individual players using their own musical instruments. Think of ways of making musical sounds as different as possible from those normally expected from the instrument. Make a piece of music using only those unexpected sounds.

Assignment 2

For four string players (preferably the conventional string quartet). Listen to a number of Classical and early Romantic string quartets (e.g. by Haydn, Mozart, Schubert, Mendelssohn). Make a note of features that are characteristic of the string quartet sound. Think of ways in which those features could deliberately be avoided (i.e. ways of playing the instruments that would prevent the players from making the conventional sounds). Using these controls, make a piece which has an overall *new* 'string quartet sound', unlike anything that could have been composed in the eighteenth or nineteenth century.

Assignment 3

Make up the most unlikely combination you can think of with any three instruments available to you. Improvise together (to discover the musical possibilities), and then compose a piece of music for this unusual sound.

Continued

Assignment 4

Make up a melody that is not 'tuneful'.

Assignment 5

Make up a piece of music for drums that is not 'rhythmic'.

Assignment 6

Make a piece for any combination of strings, wind and keyboards in which every instrument is treated as a percussion instrument.

Assignment 7

Make a piece for singers in which the voices are always used like percussion instruments—except at one point only, where they produce the kind of sound usually expected of them.

Fig. 5 Project 9: New ears, from *Sound and Structure*

I suggested that such projects could be led either by instrumental teachers or schoolteachers. They could also involve students who are not learning to play an instrument, and could include teachers, including music teachers, among the participants.

Here is an example of a short project that was led by a primary class teacher:

Two [9-year-old] pupils who had recently started cello lessons had brought their instruments to the lesson. The teacher organized them to provide a demonstration of *high, low, higher* and *lower* on cellos. Next, there was demonstration and discussion of *steps* and *leaps* on cellos. This led to a composing activity. In pairs, the pupils composed question and answer phrases, thinking about their use of *steps, leaps, high, low, higher* and *lower*. The teacher circulated round the pairs, helping them to develop their ideas. The lesson ended with detailed appraisal, discussion and development of two compositions in front of the class.

During this lesson, the pupils appeared to grow musically in front of your eyes. They already had reasonable skills in playing tuned percussion with two mallets, and they understood that *high* and *low* are relative terms, that what is *high* for a cello might be *low* for a violin. The teacher elicited demonstrations from pupils, and used them constructively when instructing the whole class. She encouraged pupils to lengthen their *questions*. She developed their verbal analysis of their peers' compositions. She expected pupils to remember their compositions, and repeat them so that others could analyse what they were doing. There were no short cuts, such as 'safe' use of pentatonic scales, or giving some pupils untuned instruments. The teacher's expectations were very high, and proved to be realistic.

The optional instrumental curriculum (from Mills 2005*b*: 80–1)

Instrumental lessons are optional, and students have the option of giving them up, as well as continuing them. In the past, giving up was sometimes viewed as entirely negative—as 'wastage'. Certainly, it is a waste when students decide to give up instrumental lessons because the lessons that they have had were unsatisfactory in some way, perhaps because the teacher was not very well organized, or was not sensitive to students' interests, and styles of learning. However, 'wastage' was usually viewed as the students' fault, and considerable efforts were made to select instrumental students who were thought to have 'stickability'. I find the notion that 'stickability' is a virtue that applies in all circumstances a somewhat troubling one. I would prefer children to learn to be critical about what it is that they wish to stick with. The desire to 'stick' with instrumental lessons can—ideally does—result from the very high quality of the experience that is being offered through them.

Gary McPherson (2000) found that, among a sample of 133 children in Australia, students who told an interviewer, before they started lessons, that they intended to play for many years, were more likely still to be playing nine months later. Yes, but was this cause or effect? The children did not volunteer that they were going to learn for many years: they were asked. Could the split-second decision about how to answer this question, if one has not thought about it before, help to determine how long one continues lessons? I find this a fascinating, but rather worrying, thought. It suggests that, as teachers, we need to be careful not to put ideas into children's heads that could lead them to lower their expectations of themselves.

Having hobbies, and exchanging them for new hobbies, is part of growing up. Children should be able to give up instrumental lessons, with dignity, simply because their interests have changed. When children give up collecting stamps, or roller blading, for example, they are not typically viewed as 'failures', or 'letting their teacher/parents down' even though both these activities, like learning to play an instrument, require some financial investment and are ones that some people continue well into adulthood. Moreover, a child who is allowed to give up learning an instrument with dignity may be better disposed to look back on their experience with pleasure, and to apply their skills by taking up another instrument, or looking favourably on the wishes of their own children to learn an instrument, at a later stage.

Some instrumental teachers believe that students who are not making good progress should be 'counselled out' of continuing instrumental lessons. Sue Hallam (1998) writes of 'sensitively negotiating children giving up playing'. I am not sure why one should do this. The sheer fact that a student is enjoying the lessons may be a good enough reason for them to continue with them. We do not suggest that a young person stops taking tennis coaching when it is clear that they are not going to make Wimbledon, or stops going to a voluntary painting class on Saturdays for fun because their teacher thinks they will not get a Grade A* in art and design at GCSE. Why should instrumental lessons be any different?

I recall a girl, aged 12, whose cello lesson I observed. She had been learning for five years, but was still playing very simple pieces. At the end of the lesson, the teacher set her exactly the same homework task that she had had the previous week, as he did not think that she had made enough progress to try a new piece—or even try a new way of playing the same piece. I looked back through her book and discovered that the teacher had actually set precisely the same homework task for the last six lessons! Yet this student persisted with her lessons, and showed signs of enjoyment during them. I feel sure that had the student been better, and more imaginatively, taught, she would have made more progress. But, even without the progress, she showed pleasure in simply playing cello, and working with a teacher on playing cello.

I recall another girl, with some embarrassment. Lois started at secondary school on the same day that I began my teaching career, and I taught her once a week for three years. I remember her well as a student who tried hard, and who did not find music very easy, but who stayed behind after lessons on several occasions to ask me questions that she had been too shy to ask in class, and to tell me that she was taking piano lessons, and what she was playing. However, she did not get involved in any of the many music activities that I ran at lunchtime and after school, and it did not occur to me that music was a special part of her life. Six years after I had left her school, she somehow found out where I was working—more than 200 miles away—and wrote thanking me for getting her interested in music, explaining that playing piano was the activity that had sustained her through two years of serious illness after she left school. Now, unlike the cello teacher above, I never taught her in a group of fewer than 28 students. But I feel sure that I could have done more for her musically had I spotted how motivated she was (Mills 2005b: 80–1).

Learning that broadens

This third sub-section of 'instrumental lessons, music, and life' relates to the instrumental learning that may be derived through working broadly, or expansively.

What might I mean by this?

As a small example, I offer my modest experience of learning to play Balinese and Javanese gamelan. Although I briefly took up both of these with no motive other than learning to play them for their own sake, I found that this had a positive impact on my string quartet playing. In the gamelan I had to work entirely by ear, listening closely to the music around me, so that I could coordinate my playing with that of my peers—including performers whom I could not see, because they were working behind me. I both supported, and was supported by, these other musicians.

When I subsequently played in my string quartet, I found that I was spending less time with my head buried in my music, worrying about whether or not I could play some difficult passages accurately, and more time listening to my peers and playing with them. It sounded, and also felt, much better.

My second example of expanded or expansive learning relates to the enhancement of listening, rather than performing, in this case through experience of composing. Before the national curriculum for music in England was introduced in 1992, so that composing was not yet compulsory in schools, I was invited to evaluate a composer in residence scheme being run by a local authority (Mills 1989a). At the time, some secondary teachers did not feel confident to teach composing, and a few thought that doing so would be a waste of time. The idea of the composer in residence scheme was that giving teachers a composer to work with would raise their confidence in teaching composing, persuade them of its value, and give young people direct experience as composers.

Nearly all the schoolteachers were very enthusiastic about the project, or soon warmed to it. (However, there was a least one exception. A basic principle of the scheme was that schoolteachers stayed in the teaching room, so that they could work alongside the composer in residence, and learn—or work out—how to teach composing more effectively. But when I entered one of the teaching rooms with the music inspector organizing the scheme, it took us some time to locate the schoolteacher, as she was hidden behind the piano knitting! I wonder what that teacher is doing now!)

Turning to the scheme more generally, it was soon clear that the experience of working with the composer was leading the students and their teachers to compose—and in the case of teachers also teach composing—more effectively. But, in order to gauge the wider benefits of working with the composer, I visited a school at the beginning and end of the project, and set the students the same listening test. Essentially I asked the students, on both occasions, to listen to 'Jupiter' from Holst's *The Planets*, and write about what they 'had noticed'. *The Planets* was not linked, in any conscious way, to the composer in residence's work, and he did not know that the same piece would be played at the beginning and end of his project. The accounts that the students wrote on my second visit were longer, and also contained much more detail than I had found on my first visit. Here was an example of expansive learning working well: students had learnt, through experience of composing, to increase the quality and length of their writing about music.

A third example relates to the enhancement of learning in composing through the raising of self-esteem—self-esteem that was raised through experience of performing. Fred Seddon (2004) asked 32 10-year-old students to use computers to create individual compositions that they, and their school-teachers, would evaluate. Sixteen of the students were taking instrumental lessons, and the others were not. The teachers' evaluations of each of the compositions were no higher for one group than for the other. But, as in some related research carried out with Susan O'Neill (see p. 45), the students who were taking instrumental lessons gave themselves higher marks than the other students.

Expansive learning, of course, is not only about music. However, conservatoire teachers emerge from earlier research (Mills 2004*d*) as examples of the type of expert that Bransford and Brown (2000) denote as 'accomplished novices', rather than 'answer-filled experts'. I explained in Chapter 2 (see p. 25) that 'accomplished novices' are rightly proud of their achievements, but constantly strive to know more, and to push out the boundaries of their expertise. In the case of instrumental music this can be seen, for example, when a performer strives to revitalize a piece in their repertoire by reading, listening to recordings of other artists, or even teaching. By contrast, 'answer-filled experts', Bransford and Brown's other form of expert, know everything that is to be known about the subject of their expertise, and hold and communicate this information in a more self-contained way.

The idea of 'answer-filled experts/accomplished novices' is related to that of expansive/restrictive learning (Engeström 2001). 'Expansive' learning looks outwards from an activity or skill, for example, in order to develop or improve it; 'restrictive' learning looks inwards. Thus a 'restrictive' approach to improving the performance of a tricky phrase of an instrumental piece might involve slowing it down to a tempo at which it can be played accurately, and then progressively speeding it up, while an 'expansive' approach could involve a multimodal strategy (see p. 83) such as singing the phrase as one would like to play it, and then seeking to transfer this finished result directly to the instrumental performance. This approach is similar to that which I describe being used very effectively for a class of secondary students who were learning to play *In the Mood* on keyboards (see p. 170).

It would be simplistic, and deeply unhelpful, to suggest that accomplished novices and expansive learning are 'good', whereas answer-filled experts and restrictive learning are 'bad'. Both types of expertise, and strategies for learning, can have their place—although their place(s) may vary between people.

However, when observing instrumental lessons in conservatoires, I have occasionally been aware that lack of awareness, by some students, that a teacher is offering the expertise of the 'accomplished novice', or an opportunity for expansive learning, could limit what the student learns. For example, in one singing lesson, I saw a teacher explicitly offer a student three different approaches to improving a particular aspect of her performance of a specific song, and invite the student to return to her next lesson ready to explain which way forward she had chosen, or to have thought of a new way forward for herself, and be ready to justify this. I distinctly saw the student write down only the very first suggestion made by the teacher! It was difficult to escape the interpretation that, at least on this occasion, this particular student wanted her teacher to provide ready-made advice that she could simply enact. An opportunity to learn, from her teacher, more of how to evaluate and improve her own performances more autonomously in future, was being missed.

A further model of expertise relates to 'surface' and 'deep' learning, and was developed originally with higher education in mind (Entwistle 2005*a*; 2005*b*; Entwistle and McCune 2004; Entwistle and Tait 1990). The model is based on the idea that learning becomes deeper as the learning skills of learners become more advanced. Or to put it another way, students who learnt to learn deeply are more likely to favour teaching that challenges them to think.

Music helping other learning

> Susan was zipping through foster homes because her mum had decided she couldn't cope with living with her any more . . . We were able to get her mum involved in some DJing in the showcase and she showed her mum how to do it . . . her mum came back to us and said 'I can't believe she's doing something useful. I never thought I would see it.' Now she's back living at home and going back to the same school she was at before her mum threw her out.
>
> Unpublished Youth Music paper 2006

> We enrolled Kim into another music course and things got back on track.
>
> Unpublished Youth Music paper 2006

Susan was enabled to return to her home, and to her school, through her participation in a music project. Kim was at risk of being excluded from her school, because she was disruptive and reluctant to learn, but she became cooperative and a good student—across the curriculum—when enrolled on a music project. For some students, including Susan and Kim, music is literally life-changing.

We read, at the beginning of this chapter, Stewart MacPherson's cautious and carefully expressed claim that learning in music also promotes learning in other contexts. Over 80 years later, we still have no scientific proof that it does so. This may simply be because of the complexity of what researchers would need to measure here. How could we hope to isolate, for sufficiently long for it to be worthwhile, two matched groups of (probably) school students—while we gave one group a programme without music, and the other the same programme with an added (and doubtless much disputed!) additional component of music, so that we could measure some non-music skills of both groups at the end of our experiment? And if the students had been isolated from the rest of their lives to carry out this experiment, could its findings be said to be related to normal life (whatever we mean by this)?

In 1998, sixty years after Stewart MacPherson's claim, Katie Overy (1998) used the pages of the academic journal *Psychology of Music* to invite readers to contribute their responses to the question 'Can music really "improve" the mind?' Several people, from different walks of academic life, had their responses published in a subsequent issue of the journal. Mine ran as follows (Mills 1998*a*):

Katie Overy asks, 'can music really "improve" the mind?'. Note that she asks '*can* it?', not '*does* it?'.

These are two very different questions. As I understand it, Katie Overy is asking whether there are circumstances or conditions, perhaps a particular sort of music or a style of music teaching, under which music may improve the mind. She is not asking whether any sort of experience that could sit under the general heading of 'music' always improves the mind.

The 'does' question has recently attracted considerable interest in educational circles in England. Rightly or wrongly, some musicians and music educators have thought that the place of music in our National Curriculum was under threat, and have sought to defend it by arguing that music offers psychological benefits that extend beyond the realms of the subject. Some of this defence has been responsible, careful, and thoughtful. However, there have been examples of carefully crafted research findings being taken out of their context and over-generalized to the point that music, any music, has been portrayed as a panacea. Researchers have been commissioned to investigate whether or not music is a panacea. In fact the 'does' assertion is easy, and not costly, to refute. One just needs to find a single counter-example of music failing to improve the mind, an example of 'does not' and it has bitten the dust. I suspect that we can all think of an example of 'does not' from our own experience. Depending on our prejudices, we may need to look no further than the nearest rave, radio station, supermarket or crush bar for our counter-example. The 'can' question is much more interesting.

Katie Overy mentions a study in Switzerland (Spychiger 1993) [in which the curriculum of a school was adjusted so that some students did more music, and less of some other subjects]. This is an appealing study if only because of the audacity, given the usual hierarchy of subjects, of the finding that the children who did more music in school, at the expense of language and mathematics, became better at language and reading and no worse at mathematics. Educationally, I do not think that it matters much whether motivation played as great a part as music in securing these results, because the motivation was bound up with the music. Spychiger showed that, in the particular circumstances of her investigation, the answer to the 'can' question is 'yes'. However, common sense tells us that this specific 'can' finding cannot be extended into a general 'does' finding. Were we to require all the schools in England to give children more music at the expense of mathematics and English we would soon find rather more than one counter-example of a school where standards in mathematics and English plummeted, if only because the teachers would not have been persuaded that this experiment was likely to work. Spychiger's study is interesting, not because it is generalizable, but because it questions the educationally unquestionable. It provides plenty of food for thought. For example, do mathematics teachers sometimes waste some of the relatively large amounts of the time that they have at their disposal? And there may be aspects of Spychiger's study that are generalizable, if only we could isolate them. For example, what was it that led to improvements in language and reading skills, despite less time being available?

To return to Katie Overy's question, I have little doubt that music can, under particular circumstances, improve the mind. One need do no more than sit in the classroom of a really good music teacher who believes that music can improve the mind, and observe the children grow intellectually in front of your eyes to be convinced of this. What I am sometimes less certain about is what, exactly, this teacher is doing that leads to this improvement, and whether other teachers could be trained to do it too. If we are to exploit the potential of music to improve the mind, we need researchers, perhaps including inspectors, to help isolate the conditions under which this happens. Perhaps it helps if teachers have a particular sort of commitment. Perhaps it helps if the teaching is particularly sequential. Perhaps it helps if children are taught to perform from memory, or to sing at sight, or to try to refine their compositions through thought experiments, instead of always reaching for a keyboard. Doubtless there are a host of other musical factors. Perhaps we need just one of them to be in place. Perhaps we need them all. Once we know more we will need to establish whether these factors can be packaged in a music education that is excellent musically. If they cannot, then the investigation may have added to the sum of human knowledge, but will not be of educational value. Whatever the potential of music to improve the mind, the main purpose of teaching music in schools is excellence in music. (Mills 1998a: 204–5)

Nine years later, in 2007, I still hold by what I wrote at that time. But now that I am addressing musicians including music teachers, rather than research psychologists, I would wish to frame my points about quality rather differently. While it may (and this is a question!) be acceptable for psychologists to seek ways of using music as a sort of education tool that promotes something extra-musical, without minding whether the music provided is educationally excellent, I am very clear that this is not acceptable as part of a music curriculum in schools. Stewart MacPherson suggested that music will only improve students' 'mental faculties' if it is 'properly carried out'. I would suggest that, whether or not this is the case, this is the only way in which we should be seeking to teach music.

Unfortunately, since 1998, the use of music as a learning tool has become something of a bandwagon. When I was writing *Music in the School*, in 2004, there was a vogue for playing western classical music quietly in classrooms for any subject in the mistaken view that this would be helpful to children. I wrote of an inspection visit that I had made to a mathematics lesson in a primary school inspection (Mills 2004*b*: 228–9):

I enter the classroom. Pachelbel's *Canon* plays quietly in the corner. The children are working silently on number problems. I smile 'good morning' to the teacher, sit down by the files of lesson plans, individual education plans and assessment records that she has laid out for me, and begin to fill out my form:

Year 6. Mathematics. 13 boys, 16 girls. Attainment target 2, levels 3–5.

Pupils seated boy-girl in attainment groups with differentiated worksheets . . .

I can barely think. The Pachelbel is approaching the height of its beautiful, long, crescendo. I know this piece inside out. It draws me in . . . Get a grip on yourself, Mills. The teacher is playing this stuff because she believes it will help the children. They are coping. So can you.

But are they coping? It is the Minuet from *Berenice* now. A boy seated away from the CD player starts to caterwaul quietly with the melody. A girl nudges him to be quiet, with a worried look at me. I smile reassuringly. The boy looks to be in pain. He is struggling to complete his level 5 mathematics—at a fast pace, neatly and accurately—while this drug that is music courses through his mind. He is battling to concentrate, to do his work, to please his teacher, the girl, me . . .

A few minutes later, midway through a phrase of a Mozart horn concerto, the teacher turns off the music, and explains something mathematical to the whole class. She turns on the music again. It is the first movement of Vivaldi's *Winter*.

What is going on here? Why is this keen, experienced, and very able teacher making it so difficult for at least some of her class to do their mathematics? Why is she polluting their learning environment with music? What is her evidence that this use of music is helping anyone with their mathematics? Let alone helping them to develop as musicians?

Fortunately, this particular bandwagon appears now to be less prevalent in schools. Clearly I was not the only confident adult who was finding it difficult to concentrate on their mathematics while music played, and was prepared, in the spirit of the Emperor's New Clothes, to speak up for the students who were also having problems, and say so.

Another bandwagon that has lost at least one of its wheels in recent years relates to the notion that the human brain consists of two hemispheres that deal with different types of activities. For example, it is sometimes stated that music takes place on the right hand side of the brain. Cognitive scientists have known that this is not the case for some decades and, in more recent years, brain scans that show several areas of the brain being activated during musical activity have been published, and shown at music education conferences (Gruhn, Altenmüller, and Babler 1997).

We still know very little about how the brain, and the mind, work. But we do know that musical activity is not confined to specific 'zones', and also that the mind can expand, or adjust, to take on—or reinforce—new musical demands that are made of it.

Instrumental teachers wisely ensure that students engage in a range of creative and inspiring musical activities, and do not spend their whole time working on narrower activities such as protracted preparation of pieces for graded performance examination. By broadening their instrumental curriculum in this way, instrumental teachers may help their students develop their minds, as well as their musicianship.

Chapter 7

The first lesson

It is not our abilities that show what we are, it is our choices.

Professor Albus Dumbledore (Headmaster: Hogwarts School of
Witchcraft and Wizardry) congratulates Harry Potter and Ron Weasley on
the loyalty that saved the day in the Chamber of Secrets (Rowling 2002)

It's not really that I think I'm gonna be a pop star or anything,
though that would be nice, it's just that I can see now that I've got
choices.

Dean in unpublished Youth Music paper 2006

Dean, aged 15, lives on an estate with mass unemployment, violence, and a very high rate of teenage pregnancy. He says that he will be the first person in his family to work for three generations. He became involved in music as part of a Youth Music Action Zone.

Professor Albus Dumbledore requires no introduction.

In this chapter we consider 'first lessons' under three headings:

◆ Choices

◆ Ethos

◆ On reflection.

Choices

We face many choices when deciding how to structure our first lesson for any student(s). This is the case whether we are the first, or twenty-first, teacher that a student has had on our instrument.

What do you remember of the very first lesson that you received on the instrument that you now think of as 'main'? And of the first lessons that you had from any subsequent teachers of the same instrument?

For me, that instrument is the violin. And while I had a succession of four violin teachers over the years I am, for simplicity, going to write only about my first teacher here.

While others teach themselves violin, or teach themselves the very first few stages of violin, my first violin lesson was also the first occasion on which I ever picked up, or tried to play, the instrument. This was although there was—in a sense—already violin in the family. This took the form of two (literally) wood-wormed, string-free, and sound-post-free violins secreted in the attic of my paternal grandfather's home. My father recalled using a matchbox as a substitute for a bridge when playing around on one of the violins as a child. But fortunately no one suggested that I 'try them out' or, worse still, had one 'done up' for me to play. Had they done so, I doubt that I would still be describing the violin as my 'main' instrument. Not only were our family violins in dreadful condition, they were so heavy that they would always have been discouragingly difficult to play.

Back to my memories of my first violin lesson.

This was in May 1965, and I had just had my eleventh birthday. My mother, who played French horn, had chosen violin for me because she thought that I wanted to play violin with a drove of other violinists in an orchestra, and she was mindful that there were more opportunities to play orchestral violin than horn. (In fact, I had expressed interest in playing violin because I had seen Martin Milner playing a Mozart violin concerto in the orchestra where my mother played horn, and I thought that his role looked more exciting than hers.) My mother chose a violin teacher for me who lived locally, and who was drawn from among those who taught at the secondary school where she had been a student. My teacher had chosen a wonderful-looking three-quarter-size violin that cost £6 10s., and a less visually exciting bow that cost a seemingly extortionate £1 30s. My violin lessons cost 6 guineas a term. By the end of my first lesson I had learnt, through following the example of my teacher and also through listening to what she said, to:

- tune my violin (using pegs not namby-pamby adjusters)
- play all the open strings pizzicato 'banjo style', and with the violin support-ed in playing position, in both cases with attention to the quality of sound
- play a sequence of open strings called out by my teacher, while she added an accompaniment on her piano
- bow the D and A strings, using up and down full bows, again with atten-tion to the quality of sound
- recognize the four open notes on the stave
- look after my violin, for example by letting down the bow, adding resin, and dusting the instrument.

I left the lesson with a written record of what we had done, intended mainly so that my mother could support my practice over the next week. By the time that the schools broke for summer in July, I was bowing my way cheerfully through first position using full and half bows, making a reasonable sound as I did so, and playing scales and simple melodies that my teacher and mother accompanied on violin or piano. Some of the melodies were composed by my teacher and written by her in my notebook; others were from published resources.

This is not the only way of giving someone a first lesson, and it will not have been the only way of giving a first lesson that would have worked for me. And doubtless other students receiving the 'same' lesson might have emphasized different features in their accounts. My lesson lasted 45 minutes: I have doubtless left out aspects of it in what I have written above.

However, I would suggest that my first lesson, as I have recalled it, had several characteristics that are—or at least nearly—essential:

- I made music.
- My teacher made music.
- My teacher planned the lesson to build upon my previous musical experience, which she had researched through discussion with my mother (and possibly also with me—I think that I can remember this conversation).
- My teacher adjusted the lesson 'vertically' as she found that I knew more, or less, than she had expected (and possibly also 'horizontally' as she found that I had interests, with which she could link my instrumental learning, that were broader or narrower than she had anticipated).
- My new violin knowledge was linked with my existing knowledge of music. (For example, I was already familiar with the stave, and so I was shown how the violin notes that I had learnt were placed on it.)
- I was taught to attend to, and improve, the quality of my sound.
- I was sent away with an instrument that I could maintain so as to carry out the practice tasks that I had been set. (You would be amazed by how many violin and other string students are sent away with '2-string' melodies to play on instruments that they have not learned to tune!)

As I reflect on this lesson, more than 40 years after it took place, I feel disappointed that it did not have a further characteristic:

- I did something imaginative or creative. (For example, perhaps I could have composed/proposed a series of pizzicato open string notes for my teacher to accompany, and then commented on whether there were ways that my melody, or my teacher's accompaniment, could be improved.)

But perhaps my teacher did this, and I have forgotten.

Not all first instrumental lessons are organized as constructively as was my first violin lesson. For example, here are some other children receiving their first violin lesson:

So enthusiastic were the 7-year-olds that they seemed to float into their lesson, their eyes and faces ablaze. They gravitated towards the shiny new violin cases at the side of the room. 'Don't touch those', the teacher said. By the end of the lesson, the children had learnt to open their case, take the violin out, and put it back 'properly', without making a sound. (Mills 2005b: 70)

I sometimes wonder why students return for a second lesson, when a first lesson has been quite as discouraging and irrelevant as this one. It did not meet any of the conditions that I suggested were essential. This was not simply because students were being taught as a group: I have observed many first group lessons that met all these conditions. But I have also seen a first violin lesson, for just one student, that consisted only of teaching him to hold his bow. He learnt to hold it very nicely, but I struggle to think how he was going to follow the teacher's instruction to practise this skill over the next week, as he had not been taught to make any sound that could be used to judge the quality of the bow hold. And what would he be able to show his family and friends when he went home, keen to share the excitement of his violin lesson with them? Might they even laugh at him? And was his enthusiasm for playing violin likely to wane given that he had not learnt to play a sound on it? There were so many missed opportunities in this lesson. If it does, indeed, make sense for a student to learn how to hold a bow before being taught how to hold the violin across which it is drawn—and I have my doubts about this—surely time could still be made, within this individual lesson, for the student to learn to play the opening four (or even eight) notes of *Twinkle, Twinkle Little Star,* 'banjo style', starting on the open G, D, and A strings. The student might return to their next lesson having worked out how to continue the melody a little, or possibly having thought of how to compose an extension to it. Or the teacher might take their violin out of its case, tune it, and craft an accompaniment to the student's playing. The possibilities verge on limitless . . .

I have recently heard a bassoon teacher defend his 'first bassoon' lessons, during which students simply assemble their instruments, and then take them to pieces and put them away again. They then leave their bassoons in their cases until the teacher's next visit. This teacher speaks of giving this standard lesson to all his students, no matter how old, or experienced in music, they are, and regardless of whether they are taught individually or in groups. I would question whether there are any circumstances in which it would be appropriate to give this lesson. I have attended a 'first bassoon lesson' where four 10 year olds arrived to find their bassoons had already been assembled, and

Table 14   A first bassoon lesson

1.	The student(s) made music	By playing simple patterns on their reed
2.	The teacher(s) made music	By improvising two keyed melodies based on the reed patterns
3.	The teacher(s) planned the lesson to build upon the previous musical experience of the students	The teacher had included a brief meeting of the students during an earlier visit to the school
4.	The teacher(s) adjusted the lesson on finding that the students knew more, or less, than was anticipated	The teacher gave particular attention to two students who initially found it hard to produce any sound from their reed
5.	The teacher(s) linked students' new learning with their existing knowledge of music	The teacher suggested that one reed pattern reminded him of a well-known TV theme tune and—while the teacher sang along—the students developed their performance of the reed pattern to match the theme tune more closely
6.	The student(s) were taught to attend to, and improve, their quality of sound	This was a constant feature of the teacher's advice and praise to students, and modelled through his own performance
7.	The student(s) learnt how to maintain their instruments, so that they could carry out the homework tasks they had been set	The homework task related only to the reed, and so the limited advice on assembling and disassembling a bassoon was sufficient
8.	The student(s) worked creatively	Through the composing of the reed patterns

then worked mainly on blowing their reeds before listening to their teacher give a more accomplished and developed performance. Finally, they learned how to dismantle their instruments, and put them away. This lesson provided a markedly more constructive induction to life as a bassoonist. It also had all the features of a first lesson that I suggested might be essential when reflecting upon the first violin lesson that I ever received (see Table 14).

This lesson was, so far as I know, planned independently by its teacher—but it is aligned with an introductory unit of five lessons for bassoonists that was published in *A Common Approach*, shown in Table 15.

Further, the parlous state of some 'first lessons' cannot be attributed solely to the short amount of time available. The stunning first keyboard lesson that I described earlier at the end of Chapter 4 lasted only 15 minutes.

Ethos

The quality, content, and ethos of first instrumental lessons must have an enormous impact on how students feel about themselves as instrumentalists.

Table 15   An introductory unit of five lessons for bassoonists

Unit of work		
Specimen for Bassoon		
Title of unit: Introducing the bassoon	Focus of unit: In this unit, guidance is provided in introducing the bassoon to pupils, enabling them to master the basic requirements needed to play simple three-to-four-note tunes	Where the unit fits in: The unit is for the initial stage of learning
Learning objectives	**Possible teaching activities**	**Points to note**
Pupils should learn: • how to assemble and disassemble the bassoon correctly • how to develop a good basic posture and embouchure, with some diaphragm support • how to play simple long notes with a steady tone • how to demonstrate basic tonguing • how to maintain a steady pulse • how to play simple pieces, making the links between sound and symbol • about the importance of acquiring a basically weekly practice routine • how to compose their own tunes and play them with others	• Ask pupils to put the bassoon together, copying the teacher in a safe routine; reverse the procedure. Ensure that they dry out the bassoon after each playing • Assess with pupils whether they are more comfortable holding the bassoon standing or sitting, and work with them to adopt a relaxed basic posture • Demonstrate a good embouchure and ask pupils to copy. Together, blow long notes on the reed, helping pupils to maintain a steady tone. Transfer this to the bassoon, checking that the airflow is sufficient for the whole instrument • Ask pupils to place the tip of the tongue gently on the end of the reed and then, as they blow, to take the tongue away and replace it again slowly two or three times, whilst keeping a steady flow of air • Clap an even pulse and ask pupils to transfer this to the reed, whilst the teacher sings or plays a simple tune over the top • Ask pupils to say the names of the notes of the chosen piece over a steady pulse (C/D/E/F). Perhaps begin by using minims and minim rests on the note E. Next, ask them to clap the piece	• A free-blowing reed with a good tone is important • In the early weeks, use the reed alone, whenever possible. This gives pupils a break from the weight of the bassoon and the complications of balance and posture • Five minutes' practice on the reed is better than no practice for that day • Encourage the use of a mirror to check embouchure and posture • Links between sound and symbol can be woven into the teaching in an enjoyable and relaxed way where appropriate

Continued

Table 15 Cont.

Learning objectives	Possible teaching activities	Points to note
	and then play it. Each note can be introduced in this way still using 'say, clap, and play' and adjusting the amount of material used for the needs of each pupil • Help pupils to acquire effective practice routines and encourage them to maintain a daily record • Provide opportunities for pupils to play by ear and from memory and have fun listening to the sounds whilst making up tunes and playing copycat games. The more [advanced players] can take the lead in question-and-answer activities and in experimenting with simple improvisations. Help pupils to achieve expressive outcomes, e.g. dynamic contrasts	
Repertoire and resources* 'Merrily' 'At Pierrot's Door'	Expectations: by the end of the unit **All pupils will:** be able to put the bassoon together safely; use a functional embouchure and be able to recognise and play at least three different notes from [staff] notation **Most pupils will:** sit or stand with good posture and have a good basic embouchure; read simple [staff] notation accurately and be able to play, as tongued minims and crotchets, the notes C, D, E and F; maintain a steady pulse **Some pupils will have progressed further and will:** tongue clearly, playing the notes C, D, E and F in tune, with focused tone; take the lead in copycat games and play a simple duet part with the teacher	

Source: Federation of Music Services 2002*d*: 64
*Here, the 'unit of work' named two melodies that could be used as the 'chosen piece'.

As I asked earlier, why should students who spend an entire first lesson doing things other than make music bother to come back at all?

I am reminded here of what mathematicians refer to as 'sensitivity to initial conditions', or Chaos Theory. The notion is that a very small change at the beginning of something can lead to an enormous difference later on. Scientists sometimes give the (theoretical) example of a butterfly flapping its wings somewhere near the Himalayas, and this causing a huge storm on the other side of the world (Gleick 1996; Stewart 1997). Here I am suggesting—without an equation in sight—that the ethos and content of students' first instrumental lessons can make a great deal of difference to how they feel about their lessons, and make progress, in future. As music educators, we are fortunate that music students, particularly children, are sometimes more resilient, and more forgiving of our lapses, than are the physical—including possibly weather—systems of the world.

It is odd how people who are experienced as music educators can fall back essentially on distant, and possibly incomplete and partial, recollections of their childhood when planning instrumental lessons.

Strangely, given my own commitment to and immersion in creative experiment in schools, when a local piano teacher first asked if I would teach her 9-year-old daughter violin privately in the evenings, it never occurred to me to structure her lessons other than in much the same way that I recalled being taught violin myself. By day, classes of 30 secondary-school students worked with me on creative projects that required them to use their memories, or perhaps—in the way of some professional composers of that time—graphic scores. By night, staff notation, rather than music, became the centre of the musical life of my growing private practice of violin and viola students. I had not been trained as an instrumental teacher, and thought simply that this was what one did in instrumental lessons. I did not actually go out and buy exactly the same books for my first student that I had ploughed through more than a decade earlier, but I did ask her to bring a manuscript book to her first lesson, and went off to the big music shop in Bradford to choose some music for her to read and play as soon as possible.

Fred Seddon (2004) describes some related disjunction in his life as a musician and his early experience as an instrumental teacher. He grew up as a creative musician of the Merseybeat era, playing in bands including The Dimensions, and later learnt to play flute (from a teacher who used a tutor book) and studied music at university:

> Throughout all my formal training and teaching I continued playing in various pop, rock and blues groups developing my aural and creative skills. Strangely enough, as I reflect on those times, it never occurred to me to employ the aural and creative skills I had acquired through my informal music education in my flute teaching. I taught my pupils in the 'traditional' way that I was taught to play the flute by my various teachers over the years. What was even stranger on reflection was that although I could and did play the piano/keyboard by ear, improvise and compose, whenever I picked up my flute it never occurred to me to play it without referring to notation. It was as though I was living in two parallel musical worlds and that they would never intersect.

However, Fred ensured that his parallel musical worlds *did* intersect. His flute teaching had emphasized the achievement of high results in graded performance examinations, a feature that was appreciated by his students, and their parents, alike. Over several years, he worked systematically with both his students and their parents to show them that they could continue to have excellent examination results, while also gaining more musical value from him:

Eventually, with the parents' support I adopted a timetable that meant I spent one term a year preparing for examinations and the other two terms developing the skills of playing by ear, group playing, improvising and composing. Adopting this new timetable meant that I was able to equip my students with a more comprehensive set of musical skills. It also meant I was breaking the 'cycle' of instrumental teaching that focused exclusively on learning to play an instrument through music notation. This style of learning had been imposed on me by my previous instrumental teachers and probably on them by their previous teachers.

I subsequently received feedback from some of my former students, who had moved on to pursue their higher education in non music disciplines, informing me that they had joined various musical groups while studying at university. One former student had become a 'busker' on the streets of Cambridge in order to subsidise her finances while studying to become an engineer at Cambridge University. Prior to my change of teaching style student feedback regarding continuing playing had nearly always been negative. My earlier students didn't seem to have the confidence to join musical groups and cited pressure of university work as a reason for no longer playing their instruments. (Seddon 2004)

Fred's observation that former instrumental students who lacked the confidence to join musical groups gave an alternative explanation—in this case pressure of university work—as the reason for not doing so is reminiscent of a study of primary student teachers at Westminster College in Oxford that I carried out some time ago (Mills 1989b). The student teachers all specialized in subjects other than music, and nearly all of them were thoroughly persuaded of the value of music in the primary curriculum, but initially lacking in confidence as to their ability to teach it. But whereas 22 out of 30 students gritted their teeth and determinedly taught music on an average of eight occasions during a particular period of assessed teaching experience, the remaining eight student teachers—who included a disproportionate number of those who were least confident in teaching music—oddly found themselves placed in schools 'that would not let' them teach any music . . .

Admitting that we are not doing something because we lack confidence to do it can feel cowardly. Instrumental teachers help students to build their confidence as musicians, and their preparedness for the next stages of their musical development, from the first minutes of their first lesson.

On reflection

I have suggested that the instrumental lessons that we teach today are sometimes unduly influenced by our recollections of the lessons that we received some time ago. I say 'sometimes' because I know that not everyone teaches like that. I say 'recollections' because not everyone who participates in a particular instrumental lesson will have exactly the same memory of it. And given that you and I were among the successes of the early instrumental lessons that we received—because we went on to become instrumental teachers—it is possible that our accounts of how the lessons went may be more positive than those of other participants.

So, how might we teach lessons—particularly first lessons—more effectively today? Clearly, the lessons that we received were not all bad. But it may be helpful to insert a 'buffer' between the lessons that we may recall from (probably) our youth, and those that we are going to teach today.

I believe that we should aim for all of the following:

- An individual lesson for every individual student in our teaching group. I am not advocating a return to those awful lessons that I used to see around 15 years ago, typically when teachers were teaching groups rather than individuals against their better judgement, and the members of the group effectively just took their turn for a (very short) individual lesson. But every member of a group needs a lesson that suits them, and within which they can grow. Students differ. We should not just have one 'first lesson'. We need to have lots of them, and adjust each of them as necessary, rather than teaching to a 'one size fits all' model.

- Musical engagement of the students. This may be very simple, but should involve the students playing their instruments, and is likely also to involve the teacher playing their instrument, for example by providing an accompaniment for the students. Despite its seeming simplicity (to accomplished players), this musical experience may be one that students carry with them throughout their lives. The teacher's attention to the quality of their own sound will help to reinforce the need for students to listen, and do the same with respect to their own sound. I have occasionally heard instrumental teachers say that they do not play their instruments during lessons for beginners, for fear of discouraging them through thoughts of how much they still have to achieve. I could not disagree more strongly with this statement. Of course, teachers should not spend the whole of lessons playing, or 'show off' to their students But to have your teacher playing beautifully with you in your very first lesson is inspirational.

- A focus on the quality of sound. As well as improving the quality of musical engagement, this helps students to focus on listening, rather than simply coordinating their bodies and instruments.

- An opportunity for ensemble playing. This could be a simple duet for student(s) and teacher, in which the teacher improvises a simple accompaniment, or it could be more elaborate, or involve students' playing as a body. But ensemble playing helps to reinforce the 'togetherness' of music-making, and opens whole new sound worlds to students. Ensemble playing is as important for adult students as it is for younger students. John Holt wrote of taking up cello well into adulthood: 'One of my earliest recollections of working with Hal [his teacher] is of playing a short duet with him, just a few notes. As we did, a wonderful feeling spread through me. It seemed to say, "Yes, this is good, this is right, this is what you are supposed to do" ' (Holt 1978: 142). John Holt wrote that he was inspired to work by the beauty of this simple ensemble piece that he played with his teacher. The feeling of becoming, in a sense, a musical equal—or at least musical partner—of his teacher was also important to him.

- A lesson that begins and ends well. I say this not in the cynical sense espoused by the conductor Thomas Beecham: 'Here are two golden rules for an orchestra: start together and finish together. The public doesn't give a damn what goes on in between' (Wikipedia 2006); but with the musical integrity of Daniel Barenboim: 'When you perform a piece of music you have to be able to hear the last note before you play the first' (Barenboim 2006*d*).

   Robert Schenck (2000*a*: 218) argues that the beginnings and ends of lessons require particularly careful planning. I have observed many instrumental lessons that begin formulaically with the teacher asking a student to play through work that they were given to practise during the previous lesson, and end—equally formulaically—with the setting of a new (or a repeat of the old!) practice task. While structuring instrumental lessons in this way can, from time to time, be effective, there are also many other options. And this formula is not available during a first lesson, as the students have no practice tasks to play through!

   In all subjects taught at school, it is now rare for lessons to begin with 'taking in' of homework, and end with setting of the next homework task. Similarly, instrumental lessons can start and end in different sorts of ways. Students who have had opportunity to warm up are more likely to be able to play through their practice tasks to a high standard. Where practice tasks—homework—are set before the end of a lesson, students have more opportunity to realize, and say, if they have not understood. Instrumental lessons can end and begin in many different ways. They can even end and begin with the same task, so that students can consolidate their learning, or assess their improvement during a lesson.

- An opportunity for everyone to get to know each other. As well as the teacher getting to know students, and vice versa, the students in a group lesson need to get to know each other. But this should be through a musical activity, rather than through an 'ice-breaker' that has no musical purpose. Time is so precious in music lessons!

◆ Lessons need to hang together, and take account of the way that students—particularly children—learn through all their senses. In the words of Lucinda Mackworth-Young:

> Pupils learn through total immersion and interaction with learning materials, using all of their senses and faculties. They learn using [the whole of] both hemispheres of the brain, and they learn aurally, kinaesthetically, visually, intellectually and with their whole bodies. Through these means they build up their own internal structure of concepts and skills, linking each new concept or skill into a pre-existing internal structure. It is this internal structure which constitutes their learning. (Mackworth-Young 2004: 98)

◆ Plenty of praise, achievement, and 'can do'. This is what Robert Schenck refers to as 'hey I'm good at this' (Schenck 2000a: 50). It is also related to what John Holt felt, as an adult, when he realized that he could work out how to sing written parts that he was given in choir: 'Like the little kid for the first time tying his shoes, I wanted to shout, "I can do this for myself!" ' (Holt 1978: 98). Linked with this, students need to know what progress they have made, and to set targets for future improvement. For reasons including the fact that instrumental lessons are often quite brief, assessment is often organized as an ongoing part of lessons, rather than separately. Teachers will typically find that students are already accomplished in assessment, because 'being an assessor' of oneself and others is a significant part of other school subjects. Instrumental teachers may wish to save time spent on assessment by aligning their approach with that to which students are already familiar from school

◆ 'First lessons' need to be organized so that students will continue to learn their instrument, and continue to make progress in learning it forever. Students who think that they may give up lessons set up an expectation for themselves that this is what will happen. We have already read (p. 124) of how school students who are asked, before beginning instrumental lessons, how long they expect to continue lessons, and choose a relatively short period of time, generally 'give up' sooner. Particularly given the current popularity in the UK for organizing initial instrumental tuition as short courses, sometimes known as taster courses, students need to know that their lessons can, and will, continue, if they wish, so that they do not assume that their lessons will end, and drop their expectations accordingly.

First lessons that aren't

Finally, I return to the students who are having their first lesson with us, but who have learnt from another teacher, or taught themselves, previously. The first time we teach them may feel like a first lesson to us, but feel very different to them.

Occasionally we may feel that students who are new (to us) have so many technical weaknesses that we need to 'start again from scratch' with them. This would rarely be wise. Lessons and learning need to have a forward momentum to them, or students will soon become discouraged. Any technical problem that a student has developed can virtually always be addressed through playing worthwhile music that does not insult a student's intellect or musical development. Pieces that a student learnt with their previous teacher can be drawn upon.

Did any of us ever pass on a student who, in our view, needed to be 'taken back to the beginning?' I rather doubt that this was the case! What an unpleasant reflection this would be upon our teaching!

We may also wish to bear in mind that students often do not appreciate being 'taken back to the beginning', so that this practice may rebound upon us, rather than upon the former teacher, whose work we have implicitly done down.

Here, Hilary du Pré, sister of Jacqueline du Pré, writes of a flute teacher who sought to have her 'start again from scratch' after she was already playing well enough to have gained a coveted place to study at the Royal Academy of Music:

[My flute teacher] explained that I needed to alter every aspect of my technique and, in order to do this, would have to go back to the beginning. It would mean giving up concerts until my own technique was established . . . [He] told me that the most secure note from which to launch my journey was B♭ . . . Each week I returned to my room with that dreaded note . . . I struggled for four hours a day to produce the perfect B♭ with exemplary technique. (du Pré and du Pré 1997: 90)

It is clear, from the published context of this quotation that Hilary du Pré neither respected, nor felt that she benefited from, this teaching.

I think that most of us would be devastated were we ever to receive a published report on our teaching that resembled the quotation stated above. 'Starting again from scratch' is an (un)educational practice that I revile mainly for educational reasons. But abstaining from it may also help to protect our individual and collective professional reputation as teachers.

Chapter 8

Planning a programme of lessons

I really enjoy it. It gives me something to do, something to achieve. It's something I wouldn't normally have chosen to do.

Gareth Williams (19), baritone horn, Thorn Cross young offenders' unit

I've only been playing two weeks and I couldn't get a note out of the cornet at first. But now things are getting easier. It gives me something extra to say I've done.

Mark O'Kelly, cornet, Thorn Cross young offenders' unit (Ward 2006)

As inmates of a unit for young offenders, and participants in a seemingly inspirational brass band run by Steve Pickett of the Hallé, Gareth Williams and Mark O'Kelly are part of a programme of instrumental tuition, coupled with ensemble work, which promotes rapid progress, a sense of achievement, and fun.

I have not observed this programme at first hand, but it sounds to me as though it is very well planned. Students who are inmates at a residential unit presumably do not have as many options as their peers as to how they spend their time. But, even so, these young men sound as though they are very pleased to be in the band, and are making progress at a rate of knots. Implicitly, and frequently also explicitly, instrumental teachers including Steve Pickett spend time planning their instrumental teaching. Like class teachers working in schools, they plan every lesson for every student (short-term planning), thinking how this relates to their planning over, say, a month or a term (medium-term planning), and how this medium-term planning contributes to what they intend for the future (long-term planning).

What is the 'long term' over which instrumental teachers should plan? I would suggest that instrumental teachers should travel in hope that their students will wish to continue playing their instrument throughout their lifespan. We know that not all students, even those who receive the most sensitive teaching in the world, will wish to do this. But if we don't entertain the possibility that they will all want to continue, and plan our teaching to promote this, the chances are that only a few students will continue for more than a few months. I am reminded of that advertisement, now a cliché, that the RSPCA used to place on television each Christmas: 'A dog is for life, not for Christmas.'

The parallel is not exact. But I do believe that it is important for instrumental teachers, like the dog owner, to aim high when considering how long their students will continue to engage with instrumental learning. Teachers working in schools and music services take particular care to ensure that students on the currently voguish 'taster' (see p. 104) experiences of instrumental lessons are not just offered a few lessons and then ditched. The teachers provide a healthy diet of musical tuition that includes instrumental tuition, but is not confined to it. They ensure that students who want to continue learning their instrument when the 'taster' ends can do so.

In this chapter we consider two aspects of planning a programme of lessons:

◆ Planning—what?

◆ Planning—how?

    ○ Teaching of skills

    ○ Focus on music

    ○ Repertoire

    ○ Avoiding obstacles

    ○ Trying different strategies

    ○ Drawing on relevant research.

Planning—what?

Piano lessons are, of course, planned primarily to promote students' progress on piano. Bass guitar lessons are, of course, planned mainly to promote progress on bass guitar. And so on. But they also are planned so that students are likely to want to 'stay the course': continue lessons so that they can make this progress. We need to motivate students, and help them to remain motivated, if they are to carry on playing.

Confidence is an important facet of motivation. Lucinda Mackworth-Young writes:

[Students] who have heard, internalized and so say to themselves 'You are clever! You can succeed!' are more likely to keep trying when faced with difficulty than those who say to themselves 'You'll never be able to do this, the others are much better than you.' Moreover, through the projection of their internalizations, what [students] hear from us depends upon what they are already saying to themselves. That is why some [students] are relaxed, smiling and sure of our appreciation, while others are tense, worried and able to hear only criticism, whether or not we have said a word! (Mackworth-Young 2004: 97)

To put this another way, students who have learnt to see themselves as successful are, as a consequence, programmed for success. They hear—i.e. receive—

more of the messages of success that their teachers actually present to all their students. They are already thinking of themselves as continuing, rather than 'giving up', instrumental music.

In all fields of human endeavour—not only in instrumental music—it is now generally accepted as educationally prudent to seek to motivate students positively rather than negatively. Teachers motivate students positively by singing their achievements, and then turning to what needs to be done to make their work even better. Teachers who seek to motivate students negatively—if such teachers exist—would begin by telling students they are hopeless, and possibly also tell them to 'pull their socks up', before listing—perhaps—what students need to do in order to improve. A degree of negative motivation of students in school was once considered more acceptable than it is now, although this has always had its dissenters. Charlotte Brontë may have reflected her own views when she cast Jane Eyre (Brontë 1847) as insisting she set up her girls' village school humanely, positively, and 'with no beatings'. When I wrote *Music in the Primary School* in 1989, I acknowledged that teachers generally sought to encourage students, but quoted a politician as follows: '[7 year olds] had better learn from the earliest possible age to come to terms with their own capabilities' (Mills 1991*a*: 5). This particular politician has now changed his tune, so to speak, but—here and there—traces of negative motivation remain in instrumental music. The legacy of selecting students for instrumental lessons according to how 'musical' they are thought to be may still be present in the dustier corners of a few instrumental teachers' thinking.

Robert Schenck offers some suggestions as to encouraging instrumental students of school age to think 'Hey, I'm good at this' (Table 16).

There are several ideas here that I would like to use to strengthen my instrumental teaching.

Why is so much time during instrumental lessons spent on music that is difficult? Why don't we spend more time on music that everyone can play—and enjoy? Why is so much of the repertoire of instrumental lessons chosen by us?

When I sit down at the piano at home I spend some time practising music that is very difficult for me, given my limited technique, but also enjoy playing—performing—music that is easier to a much higher standard. And all the difficult music that I try to play is music that I want to be able to play, so that struggling away at it feels to have a purpose. And this control that I have over my repertoire gives me an experience of teaching myself piano (although I would not dream of offering piano lessons to a third party because of my parlous technique). And when one of my pianist friends, or my mother, visit and say that they would like to play a piano duet with me, that is just great.

Table 16   'Hey, I'm good at this!'—some practical tips

Find a good balance [when choosing music to play during lessons] between old favourites and new challenges
Use fun and stimulating music 'below' the technical challenge of your students
While progressing forward, also provide suitable contexts for the use and enjoyment of previously acquired skills. Supplement your student's book by offering additional pieces and creative activities on an easy-to-manage technical level
Provide time and ideas for students to provide their own music
Switch roles with your students so that they too get to lead the group, for example at imitation sessions, guessing games or small 'performances' at lessons
Provide natural opportunities to revisit repertoire. Enjoy the music together!
Let music at lessons and assignments be the 'student's choice' at regular intervals
Let students and groups who normally don't meet one another play pieces together they all know
Make music *together* (from duets on upwards), choosing music that reinforces self-confidence, offering the feeling of success and giving the opportunity to experience the music
Improvise, making it easy for all to participate
Nothing succeeds like success

Source: Schenck 2000a: 63

But aren't all these activities ones that it would be good to include in instrumental lessons as a matter of course, not only because they will encourage students of any age to believe 'Hey, I'm good at this', but also because they are enjoyable and improving activities that musicians do?

In 2006, a mathematics teacher—with the possibly apt name of Zoë Fail—acquired a degree of notoriety by allegedly asserting that students needed more boredom in their academic lives. She took the view that students' lives were 'over-stimulated': 'Too often pupils and parents expected lessons to be "all singing and all dancing" when the reality was that some learning could be tedious and hard work' (Lightfoot 2006). The perceived topicality and resonance of her view were illustrated through its publication on the first page of the *Daily Telegraph*.

But instrumental music does have a particular reputation for demoralizing students. When the *Guardian* columnist Armando Iannucci advised: 'If I was Tony Blair's adviser, I'd tell him to take up the piano' (Iannucci 2006: 48), this was not the positive endorsement of piano playing that it might have seemed. Iannucci had recently begun piano lessons as an adult learner, taken a Grade 1 piano examination, and found this experience to be somewhat demoralizing.

He was unable to settle himself during the short standard time that is set for Grade 1 examinations. Consequently, the music that emerged from his fingers 'turned out to be completely strange music . . . because, for some reason, my hands had been suddenly replaced by two packets of fish fingers, neither of which could be controlled by signals from the brain. Sounds came out that have never been categorised before.' Consequently, Iannucci recommended piano lessons for Tony Blair on the assumption that Blair would soon take an examination, and find this a negative experience:

All of us, especially those of us who have a particularly high regard for ourselves (for example Tony Blair), would benefit from being thrown into a short, relatively trivial but deeply embarrassing, situation over which we have no control and throughout which we are mercilessly judged.

There are, of course, many misunderstandings about piano examinations here. Nobody has to learn piano, nobody who learns piano has to take piano examinations, and everybody who is thinking of taking a piano examination can find out well in advance what would be expected of them, and seek the guidance of their teachers or others in preparing effectively for the challenges involved. But the sheer fact that this article could be run in the *Guardian*, safe in the knowledge that it would be appreciated by *Guardian* readers, illustrates the association between instrumental lessons and negativity that is found in at least some groups of the population.

Planning—how?

There are, of course, many ways of planning a programme of instrumental lessons. *A Common Approach* (see p. 9) (FMS et al. 2002*a*), which is a framework for instrumental teaching that was developed by a large collaborative group of UK instrumental teachers over several years, sets out an integrated collection of 'generic' documents for all instruments that it supports with more specialized writing for 'families' such as strings. It also includes, as appendices, some exemplar 'units of work', of which one, relating to the early stages of learning bassoon, is given in Table 14 on p. 137. Moving beyond the exemplar units of work, *A Common Approach* is such a comprehensive and thoroughly thought through piece of writing that summarizing it in a short book such as this risks accidentally trivializing it, or inadvertently giving the impression that the document is less coherent than is the case. Here, I simply quote two of the generic passages that underpin all of the writing about instrumental 'families': the 'generic framework' and the 'holistic approach to teaching and learning'.

The Generic Framework

Pupils[1] should be offered broad and balanced programmes of study that promote and develop musical playing and singing.

They should be given opportunities to:

◆ Express their musical ideas and feelings
◆ Use their creativity, imagination and intuition
◆ Develop their skills, knowledge and understanding
◆ Reflect on and evaluate their progress

through the interrelated areas of:

A. listening and internalising including:

○ listening to music with concentration in and out of lessons, building on their experiences
○ having a clear aural perception of the music to be played/sung
○ recognising and discriminating between the musical elements[2] of pulse, pitch, rhythm, tempo, dynamics, texture, and tone colour
○ making links between sound and symbols when using notation

---

[1] There are some slight differences in the terminology used by *A Common Approach* and this book. For example, in the passages quoted here, *A Common Approach* writes of 'pupils' rather than 'students', 'instrumental/vocal' rather than 'instrumental', and 'pieces/songs' rather than 'pieces'.

[2] In writing of 'musical elements', *A Common Approach* employed vocabulary that is used frequently in English music education. However, the list of elements that was chosen differed from that in some other publications. I take the view that 'musical elements' is not a helpful term to use in music education. While it is, of course, crucial that students work with, and understand, pitch, duration, pace, timbre, texture, dynamics, and structure, and so forth, the nomenclature 'elements' for such lists in these, and other, documents is, in my view, unhelpful and potentially misleading to teachers and students. The notion that there are 'musical elements' became prominent in 1990, when the National Curriculum Working Group argued that they have a parallel function in music to the chemical elements in science. However, this is clearly not the case. First, the chemical elements are distinct from each other (e.g. oxygen is different from polonium), where as 'musical elements' such as rhythm and tempo clearly overlap. Second, the idea that the musical elements 'react' to give music in the same way as the chemical elements react to give chemical compounds is misleading. Some chemical elements, such as oxygen, exist on their own, whereas none of the musical elements listed above comprises music.

Students who are at school typically study science as well as music. When music educators adopt vocabulary from other subjects, it is worth checking that their original meaning has been understood. How many students, over the years, have been confused by the different—but typically unexplained—usage of 'element' in music and science? 'Element' is a term that appeared in science long before it appeared in music education. In my view, it would be educationally helpful for music educators to back off from using this term in their documents, and find—or devise—a new term if one is needed.

B. making and controlling musical sounds: developing technique including:
    ○ posture and freedom of movement
    ○ tone quality and intonation
    ○ articulation and coordination
    ○ breathing, fingering, embouchure and diction, etc.
C. creating, developing and interpreting musical ideas including:
    ○ improvising expressively
    ○ applying their instrumental/vocal skills in composing
    ○ interpreting music, developing a personal response
D. playing/singing music including
    ○ working out how to play/sing music by ear
    ○ repeating musical patterns and phrases accurately from memory
    ○ playing/singing pieces in a variety of styles with fluency, expression and under-standing
    ○ memorising pieces/songs that have been learnt
    ○ reading and playing/singing music at sight (where appropriate)
E. playing/singing music with others including
    ○ listening, watching, responding and leading
    ○ contributing to collective decisions, including interpretation
F. performing and communicating including
    ○ interpreting and communicating the character of the music
    ○ evaluating their performances and making improvements.

(FMS et al. 2002*a*: 12)

An holistic approach to teaching and learning

There are many valid ways of categorizing musical experience. The six interrelated areas identified above [i.e. A–F above] however, should be viewed as whole and not as hierarchical. The intention is that together they offer teachers sufficient flexibility to plan interrelated activities that are true to the intrinsic nature of music. This holistic approach to planning is central to *A Common Approach 2002* and is reflected through-out the documentation.

An example of teaching a piece holistically:
◆ perform the piece to pupils and discuss with them the overall effect
◆ jointly analyse the piece, i.e. in relation to mood, character, style, structure
◆ teach the piece to pupils, breaking it into manageable chunks, so that a little is learnt at a time
◆ demonstrate aspects of the piece to pupils, e.g. shaping of phrases, expression marks, and encourage them to use their aural and reading skills as the piece is absorbed
◆ make use of and devise (as necessary) appropriate exercises and scales to help pupils acquire technical accuracy and control

- encourage pupils to explore expressive possibilities from the outset
- assess progress and identify achievement and areas for improvement so that pupils learn to identify what needs attention, how to identify tricky passages and how to make improvements
- set short-term targets for practice at home, structuring the amount of time to cover technical and musical skills and establish a daily routine for pupils
- build on pupils' fluency within a realistic time-frame (according to individual needs)
- revisit technical and musical problems in lessons and suggest ways in which pupils can practise independently
- help pupils to refine their musical performance and convey the character of the music
- teach pupils how to improvise/compose a short piece based on ideas from the original piece
- where possible, listen to performances of music in the same genre and discuss
- arrange an informal and/or formal assessment as appropriate, e.g. pupils perform to teacher or to others in a concert or examination. (FMS et al. 2002a: 13)

A Common Approach, excellent as it is, does not provide the only structure through which one could plan a programme of instrumental lessons. Neither was it intended to do so. There are other publications, and teachers have their own ideas. Whatever the structure that teachers use for planning their curriculum, there are some overarching principles that affect their organization, and teaching, of it. I would suggest that these principles include:

- teaching of skills
- focus on music
- repertoire
- avoiding obstacles
- trying different strategies.

I address each of these themes, in order, below. In each case, there are subheadings, each with at least one example of the point being made.

Teaching of skills

Teachers teach skills, in the broadest sense of the word, using an approach that enables students to:

- relate the new skills they are learning to the skills they already have. *Learning to 'read ahead' when using staff notation.* Learners who have reported difficulty with this include John Holt, who has suggested that this skill might be particularly difficult for adult learners, such as himself, to master. I would suggest that most of the difficulties that students—of any age—report with learning to 'read music' can be avoided by drawing on their previous learning, and using staff notation initially as an aide-memoire of pieces that they know already, rather than as a route to learning new repertoire. I have already given an example of a keyboard teacher using this approach (see p. 83) to very good effect when working with a young beginner who had a very short weekly lesson. The teacher did not use written music at all until the student had learnt a piece orally, and was ready to see what it 'looked like' while simultaneously playing it in their head. Ruth Brittin and Deborah Sheldon (2004) have observed that the 'band methods'—published curricula—used to train bands in US schools now rely mainly on new repertoire, and it is possible that this will make it harder in future for US band students to learn to use staff notation fluently.

Teaching students to use staff notation by treating it initially as an aide-memoire also has further advantages. Staff notation, clearly, has its uses but is, at best, only an approximation of music, particularly in respect of rhythm and phrasing. The delivery of pieces that are learnt using staff notation that is barely understood is typically disjointed and wooden. Using staff notation initially as an aide-memoire keeps alive students' memory of pieces that they learnt orally, and sustains the habit of playing musically. Further, it provides a way of introducing staff notation that is consistent with Robert Schenck's 'Hey, I'm good at this!'.

In *Music in the School*, in a chapter entitled 'How not to teach music musically' I wrote of Lucy and Sue, instrumental students aged 9, who were becoming woefully confused by their teachers' attempts to introduce them to staff notation. I wrote also of the thoughts of some adults whom I had asked to interpret rhythmic notation for the first time in their life. Because of its crucial relevance to the work of instrumental teachers, an extract from this chapter of *Music in the School* is reprinted as Appendix 2.

♦ Students should never need to 'unlearn' something that they have learnt previously, either because they were taught something wrongly, or because they were taught something that is incomplete. *An example of teaching that is wrong would be 'a crotchet lasts for one beat', when this is the case only in some time signatures.* Turning to examples of teaching that would be incomplete, it is not constructive for students learning a transposing instrument to be unaware that they will need to relate the names of the notes that they play to those played on some other instruments. Students who are learning a transposing instrument should know that this is the case from the beginning. It is not helpful to a student to learn to play the note 'G' during their first trumpet lesson, and then take this note home, and find that it sounds discordant when placed with the 'G' played by a friend or relation on a keyboard. Telling students that 'the note that I have taught you is called 'G' but you will find that it is called 'F' on many other instruments, including piano and keyboards, does not take up much time within a lesson.

- keep alive skills that students brought to their first instrumental lesson.
  Composing. The American composer John Cage defined composing as follows: 'The material of music is sound and silence. Integrating these is composing' (Cage 1962: 62). I find this definition helpful. Cage used the term 'integrating' literally. In his view, in order for us to have some composing on our hands, sound and silence must have been made 'whole' in some ways. Playing around mechanically on an instrument, for example, without bothering to listen properly to what results, or to judge or evaluate its aural effect, would not meet Cage's criterion.

Being creative with sound is a natural occupation of childhood, and it is an activity that we continue to do until someone—sadly in some cases an instrumental teacher—tells us to stop. Just think of the ways in which young children will explore, and make up musical patterns upon, almost any potential sound maker that they find in their homes—cardboard boxes, cutlery . . . And the comfortable way in which they 'make up' songs that frequently draw germs of melody or lyrics from material that they know already, but that are turned into something that is distinctively new. The work of Esther Mang (2001) with young Chinese girls in Canada, and of Margaret Barrett (2002*a*; 2002*b*) with young Australian children in Tasmania, provides powerful examples of this. Earlier work by Coral Davies (1986) in the UK, similarly, showed that young children naturally compose, and adapt, songs.

Like the ability to paint or to write poetry, for example, the potential to compose lies within us all, at least to some extent. It is just that some of us may have learnt to do it rather better, or receive more acclaim for our efforts. Few of us may aspire, as composers, to reap the financial rewards that the *Sunday Times* recently reported in the case of Elton John and Tim Rice at a charity event:

Elton, going for a £500,000 song
For a fan of the Rocket Man, if could be the ultimate romantic gesture. An unknown bidder has paid £500,000 at a charity auction to have Sir Elton John write an individualised love song . . . the pop star will collaborate on the song with Sir Tim Rice. (Winnett and Swinford 2006)

And few will achieve the centuries-long reputation of composers including J. S. Bach and Mozart, for example. However, this does not mean that it is a waste of time giving us all a crack at it. Painting and poetry writing, for example, are taught to everyone in school with much less fuss. And we don't expect children to copy other people's paintings or poems, for years on end, before inviting them to produce some of their own. The argument for keeping composing alive when people become instrumental students is compelling.

Expecting instrumental students to work only as performers of other people's compositions for several years—or even only several days or weeks—in their instrumental lessons, and then suddenly become creative again is not realistic, and wastes students' time. It is neither contrived nor unauthentic for composition to be an integral part of instrumental lessons, even within western classical music. In times past, instrumental training routinely included aural work and creative work, because the accomplishments expected of instrumental western classical musicians included improvisation. Robert Schenck argues that it is a crucial part of any musician's toolkit for them to: 'be able to create music "on the wing"; to respond to others and join in musical dialogues; to explore the possibilities inherent in a melody, rhythmic pattern, or harmonic, structural or extra-musical starting point; and to arrange and compose music' (Schenck 2000*a*). He also suggests that group lessons are ideal for creative work, because of the larger numbers of instrumentalists present to originate, try out, evaluate, and develop ideas.

There are many ways of integrating creative work into group instrumental lessons. However it is done, it is crucial that the students listen to, and evaluate, their work. Otherwise, they are not 'integrating sound and silence', and consequently they are also not composing. In *All Together! Teaching Music in Groups* Jo Glover and Nigel Scaife suggest approaches including two entitled 'Imagine a beginning' and 'Composing challenge':

Imagine a beginning
. . . Warm up by asking each person in the group to practise (all at once, in cacophony) a short phrase or motif. This might be a melodic or rhythmic idea, or a timbral effect (such as short sounds, a slow slide, a trill that starts slowly and speeds up).

Make a really focused 'listening silence'. Let each player in turn play his or her motif and then leave a silence while the rest 'think it'. Then follow this sequence:

◆ practise 'hear it and then think it' around the group several times
◆ ask pupils to try to 'think' one of the motifs or a new one, imagining the music
◆ ask pupils to think a motif and then play it, or to describe a motif and ask someone else to play it.

Then ask everyone to close their eyes, clear their minds of sound and listen for an idea that could be the beginning of a new piece for a solo instrument. It can help to imagine an empty stage, silence, a spotlight on the player, and so on. Try out these ideas and discuss how each might lead into a new composition. Let pupils try to develop a new composition from their starting idea, away from the lesson.

Composing challenge
Pupils set a challenge, for themselves or each other, consisting of a verbal outline for some music. For example:
- make a piece that starts low and slow and gradually winds higher and faster
- make a piece to send someone to sleep.

Pupils take the challenge away, then bring their ideas, finished or unfinished, to share with the group. (Glover and Scaife 2004: 91)

'Imagine a beginning' prepares students to compose individually, away from the lesson, using an approach that depends heavily on ideas that they, or their peers, form in their head. It leads towards the creation and performance of pieces that integrate sound and silence, and teaches students techniques that may help them to work more effectively with music aurally, i.e. in their heads, when composing, performing, and listening. 'Composing challenge' turns the sequence of composing on its head. Instead of taking a germ of an idea and working it into something much larger, individual students create an entire piece that meets particular criteria, and then bring it to the group for evaluation. The task of composing a piece that will 'send someone to sleep' will appeal to the humour of students in many age groups, and is a welcome challenge of any notion that music should always be gripping listening that energizes the listener.

There is no room in music education for 'composing by numbers' in which students are set routines that produce results that may sound superficially like compositions, but do not require students, literally, to integrate sound and silence, through choosing, evaluating, and refining their ideas, for example. I once attended a lesson for a class of 30 10 year olds, given by some very expensive consultants who aimed to cover the entire range of the national curriculum, but where the 'composing' consisted of silent reorganization of the order of some cards with rhythms drawn on them. This activity really was totally musically silent. Nobody 'played' the original sequence of cards, or the revised sequence of cards, or said anything about how one might be different from the other one. But even had the class done any of this, it would not have been good enough unless the students had been asked to engage with the sound of the piece that they had made, and think of some ways of improving, or developing, it. And even if this had been done, the task still seems rather boring and uninspiring to me.

Even distinguished improvisers may take steps to spice up their composing. Here, Larry Adler describes how an improvisation with Sting was invigorated when Adler was left free to play what he thought he should play:

In March 1993 I had an invitation from Sting to play a song of his called 'The Shape of My Heart' . . . He sent me a cassette of the song that I liked a lot. I went to his recording studio and played the required ten bars. Then Sting suggested we do it again, and I just played wherever I felt like playing. The song was included on his Grammy-award-winning CD, *Ten Summoner's Tales*. (Adler 1994: p. xi)

However, I am not offering this example as an invitation always to play 'what one wants'. Larry Adler was an extremely accomplished improviser, and 'what he wanted' was likely to make rather more sense musically than what most of the rest of us would offer in the same circumstances! The point is that even for Larry Adler, formulae for composing—in this case playing 'the required ten bars'—are not necessarily the most efficacious way forward.

Focus on music

There is no time for anything other than music in a music lesson.

- There is no point in having fun in a music lesson, unless this fun has some musical context and purpose.
  Starting a lesson with fun. Many worthwhile musical activities can be couched in a way that is fun. Excellent! But thinking of an activity that is intended to deliver fun, and then trying to graft some music on to it, rarely works.

  Many primary schools used to teach a game called 'Pass the tambourine', in which the students sat in a circle and tried to pass a tambourine round in total silence. Why? I can see that this game could be a very useful occasional warm-up for a composing activity in which students would be asked to work with very quiet sounds that they would need to listen to very carefully, for example. But I have hardly ever seen this game used as a warm-up for anything. The class has played 'Pass the tambourine', and then has gone on to an activity that has no relation to it, and that may not even involve any music or listening.

  Warm-up activities on instruments, too, need to be an integral part of the lesson that is unfolding. If they are also fun, that is all to the good. Younger students will be speeding to the lesson, and assembling their instrument without delay, in order to join in the fun. And they might even practise the activity at home as well. But 'fun' is not the *raison d'être* of the activity. Much of the fun of playing an instrument comes directly from engagement with the instrument, with music, and with other people who love their instrument and music. We do not typically start our practice sessions with a modified version of Sudoku, or some other game of the moment, and it could be confusing—and possibly also patronizing—were students asked to do this.

- ◆ Progress relates to making music more musical.
  Progress can come from playing the same piece better, or a piece that is technically easy stunningly well. Progress is not only about playing pieces that are technically difficult. And it is certainly not about playing badly pieces that are difficult.

I have lost count of the number of schools where I have heard a class singing two parts of a four-part round really well, making a lovely sound and looking at and listening to each other, and the teacher has decided to try three parts, and then four parts, both within the same lesson. The three-part singing is usually successful, but—unsurprisingly—is not as good as the two-part singing, and the four-part singing often verges on disastrous. Moreover the teacher, sadly, is often quite pleased with it. While the parts may still be synchronized, the quality of the students' sound may have diminished, they may placed their fingers in their ears, and they have often moved into huddles where they can ignore the other parts. The lesson is getting progressively worse. Perhaps the teacher could have done some more work on the three-part singing before moving on to four-parts? Or on finding that three-part singing was more difficult for the students, she might have sought to develop students' ensemble skills further in two parts, perhaps by regrouping them so that the members of the two parts stood alternately, or the performance was given a dynamic shape, for example.

Similarly, in instrumental lessons, progress can come through performing the same piece better, rather than turning to something more difficult. At a concert at the first school where I taught, a boy who played trumpet in the National Youth Orchestra of Great Britain elected to perform a piece that is often learnt within the first couple of years of tuition, and the effect on the audience, which included beginning trumpet players, was electrifying.

More mundanely, if students have learned a piece that the teacher knows is a round, the teacher has several options as to how the idea of round will be introduced. Rather than explain about rounds, and divide the group into two, the teacher could, if they wished, ask the group to play the melody several times, add the second part without saying what they are doing, and then ask the students to comment. This can be a more subtle and revealing approach: the students are encouraged to listen to what is happening around them, and the teacher finds out who is doing this. Of course, once the idea of 'round' has been grasped, the students can be given the chance to play in a round themselves.

Progress can take the form of learning to play an independent part in an ensemble. However, this is an activity that may sometimes be misunderstood. A year or so after she had taken up cello as an adult learner, one of my friends received a phone call from a violinist eager to complete his string quartet. She found that the quartet judged success simply in terms of whether or not everyone finished playing their part at the same time. And perhaps because this criterion was met rarely, the quartet would express pleasure when individuals finished their parts only a bar or so apart. The quartet had lost sight of the intentions of the composers of the works that they were striving to play. While it is difficult to imagine anything as gross as this happening with a teacher in the room, I have sometimes heard milder versions of the above taking place during ensemble rehearsals. Ensemble playing is a fabulous way of enabling students to sustain their motivation, and to make progress as musicians, over virtually any timescale. But where the musical focus is lost, so that students bury themselves behind their music stands, and do not listen to each other, ensemble playing becomes counter-productive.

Repertoire

Teachers who are planning a programme of instrumental lessons have the opportunity to include a wide range of repertoire. They have a wonderful chance, open less to class teachers who work with larger groups, to build on students' initial musical interests, and help to extend them. As part of this, teachers may find that they extend their own repertoire. There is no music that is per se unsuited to be included, in some form or other, in an instrumental curriculum.

◆ Students' one-off interests and enthusiasms, and not only their general ones, can be built upon.

My enthusiasm for the music of Larry Adler was fuelled by a performance that he gave, aged 84, seated in an arm chair that exceeded him in size, at the De La Warr Pavilion Theatre in Bexhill on Saturday 11 September 2000. More significantly, 70 years earlier, Larry Adler had been influenced by a close encounter with Gershwin, composer of Rhapsody in Blue and many other pieces that became central to his repertoire:

One night I was standing outside the stage door of the Roxy Theater in New York, playing my mouth organ at anyone who came out, hoping to hear the magic words: 'Hey, I *like* it.' . . . Frankie Trumbauer was heading past me for the stage door . . . The bandleader frowned, nodded, then said: 'Let me hear you play "Rhapsody in Blue".' Now this piece of Gershwin brilliance was far too complex for me to handle, though it would later become a favourite in my repertoire. In those days, however, no chance. But I wasn't going to admit it. Loftily I said: 'Sorry I don't like "Rhapsody in Blue".' (Adler 1994: 10)

Gershwin was so amazed by this statement that he asked to meet Adler without further ado.

The skills that students have learnt through instrumental lessons can take them naturally into a wider range of music-making. The UK Schools Prom 2006, organized as ever in the Royal Albert Hall by the seemingly indefatigable Larry Westland of Music for Youth, included a lively contribution by a folk group that is based in Alnwick in Northumberland. The folk group chose their name—NE66—to reflect the postcode of where they all live. The students had gained their instrumental skills through a varying range of routes. One of the fiddlers, the guitarist, and bassist have had some classical lessons, some of the group are entirely self-taught as folk musicians, and two of them continue to play classical instruments—French horn or trombone—in addition to their folk instruments.

The Royal Scottish Academy of Music and Drama (RSAMD), the only conservatoire in Scotland, introduced a few years ago a degree course in Scottish music, alongside its long-established courses in classical music. Since then, it has reported improvements in the facility of some of the classical string playing (Federation of British Conservatoires 2003). Violinists, for example, who were aware that their bow arm was unconstructively tense, have learnt from the more relaxed bow hold of their fiddle colleagues. Some students made progress through playing Scottish music themselves; others by observing it being played. NE66 appear to have learnt some related skills that they could transfer into a range of musical contexts, should they wish.

Moreover, NE66's item at the Schools Prom consisted of music that had been composed by members of the group, in some cases for A level or GCSE examinations. The musical experiences enjoyed by these students are linked, but to an extent and in a way that appears to enable, rather than constrain, them. Readers of *Music in the School* may have spotted the reference to Alnwick, and realized that NE66 are students at The Duchess's County High School, which established a reputation for excellent curriculum music, carried out mainly through singing when performing and composing, almost ten years ago. All the members of NE66 have taken part in the choirs that have grown out of the curricular singing. The range of music-making that underpins NE66 has been built up over a substantial period of time.

◆ As part of their instrumental education, students learn music that is new to them, including some that challenges them through its nature, and not just through being more difficult—for example technically—than music they have played previously. Students are often more open-minded than adults when asked to listen to music of a type that is unfamiliar, perhaps an example of atonal music composed during the middle of the twentieth century (Taylor 1973). But when teachers ask students to learn to play music that the teachers know, but the students do not know, something different is happening. Students may need to hear the music played several times before coming to terms with it.

In the 1970s, it became fashionable for the (very short and serial) instrumental works of Anton Webern to be played twice—one performance after the other—at concerts. I had learnt to respect this music—which I am embarrassed to admit I had originally thought sounded random—by rehearsing it on several occasions, and I feel sure that hearing the pieces twice was helpful to members of the audience. (Although I sometimes suspected that Webern aficionados with good aural skills were using the repeated performances mainly to check the accuracy of our playing!)

I recently carried out an informal experiment on myself. I wanted to reacquaint myself with some processes of learning music that were new (to me) as a listener, so that I could think further about how to present music that I knew well, but that was unfamiliar to my students. I bought a CD of some music of John Taverner that I wanted to learn, and also loaded this onto the iPod[3] that I take on train and plane journeys. I should explain that I listen with focus to my iPod—in so far as this is possible on trains or plains—I do not use it as background for other activity such as reading. Up to now, I have listened to the entire CD, and read the accompanying booklet, on two occasions, and have listened to individual songs (term equivalent to

---

[3] Research on the impact of the iPod is, as with the technology itself, still in its infancy. Phenomenological descriptions of how we use the iPod (Bull, 2006) and mobile music as way of articulating our daily routines, attempts to describe how the technology has been appropriated and how its use is one of negotiation between the physical and the virtual. Although research on the iPod has largely focused on the social effects, there have been projects that have explored podcasting and the iPod as a tool for learning. Several universities in North America have adopted the technology as part of a wider e-learning culture, although the effects on learning have received less critical attention within the literature: http://news.bbc.co.uk/1/hi/technology/2988325.stm (information provided by Anthony Phillips).

'track' on a CD) on the iPod on between four and nine occasions each. Aspects of my learning that I have noted include the following:

o The moment when I first anticipated the entry of the organ, and the sound of the chord that it would play, in *God is Good*, was magical

o Anticipating the spiky orchestral string patterns that interrupt the legato solo cello in the first movement of *The Protecting Veil* happened earlier but felt less momentous. Nevertheless, my iPod counter tells me that this is the 'song' that I have returned to most frequently, and I am looking forward to buying a further CD that contains the whole of *The Protecting Veil*

o The booklet meant more to me on the second time that I read it, when I had listened to each song on at least four occasions. When I next listened on my iPod, I realized that I was listening out for some points made in the booklet

o I have still not learnt to predict when I will hear a major or minor third in the *Song of Athene*. This is one of only two songs that I know that I had heard before buying the CD, and I have felt less excited about listening to it on my iPod. Indeed, my iPod counter tells me that it is the song to which I have listened least.

This was, as I said, informal research, and I am not in a position to say whether my findings would be shared by anyone else. But the impact of this research for me, as a teacher of startlingly new repertoire, as a result of this informal introspection, includes the observation that it can take several listenings for new music to be absorbed; individuals may absorb the same new music in different ways; there may be limited value in teaching students about music until they have started to make sense of the music itself; learning new music of a nature that is unfamiliar, and possibly even initially alien, can lead to the development of new musical interests.

♦ Using staff notation to show students how some music that they love can be written can sugar the pill of learning to read music. Teachers will recognize that the published versions of songs, in particular, are not always notated exactly as they are performed. Nevertheless, following the notation can be helpful to students, who can be asked to 'spot the difference'.
Teachers will often ask students to bring their own (legitimately acquired) examples of written music to lessons. Introducing students' materials into lessons motivates them, and avoids drawing too heavily upon the

sometimes unfashionable—and in some cases 'twee'—materials found in some published tutor books.

◆ There are many valid reasons for including music of the past, as well as contemporary music, in a repertoire for teaching.

Daniel Barenboim, conductor and pianist, writes here of western classical performance of a very high standard, but his message is relevant also to elementary students working in a range of musical contexts:

One of the questions that preoccupy many intellectuals today is why is the music of the past of such relevance to us today? And what about the music of today? And it's evident that the music of today could not have been created, and therefore cannot exist, without the music of the past. And there is a necessity to be able to play the music of today with a feeling of familiarity that seems to us perfectly natural when we play the music of the past, as if it is being written today. (Barenboim 2006c)

◆ The most unlikely music can, in the right context, become a usual part of a teaching repertoire. The performing rights, and other rights, of composers and performances must, of course, always be respected.

Larry Adler arranged Ravel's Bolero for his own use on solo mouth organ, and offered his version to Ravel for approval. Initially, Ravel was not enthusiastic. He asked Adler why he had missed out some sections, for example. But he was soon won round. Adler was given permission to play Bolero, free of charge, in whatever arrangement and wherever he wished. Ravel's generosity—or perspicacity—brought Bolero to many other audiences, for example through the ice-skating of Torvill and Dean.

On a rather less exalted musical level, during my first teaching post, I used my own arrangements to bring to life some pieces that I wanted to share with students. At the time, the school 'orchestra' comprised the advanced trumpeter whom I have already mentioned, several initially secretive pianists, a clarinettist who had been learning for three years, a tenor horn player who played and read well (but quietly), several students who were in the very early stages of learning western classical instruments or guitar, or who had learnt recorder at primary school, and yours truly on violin, trombone, anything I needed to turn my hand to. Writing arrangements for this ensemble, in such a way that everyone had an interesting and worthwhile part to play, and the whole thing did not sound like a trumpet concerto, was a challenge that I relished.

Avoiding obstacles

It makes sense to try to avoid obstacles to learning, rather than allow them to develop, and then seek means of curing them.

Robert Schenck has suggested that there are three types of obstacles to instrumental learning that can be addressed—external obstacles, emotional or mental obstacles, and physical obstacles:

Eliminating external obstacles—some practical tips

- Make sure that all instruments are of the best possible quality
- Devote time to caring for the instruments with your students, not only at the first few lessons, but continually
- Treat all instruments carefully, respectfully and fondly
- Keep abreast of developments relating to the instrument(s) you teach
- Discuss practising with your students
- Vary activities at lessons so that the musical abilities of your students will emerge with and without their instruments
- Consider music lessons in a larger context. What does the day look like before lesson time? Are music lessons in balance with other interests and activities?
- Scrutinize your teaching, and experiment with changing repertoire, level of difficulty, scheduling or the make-up of your groups.

(Schenck 2000*a*: 87)

Eliminating emotional or mental obstacles—some practical tips

- If lack of musical self-confidence is the obstacle, establish a safe atmosphere and aim for as much student success as possible
- When devoting time to musical progress—feeling the beat, singing, reading music—plan activities which do not include the use of the instrument
- Work for the availability of playful, creative music groups for all small children in your community
- Choose a playing level and include all-round activities which give your students an outlet for musical expression
- Clarify your own thoughts concerning the best age to start playing your instrument(s), what musical 'path' you recommend for small children, and also your own approach to adult learning.

(Schenck 2000*a*: 87)

Eliminating physical obstacles—some practical tips

- Increase your own body awareness, generally speaking and in relation to your music making, in order to set a good example for your students
- Become well acquainted with the specific ergonomic issues (see Table 17) concerning your instrument
- Make proper use of the body an integral part of your students' playing and singing by including ergonomic activities in the form of games, imagery, movement, eurhythmics and rituals
- Vary activities so that different playing positions, movement and 'time-outs' become a natural part of lessons. Remember that both physical warm ups and muscle recuperation do not require as much time for children as for adults

◆ Deal with removing possible existing obstacles in a positive spirit so that full playing or singing potential can be realized. Replace unnecessary tension with new, positive habits rather than struggling against the old ones.

(Schenck 2000*a*: 115)

Table 17   Principles of ergonomics

Economy of movement	Using the required muscles and strength, and no more
Awareness	Getting to know your body and its signals
Symmetry	The two sides of your body—in balance and interplay
Joints	They work best in the middle of their range
Breaks	An indispensable part of ergonomic music making
Good physical condition	Being a musician requires endurance
Take care of your hearing	Sound levels are everyone's responsibility

To be able to set a good example, it is necessary for teachers to understand these principles in relation to themselves and their own playing.

Source: Schenk 2000*a*

Performance anxiety. While performance anxiety has been researched particularly as an obstacle for adults who are advanced learners (Kokotsaki and Davidson 2003), it can also affect the learning of younger students, and beginners of all ages. Robert Schenck suggests that performances take place on a continuum from 'playful' to 'serious', and proposes that adopting a balance of these may help students to avoid developing performance anxiety that is unconstructive (Schenck 2000*a*: 146–7):

As teachers, we do not need to push our students into feeling the gravity of a performance to make them 'learn' what it feels like to be nervous. If we do so, the risk is that learning *at* play will become learning *without* play. The demands already exist within them (and their parents). Instead, we should see to it that the concert very simply takes place, and facilitate its positive atmosphere and diversity. At concerts, like at all our other activities, serious learning and playful attitudes should coexist (see Table 18).

The prospect of forgetting part, or all, of music that is to be played from memory adds to the anxiety of some performers. There is an anecdotal view that performances given from memory sound superior to those given from a score. This is sometimes said to be because the performer will have a more holistic interpretation of the music, and can be seen more clearly. Yet the aural, rather than visual, difference in these performances may be more imagined than real. When Aaron Williamon (1999) asked some university music students to listen to a series of solo performances given by a cellist, a performance that made no use of a music stand was judged to be best. Yet the music stand 'used' for another performance actually had no music on it, and had

Table 18   Concerts: learning at play

Playful elements	Serious elements
It doesn't matter if I make a mistake	The music is performed well
Everyone gets to participate; all students, at all levels, are treated equally	More advanced students, performing difficult pieces, are looked up to and admired
Proving oneself is not the important thing	Progress is to be proud of
The concert is short and informal	All forms of concerts demand respect
The recital features both small and large groups, audience singing, and imaginative accompaniments; costumes, acting, movement and/or dance are included in the programme	Some students appear as soloists
The level of the pieces played is chosen to assure success, strengthen self-confidence and ensure musical expression	The level of the pieces played is chosen to guarantee advances which would never have been possible without the recital in sight
It is an occasion to share, celebrate and have a good time.	'Now's the real thing'

been arranged so that the audience's view of the cellist was not obscured! Perhaps the stress that some performers invest in memorizing performances could be invested more profitably, at least on some occasions.

Teaching that is confusing. No teacher deliberately confuses students, but it is easy to do so unintentionally, perhaps particularly when teaching skills that we have had for a long time—such a long time that we cannot remember acquiring them, or any problems that we encountered along the way. The teaching of rhythmic notation is particularly susceptible to such misunderstandings. Teachers sometimes forget that they learnt to read music using an instrument, for example the recorder or piano, which can make a sustained sound, and try to teach children partial truths such as that 'a crotchet is twice as long as a quaver' using clapping. A crotchet clap sounds exactly the same as a quaver clap—it is only the silence after it that changes in length. A crotchet in one piece can be shorter than a quaver in another piece that is played at a slower tempo. Students sometimes find this confusing.

Some years ago, I worked with 40 students aged 8–10, and five adults who did not read staff notation, to learn more about the information that they picked up from rhythms that were clapped or played to them (Mills 1991*b*; 1991*c*). I found the results most revealing. Some students who were learning instruments were confused about rhythmic notation in ways that were likely to interfere with their instrumental progress. They followed routines taught by their teacher, often involving 'counting' and clapping, without understanding what they were being asked to do. Like the adults who did not read music, they were conscious of, and distracted by, the compromises that rhythmic notation makes when dealing with phrasing and emphasis, but that music readers somehow learn to overlook.

I wrote about this research in *Music in the School*, and a related extract from this book (pp. 101–7) is included as Appendix 2.

Trying different strategies

I suggest this for two reasons. First, it can make instrumental lessons more interesting—and hence more motivating—for students and teachers. Second, it can meet students' learning needs more effectively.

Giving students a balance of individual and group lessons. While some parents and teachers take the view that individual lessons are necessarily more efficacious than group lessons, from the earliest stages of tuition, this is not the case (Mills 2000*a*). I return to this subject in Chapter 10. However, I personally take the view that students are served best through a judicious mix of individual and group lessons from the earliest stages. This can be difficult to organize but it is not impossible, as many teachers have shown. In general, students may benefit from having a higher proportion of individual lessons as they advance, but not all students will be the same in this respect. Desmond Hunter (1999; 2000; 2006; Hunter and Russ 1996), who works at the University of Ulster, has argued that higher education students benefit from receiving a mix of group and individual instrumental lessons, and has developed means of organizing this over more than ten years.

As students become more autonomous as learners, they become more able to extract learning from different sorts of situations. I have sometimes thought that the students at the Royal College of Music who are particularly effective learners, and who enjoy an allocation of roughly weekly instrumental lessons, actually draw the potential benefits of group tuition from some of their other curricular activities. For example, a string player sitting towards the back of a section in an orchestra may learn from observing, and analysing, the different techniques that their peers are using as they attempt to produce exactly the same oral effect from the same written music; a student who attends a concert given by one of their peers—on whatever instrument—will take away ideas about presentation, and programme organization, that they can apply. Some students who have been interviewed for the *Learning to Perform* research

(TLRP 2007; see www.learningtoperform.org.uk) at the Royal College of Music have suggested that they have drawn upon these, or similar, sources of learning. These sources provide authentic contexts for developing the skills, knowledge, and understanding that the students know they will need as they build their career in music. For these perceptive students, group lessons may not be necessary, or could even be redundant. For other students, group lessons might provide a crucial part of their education.

Speeding up a performance without just shouting 'faster'. It is customary for students to be taught initially to play a piece below its intended tempo, and then gradually winch up the speed without any loss of quality. This approach is often successful, particularly where there is only a small gain of tempo needed, everyone is concentrating, and the teacher exudes confidence of success. But this approach is not universally successful. During group lessons, one or more students may reach what feels to them to be their 'top' speed some time before the desired speed has been reached. Either they stop playing, or the performance grinds to a discordant halt.

This class teacher used a different approach:

Everyone in the class (of 12-year-olds) was learning to play *In the Mood* (melody and chords) on keyboard. The teacher wanted them to play it much faster and more fluently, without feeling that they needed to read it from staff notation, checking more or less every note before they moved on. He also wanted more swing. He started the lesson with the class singing *In the Mood* to his piano accompaniment. Techniques including sharing the melody between two groups that were expected to stand to sing, and sit when they were silent, ensured the concentration of the class, and encouraged them to think of the melody as phrases, not just notes. Next, he asked the class to repeat what they had just done, but singing along with a commercial recording of *In the Mood*, which was much faster. They did. Finally, he asked them to go to the keyboards and play *In the Mood* as they had just sung it, singing along in their heads or out loud if they wished. This worked extremely well. (Adapted from Mills 2000*b*: 65)

This teacher's approach is related to what Tânia Lisboa describes as a 'multimodal' strategy. The schoolteacher used one mode—singing—to help the students in another mode: playing keyboard. Lisboa found that three of her cello students avoided the stiltedness of their performances from staff notation if she first taught them to sing the pieces that they would play. When the students were subsequently shown the notation, and asked to play it on their cellos, they played it in phrases, like they had sung it, rather than 'note-by-note'. Lisboa suggests that this is because they already had a mental model of the melody (Lisboa 2002).

The class of students who played *In the Mood* at full speed had also used singing to give them a mental model of what they were trying to achieve. They had learnt to 'chunk' the melody so that their performance was not held back by fingers and eyes that were more accustomed to working 'note-by-note'. And the performance that resulted was highly motivating for all concerned.

Drawing on relevant research

In recent years, research into instrumental teaching has mushroomed. While research studies are often carried out in specialized locations, in order to maintain their focus, they may have wider implications. Examples of such research pepper this book. Here is another one:

Planning a programme for students at conservatoires. Research at the RCM (Burt and Mills 2006) investigated the hopes and fears of students before they enter the institution, and compared these with the thoughts that they expressed in interviews carried out a term later.

While new students are often particularly enthusiastic about the opportunity to learn from a teacher who is also a working performer, they soon take this for granted. By the end of their first term at the RCM, three 'pivot points' start to shape students' development as musicians:

1. performing solo for the first time at college

2. overcoming feelings of inadequacy that arise from being taught with such an able peer group

3. receiving formative feedback on their written and practical work.

All instrumental learners of any age or stage—not only those studying at conservatoires—need to feel that they are acquitting themselves with dignity if they perform to others. They also need to develop a sense of perspective about how their playing compares with that of other people—if this is important to them. Stephanie Pitts (2002) found that some first-year music undergraduates at the University of Sheffield respond to their able peer group by setting out to prove their musical skills. Providing that this is monitored carefully, such motivation could be beneficial to musicians at any stage. And feedback that develops confidence, and assists with learning how to improve, is helpful to everyone. Don Lebler (2006), working at Queensland Conservatorium Griffith University in Australia, writes of incorporating feedback formally into music higher education. Students studying Popular Music Production at the conservatorium, for example, must act as peer-assessors. This allows them to critique their peers' work, and to receive such evaluation themselves, in an environment that ensures that the feedback remains constructive. Desmond Hunter (1999) has established peer assessment of performance by, and of, all the music students at the University of Ulster.

Chapter 9

Practice makes perfect?

I have told Miss Bennet several times, that she will never play really
well unless she practises more.

> Lady Catherine de Bourgh passes judgement on the playing of Miss
> Elizabeth Bennet. *Pride and Prejudice* (Austen 1813)

Kathryn [arrives at her violin lesson], opens her violin case and
discovers someone else's violin and music inside.

> Deborah Kemp, instrumental teacher, reflects on the possibility that a
> student has not opened her violin case between violin lessons. (Kemp 2006)

Explain your parents' reasoning for weekly violin lessons, when you
hate them, refuse to practise, and sound like a strangled cat.

> Part of a satirical test paper for 7-year-olds, written by Ted Wragg, in
> response to a government proposal to accredit the academic
> achievements of particularly able primary children. (Wragg 2004)

Mira came home to find her grandmother, who was not known for
her piano playing, practising furiously. 'What are you doing
grandmamma?', she enquired. 'Driving the moths out of the
piano', came one response.

> Reminiscences from 1950 of a family that grew up in Croatia, 2007

In this chapter we consider 'practice' under three headings:

- Why practise?
- Practice as a chore
- Practice as play

Why practise?

Elizabeth Bennet did not practise enough, Kathryn seemingly did not
practise at all, Ted Wragg's fictional students continued to take instrumental lessons

although they had refused to practise, and Mia's grandmother, who grew up in Croatia more than a century ago, practised as a form of pest control.

So why are teachers so keen on having students' practise? And why do students still make progress if they don't do as much practise as their teachers think they should?

In Chapter 6 of *Music in the School* (Mills 2005*b*: 71) I wrote about instrumental practice as follows:

'Practice makes perfect', or so we are told. Instrumental teachers typically encourage students to practise. Inexperienced students sometimes find this a chore. Some students who practise a lot do not succeed. Some very competent musicians appear not to practise. The link between practice and perfection is clearly complex.

Some psychologists believe (Ericsson and Smith 1991) that expertise in music (by which they largely mean expertise as an instrumentalist) is developed through prescribed 'deliberate' practice over many years. This belief is based on research that was carried out in fields including chess and skiing. The researchers count the amount of deliberate practice that has taken place; they do not consider its quality. While it is interesting to know how many thousands of hours accomplished musicians have spent in practice, this information is of little use to us, as teachers, because it does not help us to improve the support that we provide to students who want to practise more effectively. One thousand hours of the wrong sort of practice is (at least) one thousand hours of wasted time. Some instrumental musicians may have done so much practice because they enjoyed doing it, rather than because they needed to do it. 'Lots of practice' is an indicator, rather than a cause, of students' progress as a performer.

More recent research has addressed also the quality of practice, particularly practice for performances that musicians will give from memory. Some of this has focused on the extent to which musicians learn 'chunks' of a piece, and then join these chunks together. Aaron Williamon and Elizabeth Valentine (2000) asked 22 pianists to learn one of four pieces of J. S. Bach, and found that the pianists who gave the most successful final performances were those who had worked on longer segments from an earlier stage. It made no difference whether the pianists were elementary or advanced.

Does this mean that we should teach students to play longer segments of pieces earlier in their practice? In my view, the answer is both 'yes' and 'no'. It is 'yes' because students who can play longer chunks of a piece are better placed to work on producing a performance that is coherent and convincing. It is 'no' because it would probably be unconstructive for students repeatedly to play longer passages that they stumble over. That would be similar to learning to play the piece wrongly! One of the lessons of this research is that students should be encouraged to structure their practice so that stumbling is eradicated speedily, and then taught to lengthen the segments on which they work as soon as possible. This is an approach that teachers could try out with all their students, although it is possible that some of them will find it more useful than others.

The researchers also counted up the total time that the student pianists spent on practice. Unsurprisingly, the students who were playing more advanced pieces spent more time practising them. However, the more advanced players also practised more efficiently; they required less practice 'per note' than their peers. They had learnt how to work more economically. The more advanced students also had more effective strategies for memorization. In *Music in the School* I wrote:

While the starts and stops during the early stages of pianists' practice related mainly to bars that they found difficult, the more effective memorizers soon mastered these bars and stopped strategically, according to the way that they had divided the piece into segments. And in due course they did not need to stop at all, but still moved from playing the whole piece to playing segments of it from time to time, thus providing themselves with further 'copies' as insurance against memory loss. (Mills 2005*b*: 73)

The points at which the pianists divided their piece into segments did not always accord with the divisions that might be made by a musicologist, but worked for the individuals concerned.

How had the more advanced pianists learnt to practise more effectively? In particular, how had they learnt to memorize? Were they taught, or did they just find out somehow? And, if the latter, are they aware of what they do, so that they could—for example—teach someone else to do it?

Some musicians may be less aware of the strategies that they use when practising than we might expect. The findings of research carried out by Roger Chaffin and Gabriela Imreh (2001) suggest that this may be the case. Gabriela Imreh—a concert pianist—recorded her practice as she learned the Presto of the *Italian Concerto* by J. S. Bach for performance from memory, commenting on her approach as she worked. What she said did not concur completely with what Roger Chaffin noticed. In particular, while she had thought that she began with work on fingering, 'familiar patterns of notes', and technical difficulties, and turned to dynamics later, Roger Chaffin spotted that she began working on dynamics from her first session of practice. Dynamics may not have been the main emphasis of the early practice sessions, but they were strongly evident.

I do not know if Gabriela Imreh ever teaches beginners. But, if she does, might she teach them to get the notes right first, and add the expression later, under the mistaken view that this is how she works when learning pieces as a performer? And if Gabriela Imreh is not alone in thinking that she deals with the notes first, and adds the expression later, when she doesn't—and I doubt that she is alone in this—is there a danger that many instrumental students are being taught to work in this disjointed way, so that they might find it difficult to produce performances that are shaped and coherent? Are accomplished instrumental students, such as Gabriela Imreh presumably was as a young woman, survivors of an instrumental teaching system that tells students to get the notes right first, but where the high achievers—deliberately or intuitively—overlook this instruction? And does this emphasis on accuracy before expression contribute to the view of some parents of younger students that creative or expressive approaches to instrumental learning might delay their children's progress (see p. 80)?

Practice as a chore

It seems to be *de rigueur* for practice, or 'homework' as it is now sometimes called, to be viewed—by teachers (and parents in the case of younger students)—as something that students will not want to do, or will not want to do enough of. Practice is portrayed as drudgery, or duty, or an unpleasant chore that few students do enough of, unless someone is sitting over them and making them do it. Why should this be? It may be partly because many of us, as teachers, grew up doing less practice than our own teachers had told us to do. So we expect our students to do the same. But if all this practice that we were told is necessary actually isn't—because we still got good enough to become instrumental teachers—why are we trying to make the next generation of students do lots of practice too?

I, for one, generally did rather less daily violin practice than my first violin teacher wanted me to do. This wasn't because I did not want to practise, but because there was not much time left, of an evening, once I had cycled home from school and completed the monstrous amounts of homework that this fiercely academic institution expected of me, and which my parents expected me to prioritize above playing the violin. But my violin teacher was no more persuaded of this argument than you probably were as you read it just now, and 'practice'—in particular time spent practising—was something that we soon learnt not to talk about too frequently. In any case, I came to realize that my teacher could not necessarily tell how much time I had spent practising through listening to me play. This said something constructive about my learning. Surely the positive effects of practice are supposed to accumulate over the years; we do not start to play our instrument anew after every lesson. But, on occasion, my teacher got her assessment of the extent of my practice very wrong. I recall a lesson when I tuned up my violin, and realized with horror that I had not played a note since my teacher and I last met, a week earlier. That lesson went well. And a week before, my teacher had accused me of not practising at all, when I had actually been quite assiduous.

These stories probably say rather more about my (lack of) practise skills than they say about my teacher who—after all—still taught me, regardless of my erratic practice, to play the violin to a useful standard. When I went to university I got very serious about practice, and rose early each morning so that I could get several hours in before my first lecture began. But this never seemed to make much difference to how things went in my violin lessons. I don't think that I was the only student for whom there was what mathematicians describe as an 'inverse correlation' between doing lots of practice, and playing well. At my university there were some stunningly good players whom I did not once meet in a practice room.

When conservatoire students in England, Australia, and the US completed questionnaires about their experience as instrumental teachers, they generally showed a high level of responsibility towards their teaching, but viewed it as their 'students' fault' if they did not practise enough (Fredrickson and Brittin 2006).

What is the point of setting practice tasks that students do not do? If it is important that students do practise, perhaps it would help if we set them more tasks that they would like to do? And given that students often love to work out how to play well-known melodies by ear, and to compose, on their instrument, why not make both of these a stronger feature of practice?

I wrote, in *Music in the School* (and see p. 117 above), of a conversation that I had with a group of primary students who had just taken part in a very useful cornet lesson. When I asked the students about their practice at home, they admitted that they spent much of their practice time in creative tasks such as composing, or working out how to play melodies that they knew from other contexts. But they seemed to feel that doing this was not how they should be spending their time, and they never told their cornet teacher what they were doing, or invited him or their class teacher to listen to the results. Mightn't it make sense for composing to become an official part of cornet practice at this school, and for cornet compositions to be volunteered by students, or suggested by class music teachers, as a matter of course? There was no sense in this school of class teachers lacking interest in what happened in cornet lessons and during practice times, or of the cornet teacher having an unduly narrow view of his work. To the contrary. But the music-making that the students engaged in during class lessons, during cornet lessons, and at home could usefully have been drawn together a little more. And the same is true of many other schools.

There are so many ways in which practice time can be profitably spent. Perhaps practice could include singing—even in the case of students who are learning an instrument other than the voice? Or some time could be used for gaining, at home, un-pressured experience of playing an instrument entirely by ear? Or for watching the practice of someone who plays another instrument and seeing what can be learnt (about performing or practice) from that. This is a technique for improving personal practice skills that is found helpful by some very competent instrumentalists (Mills 2004*d*). The list of tasks that teachers—or students—could usefully set for practice time is probably endless. The issue is to find something that students *will* do, and that will also help them to make progress in music. On occasion, a teacher may feel that a student needs most to do some specific repetitive practice of a particularly dreary kind. But if the student is not going to do this, there is no point in setting it as homework. It may work better for a little of the repetitive work to be introduced in a lesson, and for the student to be asked to return with an exercise, composed by themselves, that they could use to teach the same point to a friend. Teachers will have their own ideas.

And do we teach students to use mental practice as a technique that complements physical practice? The answer is probably 'no'. I first met mental practice as an idea in my twenties, when a friend who was a businessman and who was driving me to 'gig' explained that he had done nearly all of his practice in the car. Clearly, nobody could learn all the physical skills needed to play an instrument from scratch 'in the car', but there is scope for more practice to be done in this way.

If you feel that you have never tried practising mentally yourself, perhaps start by playing a piece, or part of a piece, silently at the bus stop. 'Finger' the piece as you go. Or concentrate to the point that you do not need to do this. Stop as soon as you feel that your concentration has lapsed for one nanosecond . . . And then start again.

Perhaps students could be introduced to mental practice by being asked to think through their performance of a piece, work out what they would need to do physically to improve this performance, play through the piece in their head with the improvements added, and then see if anything had improved when they started to play their instrument. Students may need their teachers' support at this point, as their experience of mental practice may have honed their listening skills, so that they think that their playing has deteriorated when this is not the case. Over weeks and months, students may start to have their own ideas about ways of doing mental practice.

John Holt wrote of how he developed a form of mental practice for himself:

For some weeks I had been slogging my way through the first movement of the Telemann [flute] suite, one note at a time. The movement is written in 12:8 time . . . [but I did not understand compound time] and went on ponderously counting twelve beats to each measure [i.e. bar], which took all the life and bounce out of the music. I had no idea at all what the piece sounded like. I have never heard [my teacher] play it, had never heard a recording of it, had never tried to sing or whistle it for myself. If was just black notes on white paper.

One weekend I went down to visit my parents in Rhode Island. I got on the bus for New Bedford and, as we drove along, looked out of the window, thought about this and that, and enjoyed the music which my private radio or orchestra was playing inside my head. This mental music maker plays much of the time, whenever or whatever it wants. On this bus ride it was playing a tune that I couldn't place . . . the tune played on, and after a while I decided to relax and enjoy it. I had stopped wondering what the tune was, was hardly paying any more attention to it, when suddenly a voice inside my head said, 'Hey! It's the Telemann! It's that flute piece you're supposed to be playing!' My first thought was, 'No, it can't be that, I'm not playing anything like that!' But soon I realised that the sluggish tune I had been playing and this dancing music in my head were in fact one and the same. I thought in amazement, 'So that's what it's supposed to sound like.' Clearly the unconscious musician in me, a better musician than the conscious, hearing the Telemann that I was playing on my flute, said, 'No, no, that *can't* be what that piece is supposed to sound like,' and decided for itself how it *had* to sound. (Holt 1978: 126)

It seems sad that John Holt had to discover this aspect of mental practice so tortuously for himself, instead of learning it as an integral part of the teaching that he received. He could have saved a lot of time, and had rather more fun, along the way. Further ways of saving his time could have included listening to a recording of the Telemann, or listening to his teacher playing at least part of this piece.

There is a view, frequently expressed at psychology conferences, or during psychology presentations at education conferences, that aspiring instrumentalists—like aspiring 'experts' in other fields including chess and skiing, must carry out 'deliberate practice' for a minimum of 10,000 hours before becoming 'expert'. I take issue with this view. I do not dispute the fact that many expert instrumentalists did indeed practise for 10,000 or more hours before becoming 'expert', but would suggest that this was, at least in some cases, because they enjoy spending time practising (nothing wrong with that!), or had not been taught to learn as effectively as they might.

Moreover, the research studies that have suggested the 10,000 figure have generally been based on experts' recollections of the time that they spent in 'deliberate practice' many years ago. Research by Clifford Madsen (2004) in the US, however, has recently shown that these recollections can be suspect, at least in the case of instrumental music. Madsen asked alumni who had graduated 30 years earlier to recall their quantity of practice as undergraduates, and compared what they said with the practice diaries that they had completed at the time. The match between these two sources of data was poor.

Further:

1. Some individuals have undeniably achieved 'excellence' on the strength of less practice than the theory would say that they need. These individuals include some students at the RCM.

2. We can probably all think of individuals who have not achieved excellence, despite having carried out much more 'deliberate practice' than the theory says is required.

3. Some sessions of 'deliberate practice' are more effective than others; much depends on their fitness for purpose. We can probably all think, as instrumentalists, of examples of our own 'deliberate practice' that worked well, or less well.

4. Subscribing to the 'prescribed hours of practice' theory lets us, as teachers, off the hook. If students have not done as much work as we said they should, we can attribute any lack of progress to this, rather than to any imperfections in our teaching. (And this is even though we, as students, probably did less practice than our own teachers said we should . . .)

5. The theory does not allow for the many students who learn more than one instrument, and who frequently become expert on their 'subsequent' instruments quite rapidly. Examples include the lapsed instrumental students who suddenly re-emerge, chrysalis-like, as self-taught guitarists or drummers. They also include students at the RCM who have secured, before graduation, professional orchestral positions on an instrument unrelated to that for which they were originally auditioned. For example, at least two alumni of the RCM secured orchestral positions in percussion, having entered the RCM as an oboist, and a trombonist, respectively (Mills 2004d). They join the orchestral musicians, graduates of a wider range of institutions, whom I researched some years ago, and who had made transitions as striking as violin to trombone (Mills 2004d) (see also p. 106).

Practice as play

But practice is, or should be, or can be, much more than a chore. Were it only this, it is difficult to understand why anyone would continue with it—in some form or other—once they have ceased to take lessons, or once the daily practice time set by their teacher has been exceeded. Practice is enjoyable, gives us the satisfaction of learning to play something better, engages us with music, gives us some of the physical benefits of a workout at the gym . . . In other words, we feel better for having undertaken it.

Without this positive feedback that flows from practising, it is difficult to imagine how we would ever have any professional musicians. Other than for a small proportion of performers, music is not a well-paid profession, so that greater—and more secure—financial reward could be obtained much more easily in other fields. Professional performers become professional performers out of choice, because this is what they want to do. And alumni of the RCM who aspire to become instrumental teachers—traditionally known as 'professors'—at the RCM will typically first build a distinguished performing career over a period of at least 14 years, and then sustain this distinguished performing career until they retire. That would be an awful lot of practising for someone who did not find this fun! In comparison with their peers as RCM students, alumni who have returned to the RCM are musicians who:

- in general, performed more and taught less than their peers during the early years of their careers, and who still perform more than them today. However, there are wide individual differences;

- are committed to their conservatoire teaching, and generally feel that it improves their effectiveness as performers;

- are determined in their pursuit of music as a career. This determination is shown, for example, through some professors [when students] leaving the conservatoire early, without gaining a qualification, so that they could take up a post in a major orchestra. It is shown also through future [conservatoire teachers'] resilience when they encountered obstacles to their career;

- are flexible as musicians. This flexibility is shown, for example, through some of the [conservatoire teachers] changing their specialism from the one with which they entered the conservatoire. It is shown also through the thirst of future [conservatoire teachers] for new musical experiences, including various forms of teaching, in order to sustain the creative momentum of their careers. (Mills 2004a)

Robert Schenck (2000a) writes of practice as 'play at home' (Table 19). I recently saw many of these principles in action:

During an ideally autumnal Sunday walk in Blenheim Park, I was initially puzzled by a 'toot toot' sound to our left. What could it be? There isn't a mainline railway for miles, and the little train that ferries visitors from Blenheim Palace to the butterfly garden and the maze makes a different sound, and is on the right. But the 'tooting' was moving closer . . .

A couple of minutes later, and all became clear. A woman, and a boy aged around 7, crossed onto our path and walked a few feet ahead of us, towards the park gate. The

Table 19 At play at home: students' practice—some practical tips

Be open to your students' various ways of practising, depending on age, personality, level of ambition, etc.

Create contexts and different forms of concerts that spur them on

Encourage students to choose their own music and assignments

Let your students make up their own music

Make music together at lessons in the way you want your students to make music in your absence

Talk with students and parents—about practising, and about thoughts, opinion and feelings concerning making music in general. Provide information and tips regarding practice; tell them what practising means and has meant to you

Clarify assignments well. Take the necessary time to discuss them

Make sure younger students already master their assignment(s) before leaving the lesson; combine new assignments with music they already feel confident at

Use a notebook for musical notation and to write down assignments

Remember that ensemble playing is a decisive factor in maintaining motivation and enthusiasm

Remember that the same universal principles of practising apply to everyone, but that strategies differ according to personality and age

Set a good example by applying the principles and strategies of practising yourself.

Practising takes care of itself when it's fun to be playing, there is a stimulating context for the music, there are positive role models and when goals with built-in rewards are clearly in sight.

Source: Schenck 2000a: 203

woman followed a silent and orderly adult route. The boy, as is the wont of 7-year-olds, chose a course that started and ended with the woman's, but also incorporated a myriad of twists and turns.

More significantly, he had brought a white plastic recorder with him. The 'tooting'—now contextualized as an exercise in tonguing—had ended, and he was playing a phrase of a melody. During the walk to the park gate we heard further melodic extracts, practice of individual notes, and unorthodox—presumably self-directed—techniques, including flutter-tonguing that the boy demonstrated with his hands in his pockets, and seemingly unaware that he had an audience.

The woman—probably the boy's mother—did not interfere.

Couldn't more practice be like this? The boy was working voluntarily, on a Sunday, in a beautiful environment, and with his mother present for company, but not constraint. He seemed to have remembered, and be practising, everything he had ever been taught. And he added some further sounds and patterns for good measure.

He clearly loved his recorder.

I hope that he continues to love his recorder.

I hope also that nobody—for example his recorder teacher—tells him to take the flutter tonguing out of his repertoire. Even though he flutter tongued with his hands in his pockets.

In 1978 I directed Benjamin Britten's *Noye's Fludde* at the school where I was then a teacher: Holy Family School in Keighley. This was a home-grown performance. While I did import some local musicians to be the 'professional string quintet', every other part was taken by a member of the school—typically a student rather than a teacher. For example, Noye was sung by a sixth-former, his stage wife was one of the teaching nuns, and the Voice of God was played by the head of boy's PE.

So it was in character that the role of 'professional recorder', who plays the part of the dove (a palindrome, to signify her outward and return journeys) was played by a 13-year-old girl who specialized in piano, but had played recorder at primary school. To begin with, she coped with the flutter-tonguing written into this part very well indeed. But as the final performances approached, she became more anxious, and it eventually became expedient for me to say that she could miss out the flutter tonguing wherever she liked, if this made her feel more comfortable.

Why was she anxious? I think that the anxiety came from having learned to play recorder, and later piano, in ways that focused on playing music 'right'—and that would not have allowed her to walk, with her recorder, along a moor land path near Keighley, flutter-tonguing with her hands in her pockets.

What a shame!

Whatever happens musically to the recorder boy in the future, I hope that his enthusiasm for experimenting with new musical techniques stays with him.

Chapter 10

Some myths of instrumental learning and teaching

SIRE/NES or SEIRE/NES (Σειρήνες), mythical beings who were believed to have the power of enchanting and charming, by their song, any one who heard them. When Odysseus, in his wanderings through the Mediterranean, came near the island on the lovely beach on which the Sirens were sitting, and endeavouring to allure him and his companions, he, on the advice of Circe, stuffed the ears of his companions with wax, and tied himself to the mast of his vessel, until he was so far off that he could no longer hear their song (Hom. *Od.* xii. 39, &c., 166, &c.). According to Homer, the island of the Sirens was situated between Aeaea and the rock of Scylla, near the south-western coast of Italy. Homer says nothing of their number, but later writers mention both their names and number; some state that they were two, Aglaophene and Thelxiepeia (Eustath. *ad Hom.* p. 1709); and others, that there were three, Peisinoë, Aglaope, and Thelxiepeia . . . Their place of abode is likewise different in the different traditions.

(Smith 1870)

The word 'myth' has a wide range of meanings. The ancient story of the Sirens illustrates the long-standing role of music in tales about superhuman beings or supposed events during earlier ages—tales that were taken by some to represent a true account. Perhaps the story arose from a wish to explain why some ships had been lost in particular—seemingly easily navigable—regions of the Mediterranean. We will never know. The Sirens make a good story that stimulates our imagination, but which few of us, today, would take as true.

In this chapter, we focus on some mythical views about music education: views for which there is no foundation in fact, but that have become part of the folklore of the subject. Perhaps they arose because some felt a need to explain why some of us become expert instrumentalists, but others do not. Again, we will never know precisely where the stories came from.

I have already addressed some mythical views about music education earlier in this book. For example, we have considered—and I have rejected—the view that students with a particular physical shape, or personality type (whatever we mean by this) are more suited, or less suited, to play particular instruments. Here, we address a further six mythical views that have been discussed in less depth in earlier chapters, but which have the potential—where held by a teacher or student—to impact adversely on the student's education.

I cannot help noticing that all my examples here of mythical views relate to western classical music—or at least music that is recorded using staff notation. Perhaps other forms of music have no mythically based practice? I doubt this, but would suggest (as an untested hypothesis that others are welcome to research!) that mythically based practice may well be less prevalent for teachers who work beyond the realms of staff notation.

There are some pairs of instruments that a student should never study concurrently

Numerous conversations with instrumental teachers and other adults have provided me with the evidence that this view exists. Counter-examples of students and other musicians who play both parts of a 'prohibited' pair of instruments provides me with evidence that the view is a myth.

Linda's bandmaster (see p. 109) believed that she should not learn French horn concurrently with cornet. I have lost count of the orchestral brass, woodwind, and string players who have told me that their specialist instrument should not be learnt at the same time as any other. When asked for a reason, they often suggest that the techniques of the two instruments will conflict, so that the student will not learn to play either instrument 'properly'.

However, Linda succeeded in learning French horn without her bandmaster noticing that she was doing so. Any adverse effect on her cornet playing was—literally—negligible. Further, the traditions of some brass bands and wind bands involve performers playing several instruments interchangeably. And it is assumed by classical composers that orchestral woodwind players will transfer between related instruments (e.g. flute and piccolo, oboe and cor anglais) within the course of a single piece of music—or even within a few bars. Players of baroque music are also frequently expected to move between different instruments including, in the case of trumpeters, instruments with a radically different mouthpiece and pitch range.

The (frequently heard) argument against learning viola while one is also learning violin has always struck me as particularly specious. Violin teachers who hold this view have sought to explain to me that a violinist who also plays viola will play their violin flat, as violins have shorter strings. Yes, I knew about the shorter strings! But, given that all string instruments have, through their nature, smaller intervals towards the bridge, so that all string players have to learn to play in tune by using their ears, I find it difficult to understand why playing violin and viola is thought to be a particular problem.

Some years ago the Yehudi Menuhin School, in England, countered the violin/viola arguments by insisting that all its violinists learnt viola, and played viola in a string quartet. This policy also improved students' attitudes to the viola as an instrument, and some students who entered the school as a violinist left it specializing on viola. There are further examples of educational institutions seeking to scotch the myth that particular groups of instruments cannot be learnt concurrently, and indeed that learning two instruments can be enriching. For example, students who enter the Royal College of Music as specialists on an orchestral brass instrument must also learn a band instrument, and give an examined recital on it.

Clearly, the view that students should not learn some particular combinations of instruments is a myth that limits their progress in music, and potential enjoyment of it. And so it needs to be countered. It is, of course, possible that students who are learning two or more instruments may need some help with playing each of them optimally. For example, a violinist who also takes up viola may need some help with placing more weight on the bow. But the provision of advice on matters such as this is, surely, part of what instrumental teachers are for!

Instruments must be learned at a young age, or not at all

This myth is often expounded by teachers and parents. It is true that some distinguished performers did start to learn their main instrument at a very young age. For example, Yehudi Menuhin and Jacqueline du Pré are well known as performers who began to learn violin and cello, respectively, before they were old enough to go to school. But this does not mean that everyone would have to start as young in order to achieve the same success. Or that Menuhin and du Pré needed to start so young in order to become as successful as they undoubtedly did. And, for the rest of us, levels of success that are markedly lower than those achieved by Menuhin and du Pré, for example, would still feel worthwhile. We do not have to become one of the best performers in the world before concluding that the instrumental lessons that we received were other than a waste of time and money!

There are many counter-examples of instrumentalists who are successful, but who did not start to play their instrument young. When I interviewed some of the professors (instrumental teachers) at the RCM, who teach along-side their undoubtedly successful performance career, I found several who had taken up the instrument on which they now specialize only after they had become conservatoire students, typically at the age of 18 (Mills 2004*d*). The current students of the RCM include some who did not start learning their main instrument until they were at secondary school, and they nevertheless achieved the standard required to pass an RCM entry audition within a few years. Some of these students were taking up an instrument for a second time, having 'given up' another instrument, but this was not always the case. One of the students to whom I have spoken began to learn violin, in a group, when she was 12, and did not have any individual teaching until she entered the RCM. She had not learnt another instrument previously. Another such student took up her first orchestral instrument at the age of 12, having played recorder briefly at primary school, entered the college with the lowest audition score of any student admitted to the RCM in her year, and graduated four years later with a first-class honours degree, gained mainly through the high standard of her final recital. I wrote earlier (pp. 22–3) of an RCM graduate who was dismissed as 'unmusical' by his piano teacher when he took lessons briefly while at primary school; he took up another instrument at the age of 13, entered the RCM, and did very well.

Harald Jørgensen (2001) researched the progress of young performers in Norway, and concluded that it is not essential to start lessons at an early age, and that an early start can be a disadvantage should the early teaching be dis-couraging, or educationally inappropriate in any way. Jørgensen's findings charge instrumental teachers with a substantial responsibility when they take on young beginners as students. If the beginners' experience of lessons is neg-ative, they may be lost to instrumental music for ever.

When teaching students a piece that is new to them, a teacher should begin by getting the notes right, and add the 'expression' later

I think that this myth is, mercifully, becoming less prevalent. RCM students who completed a questionnaire on their attitude to being a teacher (see p. 23) gener-ally disagreed with the statement 'I believe in getting the notes right first, and adding expression later'. *A Common Approach* addresses communication and expression from the earliest stages of tuition (FMS et al. 2002*a*). Nevertheless this myth remains alive. I have heard it recently upon the lips of some instrumental teachers, and also those of some parents who learnt an instrument in their youth, but gave up at an early stage—possibly because this was how they were taught . . . This myth is reinforced by tutor books that include few, or very limited, references to any form of expression for several pages.

Music is much more than an exercise in taking a piece of paper with dots and squiggles on it, and converting it into metronomic sound. I can't imagine ever teaching myself a new piece without—at least—thinking about how I would shape my performance as it improved. When it is a violin sonata, I am soon playing what I can of the piano accompaniment, while singing the violin part in whatever octave I can manage. When it is a chamber or orchestral part, I strive to obtain a score and a recording. I cannot imagine ever feeling motivated to play a piece metronomically and at a constant volume—unless this is what the composer wanted—and I cannot imagine beginners feeling motivated to do this either. And my recollections of those music lessons where I have observed teachers 'adding the dynamics' to performances that should never have had their natural dynamics removed in the first place, are just too painful to recount right now.

I wrote earlier (p. 175) of a concert pianist who spoke of 'getting the notes right first, and adding expression later' when learning repertoire herself, but who actually attended to expression whenever she played, and just gave it more emphasis in her later practice sessions. I think that this is very constructive. It sounds as though the strategies used by at least one concert pianist who is learning a new piece, and used by many instrumental teachers to assist students in learning a new piece, are aligned. But teachers can only pass on the strategies that they use to learn a new piece if these strategies have first been analysed. And the same would be true of any other strategy that a teacher might want to pass on.

Perfect pitch—either you are born with it, or you will never acquire it

Perfect pitch—sometimes known as 'absolute pitch'—undoubtedly exists. I recall the ease with which some of my peer group at university romped through aural tests that I, like most students, found difficult. Writing down melodies, or whole Bach chorales, or fiercely chromatic pieces, just did not seem to be a problem to them. They knew the pitch name of a note—any note—as soon as they heard it. I had to work out the pitch names by relating them to those that I had worked out already.

Perfect pitch not only indubitably exists, it exists in a range of forms. Some instrumentalists seem to possess it comprehensively; others possess it only in some particular circumstances, or when playing their specialist instrument. I have never had anything approaching the perfect pitch enjoyed by my colleagues at university. But when I was doing a lot of orchestral playing, I found one day that even I could predict the exact sound of an oboe A, and tune my violin with it as though I had perfect pitch.

No, the 'myth' here is not that perfect pitch exists—it is the notion that anyone could possibly be born with it. How could they possibly be? There is nothing absolute about our choice of a wave with a frequency of 440 cycles per second (cps) as the note we call A. Instrumentalists who play baroque instruments often make other choices, and there is no theoretical reason why A should not have been set at 700 cps, or 432, for example. Nor is their anything absolute about the frequencies we assign to B, C, and D, and so forth, even after we have all agreed to call 440 cps 'A'. Different cultures make differing choices. Perfect pitch is learnt. Some of us may learn it faster than others, and many of us will not learn it at all. But I believe that we could all learn perfect pitch, at any stage of our life, if this was something that we really wanted to do, and had teaching that helped us. Whether it would be worth the trouble is another matter.

Some particularly intense aural, including musical, environments promote the development of perfect pitch in ways that others do not. I visited a school for visually impaired and blind students where more than half of the students had developed perfect pitch. Those taking A level music brailed their responses to melodic and harmonic dictation tasks without, seemingly, any difficulty. Many of the students did take instrumental lessons. But even those who did not often possessed remarkable acuity. I recall such a 13 year old who was asked to identify the key of a commercial recording, and who replied along the lines that 'it was in B, but a bit flat'!

You cannot join an ensemble until you are an accomplished player

I have not heard this mythical view expressed so frequently over the last couple of years. The recent expansion of ensemble opportunities for young people in many areas of the country has shown, by example, that the view was not well founded. The visible delight and motivation that students gain from taking part in ensembles speak for themselves. John Holt (p. 143) wrote of the fulfilment that he felt from playing a simple duet with his teacher. Over the years, many teachers have arranged and composed ensemble pieces for players of instruments that perhaps have less of an established elementary ensemble repertoire, such as piano and classical guitar. *The Singing School*, which was developed by Maurice Walsh, of the Manchester Music Service (Walsh 2006), helps primary schools to develop singing, including ensemble, skills amongst everyone—and includes some songs with parts for instrumentalists who are in the earliest stages of learning to play an instrument. The materials have been written with a view to ensuring that everyone—teachers and students—make progress and have a lot of fun.

Where the mythical view lives on, this is typically because teachers are working in isolation from each other. Perhaps they think that the repertoire for ensemble work is inevitably more difficult than that for solo playing, or that the skills needed to play at the same time as other people develop later. The rationale here is not unlike that which is sometimes used to argue for 'getting the notes right and then adding the expression'. It needs to be countered.

It is better to be taught individually rather than in groups

In 2000, Ofsted (Mills 2000*a*) found that the quality of the group instrumental lessons taught by music services was generally higher than that of individual lessons. This surprised a lot of people. It was quite usual for teachers in music services, as well as the parents of instrumental students, to think that an individual lesson was necessarily better in some way. At the time, I suggested that this might be partly because the better teachers were more willing to attempt group teaching, including teaching of whole classes, so that their individual lessons might be better too. However, from my privileged position of having observed some of the instrumental lessons that were inspected, and reading the reports of all the others, I was also aware that group lessons presented opportunities that individual lessons lacked. In a group lesson, students have more opportunity to learn from their peers, to have fun with their peers, and to learn in a range of ways. Moreover, unless they are very unlucky, they are not always the least competent musician in the room.

A few years on, perhaps mainly because of the numerous government music education initiatives that have taken place in recent years, there is now much more group instrumental teaching, particularly in primary schools, than there was in 2000. Ironically, Ofsted no longer inspects the work of music services, but my hunch is that both the group and the individual teaching are generally better now than they were in 2000. The expansion in number of lessons has been accompanied by extension in the training of teachers, although many music services would like to be able to offer training continuously—using models more like those found in school.

Group instrumental teaching has many advocates. Evelyn Glennie, percussion, writes:

group teaching allows teachers and pupils to take responsibility for their collective growth and open the doors of discovery for each other. In a group situation, teachers and pupils all tug, push and lead one another on to higher levels . . . I experienced group music teaching myself as a young girl. I was immersed in an environment of demonstration and inspiration from teachers and fellow pupils which enabled me to develop as a human being and led to my being better able to teach myself. (Evelyn Glennie (ABRSM 2004: p. ii))

Richard Pepper, a seasoned instrumental teacher, adds: 'I pity the pupil who learns on their own, who plays to the bedroom wall and sticks their examination certificates on it' (ABRSM 2004: 11). John Holt, an adult learner, observes: 'In music as in tennis the beginner needs other people to play with' (Holt 1978: 187). Daniel Barenboim writes on some of the group skills that are needed in orchestral playing:

Let us consider for a moment the example of playing in an orchestra: . . . [the] very powerful instruments, the so-called musical heavyweights—trumpet and trombone— play in such a way that they give a full sense of power, but . . . allow the other instruments, who are less powerful, to be heard at the same time. Otherwise they cover them up, and then the sound has no strength, only power. See the difference? Therefore when you play in an orchestra everybody is constantly aware of everybody else. (Barenboim 2006d)

Ideally, I would like all instrumental students to have a mix of group and individual lessons, with this mix adjusted to meet their needs at the time. I don't mean by this that the proportion of individual lessons would increase as students became older, or more advanced, but there might be an element of that—if this is what a student wants.

But if it was too difficult for a school or music service to offer this mix of individual and group lessons, I would vote for group lessons any time. For the educational reasons that I have mentioned, and not only because this would allow more students to be taught within a given budget.

What are the likely outcomes for the students who take group instrumental lessons? We already know that some of them will become very successful musically, because there are graduates of group instrumental teaching among the students at the conservatoires. And provided that the instrumental teaching can be sustained, so that students do not have any discouraging gaps in their tuition, the students' musical prospects look very promising.

A scheme in Caracas, Venezuela, which has been running longer than schemes in the UK, may provide a clue to what could ultimately be achieved in England.

In 2006, Charlotte Higgins (2006) wrote in the *Guardian* of an approach that has already stood the test of time. For more than 30 years, large numbers of children living in an impoverished area of Caracas, have spent the mornings at school, and six afternoons a week, from 14.00 to 18.00, following the so-called System by learning to play an instrument in large groups. The System includes supervised practising and ensemble experience that merge with tuition. While the System was set up originally, and continues to aim primarily, to 'punch through the poverty cycle—with the help of skills learned through music' it also produces great musicians. Gustavo Dudamel is chief conductor of the Gothenburg Symphony Orchestra, and Edicson Ruiz became a bass player in the Berlin Philharmonic at the age of 17. The System also produces many teachers and instrumentalists who enjoy the camaraderie of orchestral and other ensemble planning, and do not feel a need to be out at the front playing the solo in the Sibelius Violin Concerto.

Not all myth everywhere is bad. Myth has, I understand, helped some ancient pre-literate and pre-scientific societies to develop and function. And reading or thinking about the Sirenes, or the leprechauns, or the fairies at the bottom of our garden, can lead us into flights of fancy that are invaluable to the development of our personal creativity. The problem, in the context of this book, that is, instrumental teaching, is that dependence upon myth, or use of it, means that teachers—and hence students—may not benefit fully from what we have learnt about instrumental teaching through being a literate and scientific society. Where the practice of instrumental teaching is governed by the leprechauns, so to speak, rather than by scientific (in the broadest sense) knowledge, or even by our own common sense, this can limit the progress of, or opportunities available to, or self-esteem of, instrumental learners, or potential instrumental learners. Given that we have known scientifically since the 1930s that the theories about physical instrumental aptitude are flawed, for example, that you don't need special fingers to play a violin if you really want to play a violin, why are books that espouse such theories still being published now? Or, given that we play musically—expressively—when we first begin to learn a new piece, why do we tolerate tutor books that expect our students to play as though they were primitive robots with just one tempo, and dynamic, setting? Indeed, why do we use tutor books at all?

No matter how long we have been teaching, or how successful (in any sense) our practice, we all—not least me—need to keep our teaching under review if it is to continue to do the best that it could for our students. We continually ask ourselves questions such as 'could I have dealt with Tim's posture problems more effectively and, if so, are there lessons here for how I deal with other students?' 'Maria is making stunning progress, so is there something that I could take from this that would help my other students?'

Instrumental teachers, in general, have fewer visits than class teachers from inspectors and other evaluators to their lessons. While a class teacher may not always agree with the verdict of an inspector who visited them, the very fact that such a visit took place means that a conversation about professional practice took place. Many instrumental teachers, perhaps particularly those who work privately and in isolation from other teachers, may need to—in effect—engineer such conversations with themselves. Class teachers, like instrumental teachers, engage continually in reflection and self-evaluation. But the need for instrumental teachers to do this is, perhaps, even more pressing.

Chapter 11

So, why teach an instrument?

> . . . music,
> Which can be made anywhere, is invisible,
> And does not smell.
>
> W. H. Auden, 'In Praise of Limestone', May 1948

My first reason for opening this chapter with this extract is that I recently heard the whole poem when listening to a recording of Auden reading his own work, and was instantly struck by how musically apposite it is. The notion that music can be made anywhere reflects the open approach to everything musical—including music lessons and music teachers—that I have sought to encourage throughout this book. The reference to music—in its most literal sense—as invisible, is a reminder of the mystery, special nature, and capacity to move, of what we, as instrumental teachers, seek to share with our students. The remark about smell made me smile, and that is an important role of music, and music lessons, too.

Being an instrumental teacher is an enormous privilege, because we carry the responsibility for guiding students as they progress along their journey of instrumental musicianship. It is a joyful journey, for students and teachers. A headteacher spoke to me recently of how good music teachers take their students to 'Music Land', and I think that we will all know what she means by that. And if students decide—because their interests have grown, rather than because there was something wrong with our teaching—that they want to move on from learning with us, we let them, after discussion, give up with dignity. A student who is made to feel guilty about ceasing lessons is less likely to want to return to instrumental music, on the same or a different instrument, in the future. Students who are at school are used to changing their teachers in different subjects periodically, and we should not be surprised if they want to change their instrumental teacher occasionally too.

My second reason for opening this chapter with the Auden extract is that I soon found myself in a bit of a tangle when I tried to discover more about the poem. (This started me thinking, once more, about what it is like to try to learn music from someone who knows it well.) I know very little about poetry as an art form, and when I tried to find out more about this particular poem, I soon began to feel quite hopeless. The internet furnished me with the full text of the poem, but the sections of the web page that were headed 'analysis', 'critique', and 'overview' were all 'pending'. Auden had included a brief note on the jacket of the recording:

In praise of limestone. This poem is a kind of prelude to the series of Bucolics on Side Two. Unrhymed, the odd lines contain thirteen syllables, the even eleven. (Auden 1953)

I had listened to the Bucolics, enjoyed them, and found them comprehensible. But I had no idea how 'In Praise of Limestone' was a 'kind of prelude to them'. More worryingly, when I counted the syllables in the line:

> Which can be made anywhere, is invisible

I found that there were 12. (The lines on either side have 13 syllables, so there 'should' have been 11, instead of 12, here.) Why had my chosen line—the first line that I had bothered to look at in this detail—got the wrong number of syllables? Perhaps Auden had a special way of saying 'invisible' that only takes 3, instead of 4, syllables?

I wondered about listening to the recording again, to find out, but decided not to bother when I recalled that we were talking cassette, rather than CD or vinyl, here. I wondered fleetingly about counting the number of syllables in some more—or possibly all—lines, but soon dismissed this idea as inefficient use of time. Auden reads this poem in a way that conceals the line breaks, so perhaps the number of syllables in each line is only of academic interest? Perhaps even Auden did not care too much about this? I still do not know.

My sortie into finding out more about a poem that I planned to quote from had left me knowing no more than when I began, and even less confident in my ability to say something sensible about poetry in general.

This is, of course, similar to what can happen to instrumental students who are taught badly. They come to their first lesson bright eyed and bushy tailed. They really want to learn to make music on tenor saxophone, or flute, or cello. But, instead of this, they are taught how to take equipment out of a box and put it back again by a teacher who has not troubled to bring their own equipment with them to the lesson. Or they learn to clap rhythms written on pieces of paper using symbols that make no sense.

But this is instrumental teaching at its worst. Indeed, it is activity that perhaps does not justify the title 'instrumental teaching' at all!

Exactly where Music Land is depends, I would suspect, on who we, and our students, are. Daniel Barenboim spoke recently, in effect, of Music Land as central to everything that we do. He believes that music is holistic by nature, and that we waste it if we seek to isolate it from other activity of any sort:

This is why music in the end is so powerful, because it speaks to all parts of the human being, all sides—the animal, the emotional, the intellectual, and the spiritual. How often in life we think that personal, social and political issues are independent, without influencing each other. From music we see that this cannot occur, it is an objective impossibility, because in music there are not independent elements. Logical thought and intuitive emotions are permanently united. Music teaches us that everything is connected. (Barenboim 2006*d*)

Others may disagree.

Whatever your take on this matter, I wish you all the best of luck, and joy, as you take your students, and yourself, to Music Land, for many years to come.

Appendix 1

Nuts and bolts: frequently asked questions (FAQs)

Readers of this book will, I hope, have found answers—or at least the beginnings of answers—to some of their personal questions about instrumental teaching, as they have worked their way through its pages. This appendix deals particularly with some, mainly practical, questions that are frequently asked by instrumentalists who are thinking of starting to give instrumental lessons, or who have recently begun to teach.

Because the answers to some of these questions may change or develop over time, for example should there be new government regulations relating to contracts, the answers given here carry the name of their author, and the date on which they were most recently revised. My thanks to Charles Wiffen for preparing the answers to several questions. In so doing, he has drawn upon materials that he has developed for his work as an instrumental teacher, and materials that he uses when training undergraduate and postgraduate music students at Bath Spa University, and the RCM, who are beginning, or seeking to develop, their work as instrumental teachers.

Question: Who is 'in charge' of a child's private instrumental lessons, the parent or the teacher?

'The father of one of my private students seems to share attitudes towards music education of the parent that you wrote about on p. 80. When we first met, he spoke only of wanting his daughter to work through her graded performance examinations! He is my employer. Is it in order for me to talk to the father about the broader music education that I want to provide, and which I think will be in his daughter's best interests? It would be much easier for me just to provide the narrow instrumental education that the father has in mind.'

Answer: Strictly speaking, the father is your 'contractor', rather than your 'employer'—but let's not pursue this point for now.

Any adult who is paid to contribute to a child's education has, in my view, a responsibility to try to act in the child's best interests. Moreover, the rate at which you are being paid by the father is (probably!) well in excess of the minimum wage, so that the father is (at least implicitly) expecting a professional service from you. Were a third party to ask him whether you teach his, or your, curriculum to his daughter, he probably would insist the latter.

So, you will have gathered that I think that you need to 'bite the bullet' here, and work out a way of delivering an effective instrumental education for your student. The best way of doing this will depend on the circumstances. But my experience of parents who speak only of instrumental examinations is that they generally think that is all that instrumental teachers want to talk about! So your job of explaining may not be as difficult as you think.

On p. 140 you will find a reference to how Fred Seddon tackled a similar challenge as an instrumental teacher. There are many ways of solving educational problems, and you may wish to find a less radical way of solving this one, particularly if you have not been teaching for very long yet.

But p. 89 shows that even instrumental examiners may not think that instrumental students should spend the whole of their time preparing for instrumental examinations!

Janet Mills
November 2006

Contracts

This section was written with the needs of new self-employed (i.e. 'private') teachers in the UK in mind:[1]

Question: Should I issue my students with contracts?

Answer: Yes, any private teacher should draw up a standard written contract for students, which should be agreed to and signed by the student (or parent/carer if the student is under 18).

Question: What kind of information should I include in this contract?

Answer: This should state your name, address, and qualifications, as well as your student's name and address. You may also wish to include the agreed lesson duration and rate and any conditions for termination or cancellation.

Question: What sort of conditions can I stipulate to protect myself against non-payment?

Answer: The normal procedure is to ask for notice of one series of lessons (which may be a term) in the event of termination of lessons. In the case of an

---

[1] A teaching practice should be run as any other business: you will find that students and parents/carers will appreciate and respect efficiency and clarity in this respect. Advice on contractual issues is available in the UK from professional bodies such as the Incorporated Society of Musicians (ISM): www.ism.org.

individual lesson cancellation, it is common to ask the student to pay the full lesson fee if less than 24 hours' notice is given and if the lesson cannot be easily made up.

Question: What sort of information should I provide on my invoices?

Answer: You should make sure that you include payment, cancellation, and termination conditions, as well as dates, duration, and rates of lessons. Don't forget to include details of any extra amounts owed (such as exam entries).

Question: Obviously I should charge for lessons, but what other services can I charge for?

Answer: You should use your own discretion when deciding whether or not to charge for a particular service, and make this clear in your contract. Teachers often charge for an interview or consultation lesson, or for accompanying a student for an exam, concert, competition, or competitive festival.

Question: But are there instances when I should not charge for my services?

Answer: Yes—it's unlikely that any teacher would charge for attending a student's concert or for a lesson missed or cancelled through an understandable or unavoidable reason (such as illness or bereavement). Likewise, a teacher should not charge for time spent on lesson preparation, marking, writing progress reports, or updating students' records.

Question: How much should I charge?

Answer: Various professional bodies suggest hourly rates for their members in a particular area or region, depending on experience. (For example, the ISM suggests rates for its members in the London area). It is important to remember that such experience is understood to be in the relevant area of teaching, and that experience in a related field, no matter how accomplished (for example, as a performer), is not necessarily relevant. However, such rates are not universally accepted or appropriate, so you should bear in mind the economic status of your area (whether wealthy or deprived). If you need to visit a student, you should consider the distance and duration of the journey: if the journey is substantial, this should be factored into the fee. If you teach at home, the environment and facilities should be considered. (Your fees should take into account the cost of maintaining your studio and instruments.)

Question: What should I charge if I teach groups?

Answer: You will probably wish to offer a discount or incentive to each student in the group. This may work on a sliding scale, so that the larger the group, the smaller the proportion of your normal individual fee charged.

Question: Are there circumstances where I should consider dropping my fee?

Answer: There may well be: for example, in the event of a student suffering unexpected economic hardship (perhaps from unemployment) it may be appropriate to offer a reduced lesson duration or fee for a limited period of time. But do think carefully about, and make a note of the criteria that you are using to reduce your fee, so that you can treat all your students as equitably as possible.

Question: When do I increase my fees?

Answer: You should aim to increase your fees annually to keep pace with inflation. But do remember that an increase of fees or a change in lesson duration is a variation to the current tuition contract and that you should give plenty of notice of such changes to students or parents.

Question: If I'm self-employed, what expenses can I claim against tax?

Answer: You should consult a financial adviser for details on this, but you may be able to deduct tax for a number of expenses, including maintenance and insurance of instruments, for scores, books, stationery, CDs, advertising, subscriptions to professional associations and periodicals, as well as for business-related phone calls and answering services. Finally, you may be able to claim for studio rental costs and for lighting, heating, and maintenance of your studio. Do remember to keep all relevant receipts.

Question: What records should I keep?

Answer: You should keep copies of contracts and invoices as well as details of students. (These may include relevant medical conditions or special needs, where you have been informed of these by students or their carers, other instruments played, repertoire played/books used, exams/festivals entered, and of course goals and targets.) Remember that meticulous record-keeping and prompt and thoughtful liaison with parents/carers will always earn the respect of students and parents/carers, as well as facilitating effective teaching.

Special needs

Question: How will I recognize gifted students early on?

Answer: Read the rest of this book, in particular Chapter 4, pp. 65–71 and Chapter 5, under the section 'Is there an instrument that I could play?'! This may challenge you to reconsider what is meant by 'gifted', and whether there are ways of ensuring that each of your students has the opportunity to show you where their interests and abilities lie, so that you can help them to benefit fully from their instrumental lessons.

Question: How will I cope with a gifted student?

Answer: You will need energy and imagination in order to stimulate the interests of all your students. You will also need to communicate carefully with parents, who will benefit from informed and tactful counselling over the musical route their child could, or should, take.

Question: How will I recognize dyslexia in a student?

Answer: Your student may declare his or her dyslexia, but if not, you should be alert to difficulties in reading and writing, as well as possible difficulties with spatial awareness. Concepts of 'high and low' and 'left and right' may not be understood. Remember that a dyslexic student may disguise the condition by compensating through aural awareness or memorization. For further information, consult Sheila Oglethorpe's *Instrumental Music for Dyslexics* (1996) or Tim Miles and John Westcombe's *Music and Dyslexia: Opening New Doors* (2001).

Question: How do I accommodate my student's dyslexia?

Answer: A dyslexic student may require more time to come to terms with learning a new skill or repertoire. You may need to devise new ways of describing musical concepts or of teaching notation. You should encourage improvisatory skills and avoid overloading the student with too many directions. Finally, it may be helpful to print out notation or instructions on coloured paper or use coloured transparencies in order to cut down on the contrast between black print and white paper.

Question: The father of one of my students says that she has been diagnosed with dyspraxia. What does this mean?

Answer: A dyspraxic student may find some difficulty in coordinating speech or movement. He or she may also be particularly sensitive to sound or light, and may find planning challenging. The student may well show frustration or confusion during a lesson. For further information you should consult http:www.dyspraxiafoundation.org.uk or Maureen Boon's *Helping Children with Dyspraxia* (2001).

Question: How do I deal with dyspraxia?

Answer: This will depend on the type and extent of the condition. You should encourage movement and expression in the lesson through singing, clapping, and dancing. Above all, you should aim to make the student feel at ease—they will be far more successful when physically and mentally relaxed. Try to break information down into small chunks and maintain a logical order and structure to the lesson.

Charles Wiffen
March 2007

Appendix 2

How not to learn to 'read music'

Extract from *Music in the School*, Chapter 7: How not to teach music musically (Mills 2005*b*: 101–7)

Some years ago, I worked with 40 children aged 8–10, and five adults who do not read staff notation, to learn more about the information that they pick up from rhythms that are clapped or played to them (Mills 1991*b*; 1991*c*). As someone who learnt staff notation so young that I cannot remember life without it, I am unable to work this out for myself through introspection. I have known, seemingly forever, the convention that one uses claps to mark the onset of a sound that lasts until the next clap, and not just literally to denote the onset and duration of extremely short sounds with a lot of silence in between. I wanted to know what people who do not know this convention are picking up from clapped rhythms, so that I could work out how to teach them more effectively. I based my experiment on a simple rhythm: ♩ ♩ ♫♩ | ♩ ♩ ♫♩ that had been used in earlier research by a US researcher, Jeanne Bamberger (1982; 1988). As in the US research, I clapped the rhythm, and then asked students to draw something that would remind them of it.

The response of Lucy, aged 8, was typical of many of the children who had taken part in the US research. Lucy had recently started learning the violin. After listening to the clapped rhythm, she drew her hand and showed, through labelling her fingers from 'beat 1' to 'beat 5' that she had spotted that the rhythm repeated, and also that the repeating cell consisted of 5 'claps' (Figure 6(a)). She also showed that 'beats 3–5' were a group of some sort. I asked Lucy if she could think of another way of drawing the rhythm. She drew five teddy bears that she numbered 1–5, labelling claps 3–5 'fast'. Lucy's response seemed reasonable enough to me: there is a sense in which 'beats 3–5' sound like a group. However, the US research had judged responses like Lucy's to be immature, and to suggest that she had not heard the rhythm properly.

I decided to try to find out more about Lucy's thinking. In particular, I wanted to know how she would approach the notation of some rhythms that really did sustain. A few weeks later I returned to her school, armed with a very simple electronic keyboard, in order to work with her individually. Instead of clapping rhythms, I taught her to play them on a single note of an electronic keyboard, using a tone which could be sustained for several seconds, but that ceased when the key was lifted. Once she had learnt a rhythm, I asked her to draw something which would remind her of what she had been playing.

On learning to play Fig. 6(b) on the keyboard, Lucy drew ten pigs, which she numbered from 1 to 10. She labelled pigs 2, 3, 7, and 8 'fast'. Next, without prompting from me, she clapped the rhythm and labelled pigs 4 and 9 'fast' too. It was as though the rhythm that she was hearing had changed into one that could be written more accurately using the notation shown below the pigs.

Thereafter, Lucy gave up drawing until she had first clapped a rhythm that she had learnt to play on the keyboard. It seemed that she thought of clapping as being something that you always did when a teacher asked you something about rhythm. For Fig. 6(c) Lucy drew eight butterflies, and labelled butterflies 2, 3, 4, 6, 7, and 8 fast—which suggests a rhythm more like that written below the butterflies. For Fig. 6(d), she drew nine tennis balls. She was in doubt about whether some of them were 'fast' or not, but the rhythm that they described is less like the original than the one written below the tennis balls. For Fig. 6(e), she drew 14 triangles. She started by marking the first few 'short' or 'fast' (she did not say), but realized that this was going to take a long time and changed her strategy, instead marking triangle 11 'long'. This drawing is more like the rhythm shown below the triangles.

Finally, I returned to the original rhythm (Fig. 6(f)). Lucy economized on her drawing by producing squares instead of teddies, and wrote out the repetition of the first 'bar', but otherwise her response was the same as it had been several weeks previously, when she had not had access to the keyboard.

Lucy's final notation could be viewed in several ways:

- inaccurate, duration-based notation of the rhythms I had taught her
- notation based on something other than duration
- accurate, duration-based, notation of rhythms reconstructed from the clapped rhythms.

Given that, in Fig. 6(b), I saw Lucy change 'accurate' notation of durations following clapping, I think my third suggestion is the most sensible. A long clap is no longer than a short clap: only the silences between vary in length. So Lucy is entitled to reconstruct the clapped rhythms like this if she wishes.

Clapping seems to alter Lucy's perception of rhythms. So why does she clap? The answer is that her violin teacher has trained her to clap rhythms before playing them. When Lucy plays a rhythm, her teacher cannot tell whether any mistakes result from inaccurate rhythmic perception or technical difficulties such as plucking a string, or changing bow, at the moment intended. Asking

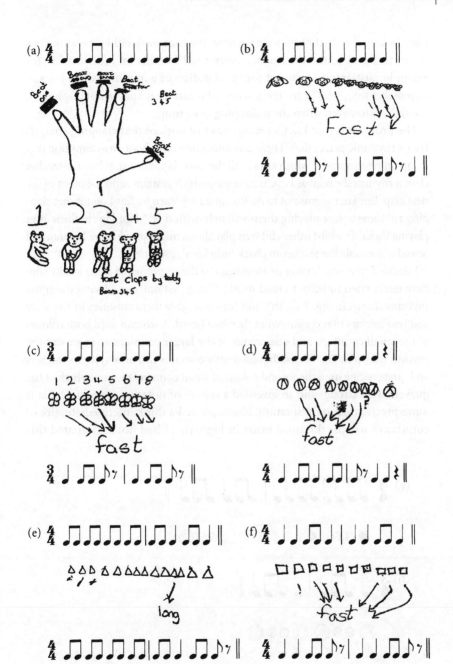

Fig. 6 (a)–(f) Drawings illustrating the notation and perception of rhythm by a student aged 8

Lucy to sing the rhythm on a single note does not work either, because Lucy learns in a group, and the teacher cannot tell whether an individual is, for example, sustaining a crotchet for the duration of a minim. Asking Lucy to clap makes things easier for the teacher, who can see if Lucy is not clapping in the right place, even when she is clapping in a group.

The problem is that Lucy's teacher has not noticed that clapping changes Lucy's rhythmic perception. There is nothing intuitive about an assumption that a clap represents a note which lasts until the next clap is heard. When the teacher claps a rhythm she may, as I do, 'hear' a tone which sustains until the onset of the next clap. But Lucy seems not to do this. She may learn to. But I doubt that clapping rhythms before playing them will help with this. Clapping rhythms after playing them, or whilst other children play them, might prove more helpful, and would still enable the teacher to check individual responses . . .

I decided to probe further by investigating the responses of some adults who have never tried to learn to read music. Using just one note, I sang them the rhythms shown in Fig. 7(a), (b), and (c)—and gave them counters in two sizes and two colours to represent what they had heard. A woman used both colours of the small counters, and one colour of the larger counters, to represent the rhythm shown in Fig. 7(a), although it only contains two note values: crotchets and quavers. She used the second colour of small counters to show which of the quavers were strong, and so invented a system of notation for herself that is more precise than staff notation. She requested a third, intermediate, size of counter to use for the third beats in Fig. 7(b). I had not anticipated this

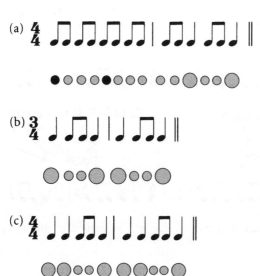

Fig. 7 (a)–(c) An adult who has not learnt to read music uses counters in two sizes and up to two colours to represent rhythms

response, and did not have a counter of intermediate size. She requested a third, intermediate, size of counter also for the final beats in both bars of the rhythm shown in Fig. 7(c). She was right, of course. When singing Fig. 7(b) and Fig. 7(c) I had phrased them by clipping the final crotchet of each bar. A child might not have challenged me.

The relationship between clapped and sustained rhythms can be different for performers and listeners, even among those who do not read music. I recall a group of students, aged 9, who composed a piece for drums and claves consisting, they said, of 'longs' (the word their teacher used to distinguish crotchets from quavers or 'shorts'). The silences were much longer than the sounds. But the performers stuck to their claim that the sounds were 'long' (as did their teacher) even when other members of the class said that they could not hear what was 'long'.

Sue, aged 9, was a friend of Lucy. She has played cornet in a band for two years. I wrote down the rhythms shown in Fig. 7(a) and (b) and she clapped them. But whenever she came to a pair of quavers, the second one was a bit early. I clapped the rhythm shown in Fig. 7(b) for her, and she copied me accurately.

I asked Sue how she knew what to clap, and she said that she tried to count (here there was a wry smile). She showed me how she counted Figs 7(a) and 7(b) and explained her strategy as follows:

It's usually 4. It's 4 in this one [Fig. 7(a)] because it looks like it's going to end on this one [the crotchet labelled '4']. In this one [Fig. 7(b)] it's 3 because the fourth one [the quaver labelled '1'] doesn't look like it's going to end.

Sue has tried to make sense of what her teachers have told her. It is, however, not the sense intended. Sue's teachers tell her to count, so she counts. But she counts the wrong thing: incidents, not a pulse. Her teachers have taught her, during music theory classes, to work out the time signature of unbarred rhythms by looking for 'endings'. Here, she applied this skill in an inappropriate situation: the performance of barred rhythms. If Sue understood what she was doing in the 'spot the time signature' exercises, she would see that the performance of a barred rhythm was a different exercise. But as she has not understood the concept of pulse, there is little chance of that happening.

John Holt, in his classic book *How Children Fail* (Holt 1984), first published as long ago as 1964, wrote of a child: 'What she needs is a broom to sweep out her mind . . . If she could only forget nine tenths of the facts and rules she has all mixed up in her head, she might begin to learn something.'

I think that Sue needs a broom too. But her problems may remain unrecognized. When Sue gets a rhythm wrong in the band, someone tells her to count, and demonstrates the finished product. She copies the finished product accurately, while trying to count the notes. The tune comes out all right, so Sue and her teachers assume the counting was all right. Sadly, the time will come when the music is too difficult to copy. By then it may be too late for the broom, and Sue will join the school leavers who have failed as music readers.

To teach music reading effectively, we must understand how the framework for music defined by staff notation looks from the outside. Those of us who have read music for a long time may not be able to apply Holt's broom to ourselves. But we can find out about this viewpoint from those who are on the outside: those who have not yet learnt to read music.

I wonder what Lucy and Sue are doing now. They will be in their twenties. Are they still playing violin and cornet? Perhaps they went to university. Perhaps they have trained as teachers. Perhaps they will be teaching some children to read music. If so, I hope that they have devised a way of doing this which avoids the confusion that they went through.

Did Lucy and Sue need to learn to read music at all? Perhaps they did, because they wanted to play music that is written in staff notation: they had just been taught badly. Peter Roadknight writes of teaching students notational systems in such a way that they believe that it is 'their' system: 'If it's their system, it will work' (Roadknight 2000: 6). Lucy and Sue needed an approach more like this, one that smacked less of the revelation of knowledge held by adults. However, I am quite sure that Sue did not need music theory lessons at this stage: she could have operated effectively in her band for several years without what was, for her, this additional source of confusion. Lucy and Sue remind us what can go wrong even when well-motivated bright children are taught to read music in a small group. The scope for getting it wrong when whole classes are taught music reading despite having no immediate musical need to read music, and possibly not wanting to read it at that stage of their development, is vast.

Suggestions for further reading

Bray, D. (2000). *Teaching Music in the Secondary School*. Oxford: Heinemann.

Crozier, R., and Harris, P. (2000). *The Music Teacher's Companion*. London: ABRSM Publishing.

Federation of Music Services, National Association of Music Educators, and Royal College of Music (2002*a*). *A Common Approach 2002*. Harlow: Faber.

—— (2002*b*). *A Common Approach 2002: An Instrumental/Vocal Curriculum*. Harlow: Faber.

—— (2002*c*). *A Common Approach 2002: Strings*. Harlow: Faber.

—— (2002*d*). *A Common Approach 2002: Woodwind*. Harlow: Faber.

Glover, J., and Young, S. (1999). *Primary Music: Later Years*. London: Falmer.

Hallam, S. (1998). *Instrumental Teaching: A Practical Guide to Better Teaching and Learning*. Oxford: Heinemann.

Mills, J. (1991). *Music in the Primary School*. Cambridge: Cambridge University Press.

—— (2005). *Music in the School*. Oxford: Oxford University Press.

Odam, G. (1995). *The Sounding Symbol: Music Education in Action*. Cheltenham: Stanley Thornes.

Paynter, J. (1992). *Sound and Structure*. Cambridge: Cambridge University Press.

—— and Aston, P. (1970). *Sound and Silence*. Cambridge: Cambridge University Press.

Philpott, C. (2006). *Learning to Teach Music in the Secondary School: A Companion to School Experience*. London: RoutledgeFalmer.

Young, S., and Glover, J. (1998). *Music in the Early Years*. London: Falmer.

References

Abeles, H. F., and Porter, S. Y. (1978). 'The Sex-Stereotyping of Musical Instruments', *Journal of Research in Music Education* 26: 65–75.

Adler, L. (1994). *Me and my Big Mouth*. London: Blake Publishing.

Associated Board of the Royal Schools of Music, The (2004). *All Together! Teaching Music in Groups*. London: The Associated Board of the Royal Schools of Music.

—— (2006). *Libretto* 3: 22.

Auden, W. H. (1953). *W. H. Auden Reading his Poetry*. London: HarperCollins Audio Books.

Austen, J. (1813). *Pride and Prejudice*. London: Egerton.

Baker, D. (2006). 'Life Histories of Music Service Teachers: The Past in Inductees' Present', *British Journal of Music Education* 23/1: 39–60.

Bamberger, J. (1982). 'Revisiting Children's Drawings of Simple Rhythms: A Function for Reflection-in-Action'. In S. Strauss and S. Stavy (eds), *U-shaped Behavioral Growth*. New York: Academic Press.

—— (1988). 'Les Structurations cognitives de l'apprehension et de la notation de rhythmes simples'. In H. Sinclair (ed.), *La Production de notations chez le jeune enfant*. Paris: Presses Universitaires de France.

Bandura, A. (1997). *Self-Efficacy: The Exercise of Control*. New York: Freeman.

Barenboim, D. (2006a). *Reith Lectures 2006: Lecture 1—In the Beginning was Sound*. BBC. Retrieved 16 May 2006 from the World Wide Web: *www.bbc.co.uk/print/radio4/reith2006/lecture1.shtml?print*

—— (2006b). *Reith Lectures 2006: Lecture 2—The Neglected Sense*. BBC. Retrieved 16 May 2006, from the World Wide Web: *www.bbc.co.uk/print/radio4/reith2006/lecture2.shtml?print*

—— (2006c). *Reith Lectures 2006: Lecture 3—The Magic of Music*. BBC. Retrieved 16 May 2006, from the World Wide Web: *www.bbc.co.uk/print/radio4/reith2006/lecture3.shtml?print*

—— (2006d). *Reith Lectures 2006: Lecture 5—The Power of Music*. BBC. Retrieved 16 May 2006, from the World Wide Web: *www.bbc.co.uk/print/radio4/reith2006/lecture5.shtml?print*

Barratt, E., and Moore, H. (2005). 'Researching Group Assessment: Jazz in the Conservatoire, *British Journal of Music Education*, 22/3: 299–314.

Barrett, M. (2002a). 'Invented Notations and Mediated Memory: A Case-Study of Two Children's Use of Invented Notations'. In G. Welch and G. Folkestad (eds.), *A World of Music Education Research* (pp. 35–44). Göteborg: School of Music and Education, Göteborg University, Sweden.

—— (2002b). 'Taking Note: An Exploration of the Function of Invented Notations in Children's Musical Thinking Processes (Ages 4–5)', *Proceedings of the 7th International Conference for Music Perception and Cognition, Sydney*.

Bentley, A. (1966). *Musical Ability in Children and its Measurement*. London: Harrap.

Ben-Tovim, A., and Boyd, D. (1985). *The Right Instrument for your Child*. London: Gollancz.

—— (1986). *You Can Make Music!* London: Victor Gollancz.

Birmingham City Council (1996*a*). *Arts Guidance for the Birmingham Primary Guarantee*. Birmingham: Birmingham City Council.

—— (1996*b*). *The Birmingham Secondary Guarantee*. Birmingham: Birmingham City Council.

Boon, Maureen (2001). *Helping Children with Dyspraxia*. London: Jessica Kingley.

Brändström, S. (1995). 'Self-Formulated Goals and Self-Evaluation in Music Education', *Bulletin of the Council for Research in Music Education* 127: 16–21.

Bransford, J. D., and Brown, A. L. (2000). *How People Learn: Brain, Mind, Experience and School*. Washington: New Academic Press.

Bridger, W. (1961). 'Sensory Habituation and Discrimination in the Human Neonate', *American Journal of Psychiatry* 117: 991–6.

Brittin, R., and Sheldon, D. C. (2004). 'An Analysis of Band Method Books: Implications of Culture, Composer and Type of Music', *Bulletin of the Council for Research in Music Education* 161–2 (Summer–Fall).

Brontë, C. (1847). *Jane Eyre*. London: Smith, Elder & Co.

Bull, M. (2006). *Sound Moves: iPod Culture and Urban Experience*. London: Routledge.

Burt, R., and Mills, J. (2006). 'Taking the Plunge: The Hopes and Fears of Students as they Begin Music College', *British Journal of Music Education*, 23/1: 51–74.

—— (in preparation). 'Pitching it Right? Selection, Equal Access and Learning at a Music Conservatoire'.

Burwell, K. (2005). 'A Degree of Independence: Teachers' Approaches to Instrumental Tuition in a University College', *British Journal of Music Education* 22/3: 199–215.

Cage, J. (1962). *Silence: Letters and Writings*. London: Calder & Boyars.

Cardus, N. (1961). *Sir Thomas Beecham*. London: Collins.

Cattell, R. B., Eber, H. W., and Tatsouka, M. M. (1970). *Handbook for the Sixteen Personality Factor Questionnaire (16PF)*. Champaign, Ill.: Institute for Personality and Ability Testing.

Chaffin, R., and Imreh, G. (2001). 'A Comparison of Practice and Self-Report as Sources of Information about the Goals of Expert Practice', *Psychology of Music* 29/1: 39–69.

Coren, G. (2006). 'Walter de la Blair: World Exclusive', *The Times*, 1 Apr.: 21.

Corkhill, D. (2005). 'A Young Person's Guide to the Orchestral Profession', *British Journal of Music Education* 22/3: 269–85.

Corredor, J. M. (1956). *Conversations with Casals*. London: Hutchinson.

Costa, D., da (1994). 'Background Listening', *British Journal of Music Education*, 12/1: 21–8.

Davies, C. (1986). 'Say it till a Song Comes (Reflections on Songs Invented by Children 3–13)', *British Journal of Music Education* 3/3: 279–93.

Davies, J. B. (1978). *The Psychology of Music*. London: Hutchinson.

Department for Education (1995). *The National Curriculum: England*. London: HMSO.

Department for Education and Employment, and Qualifications and Curriculum Authority (1999). *Music: The National Curriculum for England*. London: HMSO.

du Pré, H., and du Pré, P. (1997). *A Genius in the Family: An Intimate Memoir of Jacqueline du Pré*. London: Chatto & Windus.

Engeström, Y. (2001). 'Expansive Learning at Work: Toward an Activity Theoretical Reconceptualisation', *Journal of Education and Work* 14/1: 133–56.

Entwistle, N. (2005*a*). *Teaching and Learning in Diverse University Settings: Findings from the ETL Project*. Paper presented at the What a Difference a Pedagogy Makes: Researching Lifelong Learning and Teaching Conference, University of Stirling, 24–6 June 2005.

—— (2005*b*). 'Ways of Thinking and Ways of Teaching across Contracting Subject Areas'. Paper presented at the ISL 2005 Conference: Improving Student Learning by Assessment.

—— and McCune, V. (2004). 'The Conceptual Bases of Study Strategy Inventories', *Educational Psychological Review* 16/4: 325–45.

—— and Tait, H. (1990). 'Approaches to Learning, Evaluation of Teaching, and Preferences for Contrasting Academic Environments', *Higher Education* 19/2: 169–94.

Ericsson, K. A., and Smith, J. (1991). *Towards a General Theory of Expertise: Prospects and Limits*. Cambridge: Cambridge University Press.

Escher, M. C. (1960). *Ascending and Descending* [Lithograph]. Retrieved 4 May 2006 from the World Wide Web: *www.mcescher.com/*

Federation of British Conservatoires (2003). *Teaching Performance: The Employment of Musical Instrument Teaching Specialists: The Report of HEFCE Good Management Practice project 41*. London: Royal College of Music.

Federation of Music Services, National Association of Music Educators, and Royal College of Music (2002*a*). *A Common Approach 2002*. Harlow: Faber.

—— (2002*b*). *A Common Approach 2002: An Instrumental/Vocal Curriculum*. Harlow: Faber.

—— (2002*c*). *A Common Approach 2002: Strings*. Harlow: Faber.

—— (2002*d*). *A Common Approach 2002: Woodwind*. Harlow: Faber.

Fredrickson, W. (in press). 'Perceptions of College-Level Music Performance Majors Teaching Applied Music Lessons to Young Students', *International Journal of Music Education*.

—— and Brittin, R. (2006). 'Undergraduate Music Performance Majors' Attitudes toward Private Teaching after Graduation'. Paper presented at the 21st International Seminar on Research in Music Education, Bali, Indonesia.

Gane, P. (1996). 'Instrumental Teaching and the National Curriculum: A Possible Partnership?' *British Journal of Music Education* 13/1: 49–66.

Gaunt, H. (2004). 'Breathing and the Oboe: Playing, Teaching and Learning', *British Journal of Music Education* 21/3: 313–28.

Gleick, J. (1996). *Chaos: Making a New Science*. New York: Vintage.

Glover, J., and Scaife, N. (2004). 'Improvising and Composing for Groups'. In The Associated Board of the Royal Schools of Music (ed.), *All Together! Teaching Music in Groups*. London: The Associated Board of the Royal Schools of Music.

Green, J. (1982). *The Book of Rock Quotes*. New York: Delilah/Putnam.

Green, L. (2001). *How Popular Musicians Learn*. Aldershot: Ashgate.

Griswold, P. A., and Chroback, D. A. (1981). 'Sex-Role Associations of Music Instruments and Occupations by Gender and Major', *Journal of Research in Music Education* 29/1: 57–62.

Gruhn, W., Altenmüller, E., and Babler, R. (1997). 'The Influence of Learning on Cortical Activation Patterns', *Bulletin for the Council for Research in Music Education* 133 (Summer): 25–30.

Hallam, S. (1998). *Instrumental Teaching: A Practical Guide to Better Teaching and Learning*. Oxford: Heinemann.

—— Rogers, L., and Creech, A. (2005). *Survey of Local Authority Music Services 2005: DfES research report RR700*. London: Department for Education and Skills.

Harpor, A. (2006). 'Chip 'n' SING: The New Way to Beat Card Fraud', *The Times*, 1 Apr.: 12.

Harrison, A., and O'Neill, S. A. (2000). 'Children's Gender-Typed Preferences for Musical Instruments: An Intervention Study', *Psychology of Music* 28/1: 81–97.

Hattersley, G. (2006). 'My Next Request? Get me off this Island', *Sunday Times*, 16 Apr.: 5.

HEFCE (2000). *Funding of Specialist Higher Education Institutions*. Report 00/51. Bristol: Higher Education Funding Council for England.

Henninger, J. C., Flowers, P. J., and Council, K. H. (2006). 'Pedagogical Techniques and Student Outcomes in Applied Instrumental Lessons Taught by Experienced and Pre-service Teacher Reflections', *International Journal of Music Education*, 24/1: 71–84.

Higgins, C. (2006), 'Land of Hope and Glory', *Guardian Unlimited*, 24 Nov.

Hindemith, P. (1952). *A Composer's World*. Cambridge, Mass.: Harvard University Press.

Holmes, P. (2005). 'Imagination in Practice: A Study of the Integrated Roles of Interpretation, Imagery and Technique in the Learning and Memorisation Process of Two Experienced Solo Performers', *British Journal of Music Education* 22/3: 217–35.

Holt, J. (1978). *Never too Late: My Musical Life Story*. New York: Delacorte Press/Seymour Lawrence.

—— (1984). *How Children Fail*. London: Penguin.

Hunter, D. (1999). 'Developing Peer-Learning Programmes in Music: Group Presentations and Peer Assessment', *British Journal of Music Education* 16:1: 51–63.

—— (2000). *Peer Learning in Music: Implementing Peer Learning Programmes in Music*. Newtownabbey: University of Ulster.

—— (2006). 'Assessing Collaborative Learning', *British Journal of Music Education* 23/1: 75–89.

—— and Russ, M. (1996). 'Peer Assessment in Performance Studies', *British Journal of Music Education*, 13/1: 67–78.

Iannucci, A. (2006). 'Umbrage', *Guardian*, 25 Mar.

Joint Matriculation Board (1956). *Fifty-Third Annual Report*. Manchester: JMB.

Jones, F. W. (1941). *The Principles of Anatomy as Seen in the Hand*. London: Ballière & Cox.

Jørgensen, H. (2001). 'Instrumental Learning: Is an Early Start a Key to Success? *British Journal of Music Education* 18/3: 227–39.

Kemp, A. E. (1996). *The Musical Temperament: Psychology and Personality of Musicians*. Oxford: Oxford University Press.

—— and Mills, J. (2002). 'Musical Potential'. In R. Parncutt and G. McPherson (eds), *The Science and Psychology of Music Performance: Creative Strategies for Teaching and Learning*. Oxford: Oxford University Press.

Kemp, D. (2006). 'Thank God it's Friday', *Times Educational Supplement*, 10 Feb.: 2.

Keynes, G. (ed.) (1932). *Poetry and Prose of William Blake*. London: Nonsuch Press.

Kokotsaki, D., and Davidson, J. W. (2003). 'Investigating Musical Performance Anxiety among Music College Singing Students: A Quantitative Analysis', *Music Education Research* 5/1: 45–50.

Lamp, C. J., and Keys, N. (1935). 'Can Aptitude for Specific Musical Instruments be Predicted?' *American Journal of Educational Psychology*, 26: 587–96.

Lebler, D. (2006). *3D Assessment: Looking through the Learning Lens*. International Society for Music Education. Commission for the Education of the Professional Musician, 16th International Seminar, Hanoi, 10–14 July 2006.

Leigh, S. (2005). *Spencer Leigh's Home Site*. Retrieved 12 Apr. 2006 from the World Wide Web: http://www.spencerleigh.demon.co.uk/Feature-Cahn.htm

Levy, A. (2004). *Small Island*. London: Review.

Lightfoot, L. (2006). 'Boring Lessons are Good Practice for Life, Say Teachers', *Daily Telegraph*, 14 Apr.: 1.

Lisboa, T. (2002). 'Children's Practice: A Multi-modal Approach to Teaching and Learning'. Paper Presented at the 7th International Conference on Music Perception and Cognition, Sydney.

Mackworth-Young, L. (2004). 'The Psychology of Group Teaching and Learning'. In The Associated Board of the Royal Schools of Music (ed.), *All Together! Teaching Music in Groups*. London: The Associated Board of the Royal Schools of Music.

McPherson, G. (2000). 'Commitment and Practice: Key Ingredients for Achievement during the Early Stages of Learning a Musical Instrument', *Bulletin of the Council for Research in Music Education* 147: 122–7.

MacPherson, S. (1922). *The Musical Education of the Child*. London: Williams.

Madsen, C. K. (2004). 'A 30-year Follow-up Study of Actual Applied Music Practice versus Estimated Practice', *Journal of Research in Music Education* 52/1: 77–88.

Mang, E. (2001). 'Intermediate Vocalizations: An Investigation of the Boundary between Speech and Songs in Young Children's Vocalizations', *Bulletin of the Council for Research in Music Education* 147: 116–21.

Maslow, A. H. (1954). *Motivation and Personality*. New York: Harper.

Mawbey, W. E. (1973). 'Wastage from Instrumental Classes in School', *Psychology of Music* 1/1: 33–43.

Menuhin, Y. (1976). *Unfinished Journey*. London: Futura.

Miles, Tim, and Westcombe, John (2001). *Music and Dyslexia: Opening New Doors*. London: Whurr.

Mills, J. (1983). 'Identifying Potential Orchestral Musicians'. Unpublished D.Phil. thesis, Oxford University.

—— (1985). 'Gifted Instrumentalists: How Can we Recognise them?' *British Journal of Music Education* 2/1: 39–49.

—— (1986). 'Testing Physical Aptitude', *Psychology of Music* 14/2: 147–8.

—— (1988). *Group Tests of Musical Abilities: Teacher's Guide and Recorded Test*. Windsor: NFER-Nelson.

—— (1989a). 'Developing Listening through Composing', *Music Teacher* (March), 9–11.

—— (1989b). 'Generalist Primary Teachers of Music: A Problem of Confidence', *British Journal of Music Education* 6/2: 125–38.

—— (1991a). *Music in the Primary School*. Cambridge: Cambridge University Press.

—— (1991b). 'Clapping as an Approximation to Rhythm', *Canadian Music Educator* 33: 131–8.

—— (1991c). 'Out for the Count: Confused by Crotchets—Part 2', *Music Teacher* 70/6: 12–15.

—— (1994). 'Music in the National Curriculum: The First Year', *British Journal of Music Education* 11: 191–6.

—— (1995/6). 'Primary Student Teachers as Musicians', *Bulletin for the Council for Research in Music Education* 127: 122–6.

—— (1996). 'Is Education in Decline? A View from the Joint Matriculation Board, 1954–1965', *Research in Education* 55: 29–38.

—— (1997). 'Knowing the Subject versus Knowing the Child: Striking the Right Balance for Children aged 7–11 years', *Research Studies in Music Education*, 9: 29–35.

—— (1998*a*). 'Can Music Really "Improve" the Mind?' *Psychology of Music*, 26/3: 204–5.

—— (2000*a*). *The Quality of Provision of LEA Music Services 1999–2000: Address to Conference of the Federation of Music Services (FMS).*

—— (2000*b*). 'Secondary Singing Inspected', *British Journal of Music Education*, 17/1: 61–6.

—— (2002). 'Conservatoire Students' Perceptions of the Characteristics of Effective Instrumental and Vocal Tuition', *Bulletin of the Council for Research in Music Education* 153–4: 78–82.

—— (2003). 'Where Do Music Teachers Come From?' Paper presented at the NAME National Conference, Stone, Staffordshire, 19–21 Sept.

—— (2004*a*). 'Conservatoire Students as Instrumental Teachers', *Bulletin of the Council for Research in Music Education* 161–2 (Summer–Fall): 145–54.

—— (2004*b*). 'How to Become a Conservatoire Professor?' 8th International Conference on Music Perception and Cognition—Northwestern University.

—— (2004*c*). 'Working in Music: Becoming a Performer-Teacher', *Music Education Research* 6/3: 245–61.

—— (2004*d*). 'Working in Music: The Conservatoire Professor', *British Journal of Music Education* 21/2: 179–98.

—— (2004*e*). 'Perspectives', *Link* 2: 50.

—— (2005*a*). 'Addressing the Concerns of Conservatoire Students about School Music Teaching', *British Journal of Music Education* 22/1: 63–75.

—— (2005*b*). *Music in the School.* Oxford: Oxford University Press.

—— (2006*a*). 'Performing and Teaching: The Beliefs and Experience of Music Students as Instrumental Teachers', *Psychology of Music* 34/3: 372–90.

—— (2006*b*). 'Working in Music: The Pianist', *Music Education Research.*

—— and Jeanneret, N. (2004). 'Brideshead Revisited', *Music Teacher* (February): 29.

—— and Moore, H. (2005). 'Special Issue—Instrumental Teaching in Higher Education', *British Journal of Music Education* 22/3.

—— and O'Neill, S. A. (2002). 'Children as Inspectors? Evaluating School Music Provision for Children Aged 10–11 Years', *British Journal of Music Education* 19/3: 285–302.

—— and Smith, J. (2003). 'Teachers' Beliefs about Effective Instrumental Teaching in Schools and Higher Education', *British Journal of Music Education* 20/1: 5–28.

Moore, H., and Hibbert, F. (2005). 'Mind Boggling! Considering the Possibilities of Brain Gym in Learning to Play an Instrument', *British Journal of Music Education* 22/3: 249–67.

Murao, T., and Wilkins, B. (2001). 'Japan'. In D. J. Hargreaves and A. C. North (eds), *Musical Development and Learning: The International Perspective.* London: Continuum.

NIAS (Northamptonshire Inspection and Advisory Service) (1997). *Differentiation: A Guide for Music Teachers.* Northampton: Northamptonshire County Council.

Nielsen, S. G. (1999). 'Learning Strategies in Instrumental Music Practice' *British Journal of Music Education*, 16/3: 275–91.

Oglethorpe, Sheila (1996). *Instrumental Music for Dyslexics.* London: Whurr.

O'Neill, S. A. (2002). *Young People and Music Participation Project.* Retrieved 1 May 2006 from the World Wide Web: *www.keele.ac.uk/depts/ps/ESRC/Preportall.pdf*

—— and McPherson, G. (2002). 'Motivation'. In R. Parncutt and G. McPherson (eds), *The Science and Psychology of Music Performance: Creative Strategies for Teaching and Learning.* Oxford: Oxford University Press.

Overy, K. (1998). 'Can Music Really "Improve" the Mind?' *Psychology of Music* 26/1: 97–9.

Paynter, J. (1992). *Sound and Structure.* Cambridge: Cambridge University Press.

—— (1997). 'The Form of Finality: A Context for Musical Education', *British Journal of Music Education* 14/1: 5–22.

—— and Aston, P. (1970). *Sound and Silence.* Cambridge: Cambridge University Press.

Pitts, S. (2002). 'Changing Times: Musical Experience and Self-Perception amongst School and University Music Students', *Musicae Scientiae* 6/1: 73–92.

Presland, C. (2005). 'Conservatoire Student and Instrumental Professor: The Student Perspective on a Complex Relationship', *British Journal of Music Education* 22/3: 237–48.

Primos, K. (2001). 'Africa'. In D. J. Hargreaves and A. C. North (eds), *Musical Development and Learning: The International Perspective.* London: Continuum.

Purser, D. (2005). 'Performers as Teachers: Exploring the Teaching Approaches of Instrumental Teachers in Conversatoires', *British Journal of Music Education* 22/3: 287–98.

Rabun, J. T. (2001). *What's the meaning of this? Ye olde English sayings.* Retrieved 4 May 2006 from the World Wide Web: *www.rootsweb.com/~genepool/meanings.htm*

Ritterman, J. (2000). 'Learning What it is to Perform: A Key to Peer Learning for Musicians'. In D. Hunter and M. Russ (eds), *Peer Learning in Music.* Belfast: University of Ulster.

Roadknight, P. (2000). 'The "Time Machine" and the Voice: Looking Back on a KS3 Music Project', *NAME magazine* 4: 4–7.

Rose, J., Jones, P., Hertrich, J., Clay, G., and Mills, J. (1998). *The Arts Inspected: Good Teaching in Art, Dance, Drama and Music.* Oxford: Heinemann.

Rowling, J. K. (2002). *Harry Potter and the Chamber of Secrets.* London: Warner Brothers.

Schenck, R. (2000a). 'At Play: Teaching Musical Instruments and the Voice'. Unpublished manuscript, Göteborg.

—— (2000b). *Spelrum: en metodikbok för sång- och instrumentalpedagoger.* Göteborg: Bo Ejeby Förlag.

Seddon, F. (2004). 'My Parallel Musical Worlds'. Paper presented at the 10th CT ABRSM Course Leader and Mentor Training Conference, 10 October 2004.

—— and O'Neill, S. A. (2001). 'An Evaluation Study of Computer-Based Compositions by Children with and without Prior Experience of Formal Instrumental Music Tuition', *Psychology of Music* 29/1: 4–19.

Shuter-Dyson, R., and Gabriel, C. (1981). *The Psychology of Musical Ability*, 2nd edn, London: Methuen.

Sloboda, J. A. (2002). 'Musical Peak Experiences: What is the Educational Relevance?' Paper presented at the Annual conference of the Federation of Music Services.

Smith, W. (1870), *Dictionary of Greek and Roman Antiquities*, retrieved 25 Nov. 2006 from the World Wide Web: http://www.ancientlibrary.com/smith-bio/3173.html

Spychiger, M. (1993). 'Music Makes the School', *Die Blaue Eule.* University of Freiburg.

Stewart, I. (1997). *Does God Play Dice?: The New Mathematics of Chaos*. London: Penguin.

Swanwick, K. (1999). *Teaching Music Musically*. London: Routledge.

Taylor, S. (1973). 'Musical Development of Children aged Seven to Eleven', *Psychology of Music* 1/1: 44–9.

Teaching and Learning Research Programme (TLRP) of the Economic and Social Research Council (ESRC). *Learning to Perform*. Research Project led by the Royal College of Music. www.learningtoperform.org.uk

United Kingdom Parliament, The (2005). Hansard, 6 June 2005. Retrieved 10 Apr. 2006 from the World Wide Web: *http://www.publications.parliament.uk/pa/cm200506/ cmhansrd/cm050606/text/50606w29.htm*

Walsh, M. (2006). *The Singing School*. Manchester: Manchester Music Service.

Ward, D. (2006). 'Thorncross Young Offenders' Unit'. *Guardian*, 31 Oct.: 9.

Ward, H. (2006). 'Trouble in the Land of Nod?' *Times Educational Supplement*, 5 May: 4.

Weedon, B. (1957). *Play in a Day: Guide to Modern Guitar Playing*. London: Chappell.

Welch, G. (2001). 'The Misunderstanding of Music: Inaugural Lecture', Institute of Education, University of London.

Wiggins, T. (1996). 'The World of Music in Education', *British Journal of Music Education* 13/1: 21–9.

Wikipedia. (2006), *Thomas Beecham*. Wikipedia, 25 May. Retrieved 30 May 2006 from the World Wide Web: en.wikipedia.org/wiki/Thomas_Beecham

Williamon, A. (1999). 'The Value of Performing from Memory', *Psychology of Music* 27: 87–95.

—— and Valentine, E. (2000). 'Quantity and Quality of Musical Practice as Predictors of Performance Quality', *British Journal of Psychology* 91: 353–76.

Winnett, R., and Swinford, S. (2006). 'Elton, Going for a £500,000 Song', *Sunday Times*, p. 7.

Wojtas, O. (2006). 'People', *The Times Higher Education Supplement*, 21 Apr. 2006: 2.

Wragg, E. C. (2004). *Education, Education, Education: The Best Bits of Ted Wragg*. London: RoutledgeFalmer.

Young, V., Burwell, K., and Pickup, D. (2003). 'Areas of Study and Teaching Strategies in Instrumental Teaching: A Case Study Research Project', *Music Education Research* 5/2: 139–55.

Index of Authors

General Index